KAJ MUNK AND GERMANY

THEATER AND POLITICS

Søren Daugbjerg

KAJ MUNK AND GERMANY

THEATER AND POLITICS

"... He could interpret a German verse so
that the German language's Middle Age and
secretive nature wrapped itself around our
young hearts, and one would have to ask: How
is it possible that anyone could bear to abuse
that language by using it to make commands?"
(Kaj Munk, on the teacher L. M. Hunø, Maribo, in
"So Quietly Comes the Spring," memoirs.)

New Nordic Press
2011

First American edition 2011.
ISBN 978-0-615-55998-8
Library of Congress Control Number 2011942035 New Nordic Press
Port Townsend, WA
www.newnordicpress.com
Cover layout and design by Marita Sempio
Sequence Graphics Gresham, OR 9703Printedby Lightning Source La Vergne, TN
Printed in the Unites States of America.

Mogens Munk: An introduction to Kaj Munk and Germany

My father was, first and foremost, an artist, a poet, and a dramatist. Then he became a martyr– but that was because he couldn't keep quiet when things needed to be said. Nor could he remain passive when action was required.

During his life his breakthrough as a dramatist was the greatest thing that could have happened to him. For Kaj Munk, the stage was no less holy than the altar. And just as his life spanned over the most unbelievable contradictions, his reputation as well bridged the gulf between the aesthetic and the religious.

This is a fascinating book about a fascinating man– my father, Kaj Munk. He was born in the remote Danish countryside at the dawn of the 20th Century. He became the great Danish focal point during the 1930's. No other single Dane had in that way stood in the middle of that last decade of peace before the outbreak of WWII.

It is also the story of the working relationship between my father and the well-known translator Erwin Magnus, who was a great admirer, and who was determined to win for Kaj Munk the recognition in Germany that he had already won in Scandinavia.

Congratulations to Søren Daugbjerg on his book. With simplicity and a steady style, he describes for us those two decisive decades in the last century. He does not attempt to paint an unrealistic portrait of my father, but we feel that we are on firm ground with Søren Daugbjerg as a guide. The book clearly illustrates that it was the war that prevented his dramas from being recognized in Germany, and therefore his broader recognition internationally. If that had not been the case then his reputation would not have been subject to the partisan-political debate that surrounded it during the 1950's. Thanks also to Brian Young who with his translation has allowed the English reader to become acquainted with this important book.

Mogens Munk, Copenhagen, 2011

A note from the translator and editor:

I have been interested in Kaj Munk's poetry and dramas since 1964. In April 2009 an Internet search led me to The Kaj Munk Research Center at the University of Aalborg in Denmark (www.kajmunk.hum.aau.dk). A new project had just begun: to transcribe Kaj Munk's handwritten sermons, spanning a 25-year period (1919-1944), into digital format. My participation in that project led to a friendship with Jørgen Albretsen, and through him to Søren Daugbjerg.

I had Søren's new book about Kaj Munk sent from Denmark on the day that it appeared in bookstores. I was initially motivated by my own interest in Kaj Munk, but as I was reading the book I began to realize that there was more to it than just the story of one man, or of Denmark's occupation during WWII, and that is why I decided that it was a story that should to be told to the American reader as well.

One of the central things to understand is Kaj Munk's early fascination with German culture, and the ideal of the "Strong Man." During the early nineteen thirties Munk admired Hitler, as well as Mussolini, even at a time when many people had already recognized the true nature of the path down which these men were leading Europe.

Winston Churchill, among others, had already been sounding an alarm over the rise of Fascism in Germany and Italy, and anyone who had read Mein Kampf, Hitler's own political manifesto (Published in 1925), should have been able to see what was in store. Hitler's plans for Europe, and for Europe's Jews, were laid out in black and white.

Kaj Munk had apparently not read Mein Kampf, and perhaps there were other reasons that compelled him to look to the "strong men" of Europe. And he was not alone. Democracy and parliamentarianism can be slow, messy, and prone to corruption. It might have been an obvious conclusion for the deeply religious Kaj Munk, so sceptical of the political system, to want to believe that these strong men would lead Europe down the right path.

That is what struck me about this story. We can see the same tendencies around us in today's political debate. There is a need to have a demagogue to follow, and a scapegoat to blame society's ills on. It is easier to repeat slogans and wave flags than it is to take personal responsibility for one's own actions, or to engage in critical and independent thought and analysis.

Once a political ideology is adopted it often becomes a rut, rather than a path. Very few people will admit that they were mistaken, even when the truth is plain to see. Therefore, what was true then is still true today. That is why I thought that the story of Kaj Munk was more than just an historical account of a Danish pastor and poet. It is about having the courage to see the truth, and to act accordingly, even if it means renouncing earlier held positions, and putting one's own life on the line.

Brian Young
Port Townsend, June 2011

The abbreviation "KMF" in the text and notes indicates that the material used is held at the Kaj Munk Research Center's Archive, The Institute for Communication, Aalborg University.

The author's archives are marked "AA." Most of these will eventually be transferred to the Kaj Munk Research Centre, Aalborg University.

Translations from German into Danish are by the author, and each translation is marked by (a.t.).

NNF indicates publications by Nyt Nordisk Forlag Arnold Busck Copenhagen

WST indicates publications by Westermann Forlag

Forlag= publisher

We have not been able to find the copyright holder for several of the illustrations used. Subsequent legal demands in this connection will be paid as if there had been an agreement in place.

Translator's acknowledgements:

I want to thank the following for their help on this project:

My wife Else, for her inspiration, encouragement, patience, and careful proofreading of the text.

In Denmark– Søren Daugbjerg, Ole Opstrup, Jørgen Albretsen, Erik Kølle, Arne Munk, Mogens Munk, and a very special thanks to Eskil Irminger in Nykøbing for his many comments, corrections, and suggestions as well as for the on-going great discussions about the finer points of both Danish and English, and his energy, tenacity, and commitment to this project.

In America– thanks to Ed Valauskas at the Dominican University in River Forest for his commentary, and to Christie Gehringer in Omaha for proofreading the text.

Contents

SECOND PART- ADDENDUM
After Kaj Munk's death

Dedicated to the memory of

Th.D. Christian Eisenberg
Braunschweig
1940-1999

Preface

Kaj Munk's biographer, Th.D. Niels Nøjgaard, briefly mentioned that the play *The Word* had been performed in Schwerin in February of 1935.

The German Kaj Munk researcher, Pastor Paul Gerhard Schoenborn, had received a copy of the playbill for this German performance of *The Word* from the theater in Schwerin. As the playbill did not indicate who translated Munk's work into German, he asked me if I could find out who had.

An inquiry was made with the always-helpful Munk family, in this case Munk's daughter Yrsa Lund. The result was that shortly afterwards I had copies of letters that the German translator Erwin Magnus had written to Munk. It was apparent from these letters that he had translated *The Word* in 1933.

Through a long involved process that included going through the Sigmund Freud Private Foundation in Vienna, I was able to contact Erwin Magnus's son Michael Freud-Magnus, whose help has been invaluable during the writing of this book. Michael Freud-Magnus told me that Munk's letters to Magnus were kept at the Captain Ove Marcussen Archive at the Royal Library, from where I was able to obtain copies.

Reading the almost complete correspondence between the author and the translator– this part of the story about the Danish dramatist and the Jewish translator– and the turbulent times in the great neighbor country in the 1930's, tempted me to write about Kaj Munk and Germany.

The letters mentioned, which are listed in this book in chronological order, are supplemented with quotations from contemporary articles and books by Munk. Individual political and personal events, which were coincidental with the texts or dates of the letters, are also mentioned.

The story about Munk's infatuation with a girl from Eisenach is also a part of the story about his relationship to Germany. It was of such importance to him that he included it in his memoirs. Kaj Munk's daughter-in-law, Hanne Munk, found the four letters that Milly Erdmann had written to him, in the Munk archives.

The letters, which have not previously been made public, are reproduced in this book with the permission of the affected families.

The contents of the book have increased considerably as it has progressed, and have been brought up to date until 2007 with the information that has been available.

The indices in the back of the book contain information about dissertations, translations, publications, and short biographies of persons who had, in German, worked with Munk in different areas.

Some manuscripts and information on the translators have not been found.

I wish to express my sincere thanks to The Henry and Edith Pedersen's Family Foundation and the firm of A/S P. Hatten & Co. of Maribo, whose support has made the publication of this book possible.

Søren Daugbjerg

About Kaj Munk

Kaj Munk was born in Maribo in 1898 and graduated from the Nykøbing parochial school in 1917. He studied theology at the University of Copenhagen and took his final university exams in 1924. In the same year he received his post as parish pastor in Vedersø, where he remained until his death in 1944. He began writing poems and plays while still a student, and in 1929 his play *An Idealist* was presented at the Royal Theater. However, it was first with the plays *Cant* and *The Word* in 1931-32 that he achieved real success. Up until 1944 Munk was one of Scandinavia's most discussed authors and most often performed dramatists. Since his youth strong men had fascinated him, and this led to his admiration of Mussolini and Hitler.

But because Hitler had abandoned his own ideals,[1] Munk turned against him in the late 30s, and against the national socialistic Germany. This led to fervent criticism in his sermons, articles, poems, and plays. During World War II he continued these attacks on the occupying forces. He annoyed the Germans so much and so long that they murdered him on January 4, 1944.

Kaj Munk's play *The Word*, which had its opening night at the Betty Nansen Theater in 1932, has been part of the Danish cultural canon since.

---

[1] For example, in the article "Brændende Europa" (Europe is Burning), Jyllands-Posten, 26 March 1939. *Mindeudgave- Dagen er inde og andre Artikler* (*Commemorative edition- The Day Has Come and other Articles*) NNF 1949, p. 95.

Chapter 1

Eisenach in the Rain

Kaj Munk's first physical contact with Germany was most likely on an outing to Lübeck together with his class and the popular headmaster, L.M.Hunø, after having taken his examinations at the Maribo Private Secondary School in 1914.

In his memoirs, Munk has written about his school time in Maribo where a trip to Lübeck is mentioned. Munk recounts how one day they ran into a German police officer who gruffly yelled at them to "cross the street!" The children were frightened, but the headmaster smiled knowingly to the officer and said, "Oh shut up." And, Munk continues,

> *There we had a uniformed member of the Master Race surrounded by about 20 laughing children, and he didn't even know what they were laughing about. What could he do? Arrest them all? That would have been difficult! What then? If Muhammad could not move the mountain then at least he could move himself. The officer moved on. The Danish smile had won over the Prussian gruffness.[2]*

The expressions "Master Race," and "The Danish smile had won over the Prussian gruffness," were probably influenced by the fact that Munk wrote his memoirs in 1942 during the occupation.

The instability in Germany after World War I brought many problems with it: political unrest, high unemployment, and enormous reparation payments— compensation payable to the victorious powers. High demand for products led to increasing

---

[2] Kaj Munk, Foraaret saa sagte kommer -Erindringer (Silently Comes the Spring- Memoirs). WST,1942, p.153.

prices and to an inflation that the state tried to deal with by printing money in increasingly larger denominations. The high inflation of the German Mark meant that the Danish Crown was worth a lot in Germany, and that made it possible for Munk to travel to Berlin several times, as well as to other German towns, where he could live a life of leisure. When the market returned to a more normal exchange rate in 1923 it did not slow down Munk's travel activities. Even after that time he took many trips to Germany, right up to the outbreak of war in 1939.

On a "currency trip"[3] to Germany in 1922, together with fellow student Herluf Aagaard[4] he visited many well-known places, and experienced a great deal. Their finances also allowed for a plane trip from Berlin to Leipzig, which was not very common in 1922. The ticket price was 500 Rigsmark, equal to 2.75 Danish crowns per person.* Later they stayed at the Hotel Wartburg in Eisenach but with an almost empty purse and, for that reason, had to get home as quickly as possible. However, before they travelled home they had one more adventure that was surely conducive to Munk's budding talent. Herluf Aagaard wrote about the departure from Eisenach:

> But first we had a little incident, which in truth was the best part of the trip. We went into the currency exchange at the train station in Eisenach, and an exceptionally sweet girl of the Thüringer type served us: thick chestnut hair, clear dark eyes, a fine tender complexion, and a harmonious figure. [The two young theology students were not just interested in theology!] Munk was helplessly smitten! As there was still some waiting

---

* Germany experienced hyperinflation in the early twenties. The average exchange rate for the Mark in 1922 was 430.5 to the US dollar. At the end of 1923 it had risen to 4.2 trillion Mark to the dollar. The mark was essentially worthless. Currency reform at the end of 1923 brought the exchange rate back to 4.2 Mark to the dollar. Kaj Munk's ticket cost about $1.16 US in 1922.

[3] Herluf Aagaard in The Book about Kaj Munk, written by his friends(Bogen om Kaj Munk-Skrevet af hans Venner) WST, 1946, p. 83.

[4] Herluf Aagaard Th.D. (1894-1982), parish pastor.

time, we made another trip to the exchange office, and it was clear enough that she had also noticed us![5]

Kaj Munk, the pilot?, and Herluf Aagaard.
The flight from Berlin to Leipzig in 1922
Hans Juel Aagaard's Archive

Back at the Regensen* Munk sat and dreamed about his experience in Eisenach, and the dream became a poem: *In Eisenach*[6]. The poem describes how his bad mood and irritation over the weather disappeared when he spoke with the pretty girl in the train station's "information desk":

Back home, Herluf Aagaard believed that the story had been forgotten. He wrote:

And when I got to Eisenach
The rain was pouring down,
And bitterly I swore: "Damned
If I would live in this dumb town!"

---

[5] Herluf Aagaard op.cit. p. 86.
* A well known university dormitory in Copenhagen, founded in 1569
[6] Kaj Munk, op.cit., pp. 311-312.

And while the rain poured down
With unrelenting zest,
I turned my feet with haste
To ask the town's help desk.

With a resentful voice
And not a trace of smile,
Asked how I might most quickly get
Away from here to Kiel.
And the answer was— I can't recall
And never will find out.
There is just one thing I do recall:
A girl had told me how.

And when I walked in Eisenach
The town was full of sun,
At Wartburg flew the castle's flag,
And all the cocks did crow.
And all the people walked round and laughed
In summer's happy dreams,
And the birds chirped out aloud
And the rain flowed down in streams.

And when I left from Eisenach
The town was full of rain,
As never more should I return
To see this place again.
And never more to ask
At the town's help desk,
And find the sun to shine so bright
Amid the rain's full zest.

How can I describe my surprise when one day, some time later, I walked into Munk's room at the Regensen, and he laid a photograph in front of me and said: 'Do you recognize her?' I *readily admit that my answer was more of a Regensen's play than actually theological! The photograph was, although not very good, still a quite recognizable picture of the pretty Thüringer girl from Eisenach.*[7]

Kaj Munk had written a letter in German addressed to: "The young lady who on August 15 in the morning helped a young Dane with information about sleeping cars. Verkehrsbüro, Eisenbahnstrasse, Eisenach, Germany."[8]

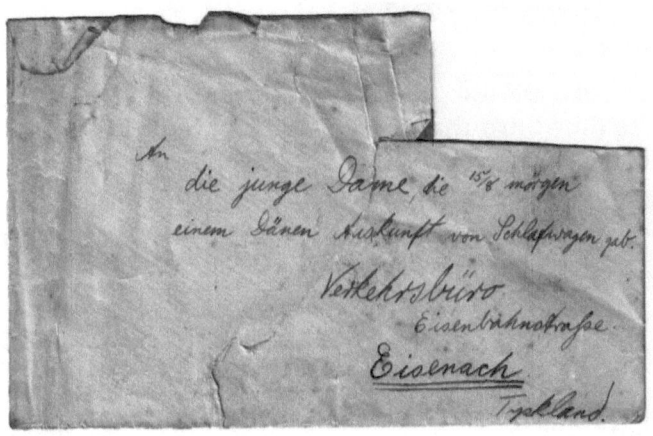

The envelope from Kaj Munk's first letter to Milly Erdmann that, despite the unusual address actually reached her.
August 1922.
Gerhard Krauss private archives

The letter from Munk, a glowing declaration of love, contained at the same time a beautifully formulated offer of marriage. When you think that he had only talked with the girl two times and that he didn't even know her name or address, you have to admit that he showed considerable audacity. In this first letter of August 19, 1922, he is very quick to state his real purpose. Here is an excerpt:

---

[7] Herluf Aagaard, op.cit. pp. 85-86.
[8] Original envelope. Gerhard Krauss private archives

You must forgive me for this reckless, this crazy letter, from a deeply serious heart, written in poor German, but I have to write to you. I must– and I have only one excuse, only one word, but the most beautiful and the strongest word in the world, and that is love... I came to Eisenach...I saw you, and I will never forget it. And it quickly became my dream, that at sometime, through happiness and sorrow, pain and joy, I would be able to love you as my wife– you are my princess– could you, perhaps– also become my queen.

With respectful greetings, Kaj Munk.[9] (a.t.)

In the letter Munk had also asked her for a photograph. He wrote furthermore that he wasn't rich, but that later he would be able to offer her a quiet vicarage in the beautiful Danish countryside.

He received an answer. The romantic girl's letters must have been balm for Munk's often torn soul:

Eisenach/ Thüringen, 27 August, 1922
Barfüsserstrasse 13

Mr. Kaj Munk, S.Th.
The Regensen, Copenhagen
Denmark
Dear Sir
I have received your letter of 19 August, but before I comply with your wishes, and send a photo to you, I must ask for a photo of you. Your words have made a strong impression on me, and for that reason I would like to know if it is that person I write to, whose picture I see faintly before my inner eye, and whose eyes that time looked so sadly at me. If I get a letter from you, then you will receive my photo. Until then, sincere greetings
Milly Erdmann[10] (a.t.)

---

[9] Munk's letter #1. Original. Gerhard Krauss private archives
[10] Milly Erdmann's letter #1. Original. KMF.

He had not been forgotten in Eisenach. He wrote again between August 27 and September 22, and sent three photos: his student photo and two photos from the last trip to Germany. One was of him and Aagaard riding on a donkey, and another standing by the airplane in Leipzig.

Herluf Aagaard and Kaj Munk on the way to Wartburg Castle, 1922. Hans Juel Aagaard's Archive

Munk's first letter is found in the original, while the following letters are found as incomplete drafts but whose text, based on Milly's answers, seem to follow the originals closely. As with Munk's first letter, quotations from the following letters are given only as excerpts.

Munk answered in a very pompous letter:

God bless you, that you would answer me. I have waited, doubted, hoped, where there was no hope, and now! — To wake in the morning and immediately be made to smile by a previously unknown feeling of happiness. And, in these unbelievable and sweet thoughts, so free and cheerful, to suspect, that in the old and beautiful town of Luther, I have a sweet young accomplice to my paramount secret, and that this accomplice is you... The eternal in woman draws us on, and I am certain that the eternal in woman can never be represented better than in your person...

With heartfelt greetings, Your devoted Kaj Munk[11] (a.t.)

That Munk had made an impression on the girl and won her confidence is evident from her next letter, where she seems to be very trusting.

Eisenach, 22 September 1922

My dear friend

And isn't it true that I can call you that, doesn't it sound sweeter and more confidential? You probably thought that I had forgotten you, but no, no, often I see your picture before my inner eye. Now after all I have your photos, which is why I thank you so dearly. I often look at your dear features and think: is it possible that I have made an impression on this man? After having read your letter, I have become more serious, and am no longer a silly and arrogant little girl. I don't know why. Can a person's spiritual empathy in that way be transferred to another person, who thereby matures, and becomes an adult? Now I believe it. I'll tell you a little bit about myself. I think that you understand me, and it will be of some interest to you. I am a child of simple people. My mother died when I was still a little girl. My grandparents on my father's side took me in, and in that way I had a home in a house with the old people. They are as fond of me as if I was their child, and I respect them and honor them as my parents. I appreciate

---

[11] Munk's letter #2, draft. KMF.

the sacrifices that they have to make for my sake. Because of the present situation, their position is such that their savings have become worthless, and for that reason my grandfather still has to work. He is the foreman in a factory here.

"Of course I have to work, too, so that I can at least pay for my board. I live after all with my grandparents and, of course, want to help a little to support them. Next month I begin in a new position where I will be paid more. I would like to work in a bigger firm, but there aren't any here, and I cannot leave my dear grandparents. Now that's enough about me. Tell me something about you. I'm happy to talk with somebody who understands me properly, and I fulfill your wishes, and enclose here a photo of me. I have changed somewhat, as the picture is from 1920/21. It will just be temporary. I'll send you another one, as soon as I have been able to get a photograph taken. You'll have to get by with this one, right?

I would be very happy to hear from you soon. Don't be angry that it took me so long to answer. I really couldn't write before.

For today I send my dearest greetings
Yours, Milly E."[12] (a.t.)

She used the expression "my dear friend," which she thought sounded "sweeter" and more "confidential." She writes in the letter about her family circumstances, that she lost her mother when she was just a young child, and therefore grew up with her grandparents under very modest conditions, and that her grandfather, for financial reasons, still has to work. She had, in other words, in certain areas, a common fate with Munk. That the photograph was "old" (one year!), and only "temporary," was also mentioned. The tone of the letter indicates that at this point she was interested in an on-going relationship with Munk. She wrote that she certainly had not forgotten how he looked, and that would not have lessened Munk's feeling of self-esteem.

---

[12] Milly Erdmann's letter #2. Original. KMF.

Emilie (Milly) Erdmann (1902-1983)
Photo ca. 1923
Gerhard Krauss, private archives.

Her remarks about having "changed" after reading Munk's letter are thought provoking. The exchange of letters with Munk matured her. She is certain that it is due to their mutual empathy. Munk read these remarks with a sweet smile on his lips. The power of words, spoken as well as written, he already knew and was master of by that time. Here the words were used as a herald in the service of love, and it wasn't just exercises in dramatic writing. Munk was in love.

He sat in his room at the Regensen, looking at her photo on the desk, and wrote:

Dear

Incomprehensible and more than incomprehensible it is for me that I can sit here in my room at the Regensen with your picture in front of me– the picture is beautiful– but you– ten times more beautiful are you, and you smile too, smile like the first time that I saw you– first and almost the last– and now, when I have your photo, I, of course, don't desire the photo, but you, just to have you. What does it help me to look at your photo when I can't hold you in my arms? Will you be the sun in my future home... and the rose in my parish garden– will you be the mild mother to my children (because I love children and I pray to God to have some)– and you will never regret all that you have sacrificed for this, and so we will thank God, forever, forever....[13] (a.t.)

The parish garden with wife and children as a theme was also used the year before in his poem "Master With the Heavy Crown of Thorns,"[14] where in his first verse he wrote:

Master with the heavy Crown of Thorns,
I cannot follow you,
When a parish, a friendly wife
And two healthy boys are calling me.

In his biography of Kaj Munk, Th.D. Niels Nøjgaard [15] places the intermezzo in Eisenach in April 1922, but it was actually in August of the same year. He also wrote that Munk brought a picture of the girl home with him, which does not agree with the letters. Nor in his description of the play at the Regensen mentioned below, *"S'mænd et Offer"(A Real Sacrifice)*, did he comment on the name of Milly Erdmann, which must however have sounded foreign: he probably did not know about any of the letters reproduced here.

---

[13] Munk's letter #3. Draft. KMF Archive.

[14] Kaj Munk: Commemorative Edition, Poems. NNF 1949, p. 59.

[15] Niels Nøjgaard Th.D. (1900-1999), has written several books about Kaj Munk, including the biography Ordets Dyst og Daad (Conflict and Conquest in Language). NNF 1946.

Niels Nøjgaard called the episode a "butterfly love affair."[16] But that concept did not exist at all for Munk. Love was for him either joyful happiness or terrible suffering. Frivolity was not in his character and certainly not in this area. The story later became a drama, portrayed in *A Real Sacrifice,* written for the freshman play at the Regensen in 1922.

Student Photo of Kaj Munk, sent to Milly Erdmann in 1922.
Photo 1917
The Munk Family Archive

---

[16] Ibid., p. 97.

The play's action was later expanded into a drama in three acts: *The Regensen's Dean had a Daughter,* but with different names. It was probably presented with the title: "Now for the Danish students we sing happily in chorus,"[17] to the Dagmar Theater,[18] and theater director Gerda Christoffersen (1936),[19] though without being performed.

The only female in the play had the name Milly Erdmann! The play takes place at the Regensen and is about the students there. One is a medical student who swears a lot, is very thirsty, and speaks with a strong Lolland dialect. He is the pastor's son Kunow, who has problems with Christianity; and it is especially the idea that Christianity requires a sacrifice that causes him a great deal of torment. But the play ends with a sacrifice: Kunow gives up his girlfriend, Milly Erdmann, the daughter of a bookseller, to his friend, the Regensen's ringer and righteous theology student Hertel, who is also in love with her. In Munk's previously mentioned first letter to Milly he expressed the wish that she might become his queen. This expression appears again in *A Real Sacrifice,* where Hertel, after reciprocal declarations of love, says: "... come now Queen Milly!"[20]

In both persons, Kunow and Hertel, Munk uses some aspects of himself: Kunow is a crass caricature whereas Hertel is the ideal of a young man who does, after all, win the girl. In fact it went the same way for Munk as it did for Kunow in the play: he had to leave Milly Erdmann to another. Did Munk suspect that it would go that way? Some things could indicate that he did, as *A Real Sacrifice* was presented at the Regensen on November 4, 1922, and Milly Erdmann's farewell letter was written November 6 in the same year; in that letter she did not use the familiar "du" (The familiar form of the 2nd person singular).

---

[17] Both editions are in the KMF.

[18] Niels Nøjgaard, op.cit. p. 118.

[19] Gerda Christophersen: *Jeg Gav Aldrig Op* (*I Never Gave Up*). Rasmus Naver's Forlag, Copenhagen 1945, pp. 133-134.

[20] Kaj Munk: Rub og Stub (Lock, Stock, and Barrel). 1923, pp. 1-16.

My dear friend

Forgive me for my long silence. I did receive your letter, and it's not easy for me to write this because I have understood and accepted your great love for me. What have I done to deserve so much? I don't know.

I certainly don't want to hurt you, but I don't think that you have asked yourself: is her heart still free, is she still free, or has she already been promised? I will tell you everything because you deserve my confidence, and that is what I will give you. I know a man here, who I am in love with, and who apparently loves me as well; it is difficult for a poor girl to follow her heart's voice, especially in this difficult time. How the future will be, I leave to Him, who controls all of our fates. I can't answer all of your questions now, but I close my eyes and experience, in spirit, a pure and heartfelt happiness.

I would like to stand in front of you, give you my hand, and thank you for the great love that I don't deserve. Be strong, don't lose courage, but have faith in Him, whose Holy Word you will spread and proclaim. It is obviously a difficult path that you have chosen. But you can always seek refuge in the Word of God, even in times of greatest need.

Therefore, we have to bear whatever burden is imposed upon us, for our sake, and for the sake of other dear people.

Don't forget me completely, and accept the most heartfelt greetings from,

Your friend, Millie.[21] *(a.t.)*

Now Millie suddenly tells him that she has a friend and adds that it is difficult to follow her heart's voice. Did her heart speak to Munk's advantage, while consideration for her grandparents and her friend pulled in the opposite direction? But why did she go along with this for so long? There was, after all, already in Munk's first letter, a glowing declaration of his love. So why did she even answer?

Instead of writing that she had a boyfriend, she asked for his photo and wrote several friendly, almost loving letters. One

---

[21] Milly Erdmann's letter #3. Original. KMF.

sentence in Milly's letter seems strangely unfinished. It says that she couldn't answer all of Munk's questions now, but that: "I close my eyes and experience, in spirit, a pure and heartfelt happiness." Was it Munk's love that brought forth the feeling of happiness? The girl seems irresolute, but despite the problems with love she finishes the letter both sensibly and lovingly.

Munk must have written an answer to her farewell letter because the rough draft of a letter has been found where he asks for an answer to his previous letter. This draft was found together with an envelope with Milly's name and address written on it. He asks politely why she had not answered his letter. He, too, no longer uses the familiar "du."

> *Dear Ms. Erdmann*
>
> *I've waited for five weeks now and longed for an answer from you. Every possible thought has gone through my mind. What is the reason? Have I been too forward, or maybe you have not even received my last letter? You must write to me. I cannot and will not believe that our friendship should have such a sudden and sad end. The beginning was too beautiful for that. I await your dear answer, and I remain your sincere and devoted friend*
>
> *Kaj Munk[22] (a.t.)*

There are no more letters between them. Did Munk give up and let his last letter stay in his desk drawer?

Munk, who had become the parish pastor in Vedersø, wrote in 1925 to his former travel comrade Herluf Aagaard, who had been granted a parish post on the Faroe Islands. In the following little excerpt from that very long letter, Kaj Munk wrote, directed to Aagaard's wife Lone, about Milly Erdmann:

> *Oh, Lone, you're a grand girl, and I probably could've been happy with you. For that reason I hate that old baldhead because he has taken you from me and has advised and persuaded me not to write to Miss Milly Erdmann in Mühlerstrasse 6, Eisenach– and I would've had three children*

---

22 Munk's letter #4. Original (or draft?),KMF Archive.

by now, with the first one speaking Danish, the second German, and the third would've been incomprehensible, as it would have been as yet too small.[23]

Was it Munk who broke off the liaison? Judging by the letters it was Milly. And why did Munk change Milly Erdmann's address?

Lone and Herluf Aagaard.
Hans Juel Aagaard's Archive

Munk never forgot people who had been close to him. They had for a time been a part of his life. Throughout his life Munk carried on an extensive correspondence with family, friends, and colleagues, and never forgot those love affairs that he had experienced during his youthful years. The just two-month long relationship with Milly Erdmann made a deep impression on

---

[23] Undated letter (1925?) in Hans Juel Aagaard's Archive.

him. In her farewell letter's last line she wrote: "Don't forget me completely," and Munk never did. She was still fresh in his memory 20 years later when he was writing his memoirs in 1942, ("*Silently Comes the Spring*"), where her photo can still be seen, together with the poem *In Eisenach*. However, he did not mention her.[24]

The only letters in this book that I did not have permission to publish were Milly Erdmann's. For that reason I tried to find her family. I thought it was an impossible task. But despite the fact that the register of names in Eisenach had burned down in 1945, Dr. Brunner, the leader of the city archives in Eisenach, by searching through other archives and following many tortuous leads, was able to help me find Milly Erdmann's son, Gerhard Krauß[25]. Gerhard Krauss and his wife Gisela have, with great kindness, through letters and telephone conversations, told me about Milly Erdmann.[26]

In 1949 Gerhard Krauss was seriously ill. His mother and his future wife Gisela were very worried. Gisela explains that during Gerhard's illness she had a long conversation with Milly about suffering, love, and happiness. During this conversation Milly suddenly pulled out a photo of Kaj Munk, together with his first letter, which her daughter-in-law read. Milly spoke, deeply touched, about the young Dane's declaration of love, which she had never forgotten. Later, when her son Gerhard, together with other children, was on a vacation in 1933 at a farm by Løgumkloster, she would wonder if it was close to Munk's parish. Later, during a vacation at Arendsee on the Baltic, she again thought about Kaj Munk and Denmark, and that again occupied her thoughts.

Gisela believes that he was probably Milly's first great love and that she broke off the connection on account of her grandparents, who had great difficulties due to the inflation, as well as anxiety

---

[24] Kaj Munk: Foraaret saa sagte kommer -Erindringer WST 1942, pp. 311-312.

[25] Letter dated 31 January 2007, from Dr. Brunner. City Archives in Eisenach. Author's archive.

[26] Emilie (Milly) Agnes Erdmann, born in 1902 in Eisenach, married grocer Richard Krauss, born in 1898 in Eisenach on 28 June 1924. It might have been him who she mentioned as her boyfriend in the last letter to Munk. The couple had a daughter and a son. They moved to Meiningen in 1959, where Richard Krauss died in 1980, and Emilie in 1983.

about going to a country where she did not understand the language. Milly did not have any knowledge of Munk's later fate. Munk's 85-year-old letter and his photo were found among her papers after her death. Now both of them are reverently taken care of by her son and daughter-in-law.[27]

This short intermezzo remained fresh in the memories of both Munk and Milly.

---

[27] Letter of 13 February 2007, from Gisela and Gerhard Krauß. AA.

FIRST PART

Kaj Munk in the European Melting-Pot

Chapter 2

Close to Heaven in Berlin

Kaj Munk wrote about his fascination with German culture and, in particular with German theater, in letters and numerous newspaper articles. For example, on February 9, 1926, in a letter to Niels Nøjgaard about plans for a trip together to Germany, he wrote:

> *Never before have I been so doubtful. That's a lie. But this round of winter frost has gotten me to ask myself again and again, why in the Devil don't I go to Rome, as it is just as cheap and I have, after all, probably been in Berlin the last seven or eight times. The answer has got to be this last point, that it's there that I meet you, and also that when I travel it's not to see, but to listen, in other words to make an acquaintance with the often mentioned living word. Then, too, Berlin is the city that I get the most out of being in– for sermons, for lectures, and for the sake of the theater, to take them in reverse order.[28]*

In November and December of the same year he was once again in Berlin; and during his stay there, according to Niels Nøjgaard, wrote the play, *In The Breakers*, which is about Georg Brandes.[29] After arriving home he wrote a letter to Niels Nøjgaard about the last evening in Berlin, where he went to the little theater known as *The Comedy*. And it there he saw a French play about a love affair between two women.[30] He didn't say much about the play's plot in the letter but rather about the two actors, who he had probably seen earlier.

---

[28] Kaj Munk: *Aldrig spørge om det nytter* (Never ask if it matters) NNF, 1958, pp. 111-112.

[29] Georg Brandes PhD (1842-1927), Danish critic and author.

[30] *Die Gefangene* by Edouard Bourdet, produced by Max Reinhardt. Program brochure, KMF.

They were Helena Thimig[31] and Ernst Deutsch.[32] He praised them highly and finished by informing Nøjgaard that not since Fjelstrup's[33] days had he been so close to heaven.[34]

That the theater-smitten Munk had felt so close to heaven that evening in Berlin could be seen by his use of Fjelstrup as a benchmark. That was because Munk, in March of 1918, had been in the Betty Nansen Theater and seen Strindberg's play *The Father* with Fjelstrup in the main role. It was divine and terrible wrote Munk, and continued:

> *In all of the misanthropical and misogynistic passion of Strindbergish rage, Peter Fjelstrup as the father— oh! Those eyes! Hell and the Devil in those eyes! What art! What incomprehensible art! What divine fury screaming, stomping, howling, groaning, and staggering in that play ... were you a devil, Strindberg, fallen from light's heavenly realm of genius?" Again and again I saw the play. After the last time I wrote: 'I get so carried away that my nerves collapse, my eyes stare, and my heart throbs.' It is an experience that you only have once in your life. God watch over Fjelstrup!*[35]

The future theater critic, and playwright, was on his way.

Munk tried several times to get away from Vedersø, and he was probably glad when it didn't work out. In 1931 he sent an application to the Danish Church Abroad for a pastor's position in Berlin. In the application's last section he gave an important reason to seek just that position:

---

[31] Helene Thimig (1889-1974), Austrian-German actress, married to Max Reinhardt.

[32] Ernst Deutsch (1890-1969), German actor. Immigrated to the USA in 1933. Back in Europe after 1945, he played in the film "The Third Man", among others.

[33] Peter Julius Fjelstrup (1866-1920), Danish actor and theater manager.

[34] Kaj Munk: op.cit, p. 137.

[35] Kaj Munk: *Foraaret saa sagte kommer -Erindringer* WST p. 245.

What would I go to Berlin for? Why, to see a good comedy, because that's an important thing for me, and you can't see one here in Denmark. And a pastor's calling down there– yes, if I actually was sent, I would believe that I was called not just by you, but by God.

Munk did not get the sought after position; but when the church council with the Danish Church in Berlin in 1987 searched their archives for material for an article in connection with the church's 75th Jubilee, they found Munk's application from back in December 16, 1931 and used it in their Jubilee publication.[36]

The magazine *Danish Folklife* will be mentioned briefly here because it gave Munk access to a new field– journalism. The magazine was published in 1930 and 1931, with Munk's colleague A. Drewsen Christensen[37] of the free congregation in Lemvig as editor. He called it a liberal, popular, and ecclesiastical magazine. It was easy for Christensen to persuade the enthusiastic writer Munk to submit articles to the magazine; and, within one year, Munk managed to write five articles about literature and theater for *Danish Folklife*. Before that Munk had only had a few articles published in newspapers and magazines, but with the articles in *Danish Folklife* his ability as a writer became clear. It was the beginning of Munk's work as a journalist. He became a sought after critic and feature writer in the Danish press, and he dealt with religious, political, and literary subjects. Of course, there were many articles about the theater.

Munk wrote a review in *Danish Folklife* on March 13, 1931 about *Success*, a novel written by the German Jewish author Lion Feuchtwanger.[38] That book critically describes Hitler's coup attempt in Munich in 1923. Despite Munk's admiration for the author, he was sceptical about many of his ideas. Among other

---

[36] The Danish Church in Berlin. 75th Anniversary Jubilee Publication.

[37] A. Drewsen Christensen, (1889-1962) Th.D., wrote two books about Kaj Munk.

[38] Lion Feuchtwanger (1884-1958), German author, in exile in France from 1933, in the USA from 1941. He wrote the novel *Jud Süss* ("The Jew Suss", Joseph Süss Oppenheimer), which was made into a film and used as propaganda against the Jews.

things, he believed that the Jew Feuchtwanger expressed harsh words about National Socialism because Jews had become disenfranchised in Germany at the time. Munk wrote that the author had made Hitler look like a clown, an empty blustering barrel. Munk believed that it was too early to dismiss Hitler and his party, and he finished his review with the following lines, where he suggested that the Jews in particular should have been more understanding for Germans and Germany's suffering after the First World War:

> When Hitler now, in reality, has again come to the front of the line, even after his God-awful and pitiable farce in Munich in 1923, can that be solely because of German madness and stupidity?
>
> Can't one think of deeper and finer reasons than that, which should after all not be completely unknown to a man whose one-liter of blood had been passed down from a people who were expecting the Messiah, and who knew so well the pain of defeat?[39]

A grant in May of 1931 gave Munk the opportunity to take a short trip to Berlin. The pastor from Vedersø travelled by plane. He was busy, and he achieved a lot. The trip resulted in a feature article in *Politiken**: "1 1/2 Days in Berlin," where he wrote about Germany, and in particular about German theater, which had again impressed him. A watchful and ready people, always on the move, he wrote, and wondered why the Lord had given Shakespeare to the English. It was the first time that Munk had reviewed German theater. He saw Heinrich George [40] in a modern version of *Tristan and Isolde*. In Max Reinhardt's[41] *German Theater* he saw one of the

---

[39] Kaj Munk: *Naar man læser "Succes"* (When One Reads 'Success') Danish FolkLife No. 6. March 1931.

Politiken, A large daily newspaper published in Copenhagen.

[40] Heinrich George (1893-1946), German actor, theater manager for Schiller Theater in Berlin 1936-1945.

[41] The actor Max Reinhardt (1873-1943) owned the Deutsche Theater in Berlin. He emigrated together with his wife, Helene Thimig, to Vienna in 1933, where he became a theater manager, until emigrating to the USA in 1938.

most talked about performances of the time: Carl Zuckmayer's[42] play *Der Hauptmann von Köpenick*. Heinz Hilpert[43] had directed the play, with Werner Krauss in the main role. Munk was fascinated by the actors and the stage technique and about the action he wrote: "I don't know how good the play is in itself, but the idea of letting a uniform be the main character in a play of 21 acts is certainly not boring."

Back in Copenhagen again, Munk spoke with Professor Einar Christiansen,[44] and asked for advice about his new play, *Cant*, a drama about Henry VIII and Anne Boleyn. Einar Christiansen told him that there weren't any rules for a drama. It was either good or not good.[45]

Throughout his entire life Munk possessed a well developed self confidence, and he knew for sure in which of the two categories mentioned by Christiansen that his play belonged: *Cant* was a good drama.

Cant premiered at the Royal Theater on October 10, 1931. It was Kaj Munk's first success, and a healing consolation for the slowly healing sores from the fiasco with *An Idealist*.[46] The Royal Theatre performed *Cant* 51 times.

The book edition of the play came out the day before the opening night.[47]

Already by October 12 Munk had received an inquiry from Yrsa Bang[48] who, together with Else von Hollander-Lossow,[49] asked for the translation rights for *Cant* in Germany.[50] Further correspondence about this inquiry is not available.

---

[42] Carl Zuckmayer (1896-1977), German author and dramatist, emigrated to Austria and later to the USA in 1938.

[43] Heinz Hilpert (1890-1967), German author and stage director.

[44] Professor, Bachelor of Divinity Einar Christiansen (1861-1939), Danish author and theater manager.

[45] Kaj Munk: "1 1/2 Days in Berlin". Feature article in Politiken, 21 June 1931.

[46] The first performance of *En Idealist* (*An Idealist*, 7 performances) in 1928 must be seen as a fiasco, but the play made Munk well known.

[47] Kaj Munk: *Cant*. NNF, 1st. edition, 9 October 1931.

[48] Yrsa Bang, no further information

[49] Else von Hollander-Lossow, German translator (1884-?).

[50] KMF

There was a run on *Cant*. A week after the play's premiere, Munk received a letter from Berlin:

Berlin-Friedenau 17 October 1931

Isoldestr. 1

Author, Pastor Kaj Munk

My friend Svend Rindom[51] sent me your play Cant, and at the same time Drei Masken Verlag (Three Masks Publisher) had, at my own request, contacted their representative in Copenhagen, Mr. Strakosch, who sent me a copy. I have read the play with great interest, and I'm convinced that it will also find its way to the German theater. It would be a great pleasure for me if I could translate Cant. I'm well aware that it's a difficult job. But for that reason it tempts me even more. As you might know, I have translated Aladdin.[52]

And I have had a great success with the book edition, as well as at the theater (Deutches Schauspielhaus Hamburg). I have, furthermore, thanks to my good connections to a series of Germany's leading theaters, managed to have 11 Scandinavian plays presented in recent years. I therefore ask you to grant me the rights to the German translation of Cant, which I would then offer first to the Drei Masken Verlag. With respect to business matters, I would suggest the same arrangement that I have with most of the authors that I translate: I'll translate the play at my own risk, though a fixed deadline is difficult to determine until I have started on the work, and perhaps have gotten into the middle of it, as it is a work that requires one's complete attention and, if I may say so, intuition. Moreover, I hope to be able to manage it within half a year, or at any rate so that it would be finished by the beginning of the next theater season. Whatever we might earn in the German language theater would be split evenly between us. I'm also quite willing

---

[51] Svend Rindom (1884-1960), Danish actor and author.

[52] *Aladdin oder Die Wunderlampe* (*Aladdin or The Wonderful Lamp*). Dramatic Tale by Adam Oehlenschläger. NNF Berlin Christiana 1920 (A handsome book with an introduction by Georg Brandes, printed in 120 numbered copies).

to send you a copy of my Aladdin *translation so that you can judge my work as a translator on your own.*
    Sincerely, Erwin Magnus[53]

The letter was a pleasant surprise for Munk. Recognized so early in his career, and already an interest abroad for his drama– and in Germany at that! For Munk, Germany was Europe's theater country above all others. Erwin Magnus was also a well-known translator of Scandinavian and English literature into German. Magnus was a Jew, and that would result in a drastic change in the course of his life a couple of years later.

The first two letters that Munk wrote in answer to Magnus have not been found. He might have written messages on the manuscripts that he sent to Magnus.

In March of 1932 Munk was again in Berlin where he wrote an article about how he had experienced the election campaign for Germany's president. The article, "The Election of Germany's Chauffeur," was printed in *Jyllands-Posten** on March 13, 1932. The question for Germany was– Hindenburg or Hitler? Munk saw the numerous campaign posters with Hindenburg's picture, bigger than life, showing a still strong and active person; hardly a person, Munk wrote, but a myth.

He was Germany's own Holger Danske.** It sounded like he was not totally convinced about the 85-year-old Hindenburg's qualifications to continue as president. Munk commented ironically on the posters of the National Socialists, modern propaganda inspired by the world of film: "And against all this the Nazis' answer is something even more emphatic: no words, just a pitch black poster, and in the middle the only light point in Germany's present situation— handsome Adolf's marble white features." In the first election round none of the candidates won

---

[53] Erwin Magnus (1881-1947), German translator. See the biographies. The original letters from Magnus to Munk are contained in the KMF Archive.
*Jyllands-Posten, a leading daily newspaper published in Aarhus, Denmark.
**Holger Danske, a heroic figure in Danish mythology, who is said to live in the subterranean vaults under the castle at Kronborg, and is expected to rise up to defend Denmark in a time of national emergency.

a majority, but in a second ballot in April of the same year, Hindenburg won an absolute majority and could continue as president.

Erwin Magnus (1881-1947)
Photo 1944
Michael Freud-Magnus. Private archive

While standing at the corner of Unter den Linden and Friederichstrasse, Munk watched the traffic of the great metropolis and, in the last section, in agreement with the article's title, he compared Germany and German politics to a car that was speeding out of control:

...As if primeval creatures had been called forth to life with a magic word and let loose on the streets of the metropolis, a whirlwind of all types of cars racing past us, with shining eyes and angry roars, leaving ugly exhaust fumes in their wake.

One of them stops with a screech right next to me, and engulfs me before again setting off with a ferocious growl. I look almost thankfully towards the man inside the monster: 'You after all have the power over it; you can control it so that it does not suddenly, in a natural eruption of power and madness, take off down through the town, smashing everything in its way.' And I shudder: Chauffeur, chauffeur, they vote on Sunday, so what about him?

What was Munk afraid of? Was it Hindenburg, who had not shown any great political abilities, or was it Hitler, who had not yet reached his political goals? Who would be Germany's chauffeur? The following year, with Hindenburg's help, Hitler was given the driver's license to Germany, and in the following years smashed Germany and Europe to pieces. In the next 12 years there would be many who would shudder.

Until the National Socialists' rise to power in 1933, both theater and film in Germany, despite the fact that Jews made up less than 1% of the German population, were marked by a strong Jewish influence. Many of these highly gifted German artists were very inspirational for Kaj Munk. They included, among others, the previously mentioned world-renowned instructor and actor Max Reinhardt, as well as the actor mentioned below, Fritz Kortner.[54]

A theater and film experience in the spring of 1932 resulted, as usual, in an article by Munk: "Kortner and Jannings in *The Patriot*". The theatergoers of Copenhagen were able to experience *The Patriot*,[55] which was played in two places, and with two great German actors: Fritz Kortner at the Dagmar Theater and Emil

---

[54] Fritz Kortner (1892-1970), German actor, immigrated to the USA in 1933 because of his Jewish heritage.
[55] Alfred Neumann (1895-1952), author of *The Patriot*, immigrated to the USA in 1933 because of his Jewish heritage.

Jannings[56] in the cinema. Both actors played Czar Paul I in *The Patriot*. Munk called them two of the world's greatest stage actors. *The Patriot* is a drama about Paul I, Russia's Czar from 1796 to 1801, a sick person who terrorized those around him. He was mean and unpredictable, and in the end was killed by officers and noblemen, many of whom had previously been his friends and advisers. The play is also about the moral qualms that his friend Count Pahlen experienced because of his complicity in the plot that ends with Paul's murder in 1801. Paul I might have been a despot, but he was God's anointed one; and for that reason Munk doubted that anybody had the right to kill him, a theme that he himself would deal with in his dramas. There is no doubt that for Munk it was stage art at the highest level.

And it wasn't just the action, but to a high degree the actors, and in particular Kortner and Jannings that interested Munk:

> *Art has again spoken to us– yes, with the eternal voice of the ages. A poetic work carried forward by two of the great– and which of them was the greater? Maybe it makes some sense to say that Kortner reached the highest, and Jannings the deepest.*
>
> *Vedersø Parish May 1932*

In parentheses Munk had rather sourly added: "Returned from *Politiken*."[57]

It cannot be seen from the letters when Munk had sent *An Idealist* to Magnus, but in the following letter it can be seen that he was working on the play. Magnus was frank enough to ask Munk to rewrite and shorten the play. Later in his career Munk would react quite angrily to such suggestions, which can clearly be seen in two letters that are quoted later in the book.[58]

---

[56] Emil Jannings (1884-1950), German stage and film actor. His most famous role was as Professor Unrat in *Den blaa Engel* (*The Blue Angel*) 1930, where he appeared with Marlene Dietrich.

[57] Kaj Munk: *Med Sol og Megen Glæde* (*With Sun and Lots of Joy*). NNF 1942, pp. 176-181.

[58] Letter from Magnus, 1 March 1933, and Munk's answer, 16 March 1933.

Küb bei Payerbach, a.d. Südbahn, Austria
31 May 1932

Dear Kaj Munk

I hope to be finished with Cant in 14 days. There are already four theatrical publishers and several theaters that are interested in the play, among them the Burg Theater in Vienna. I will also soon write to Kortner, who in fact just played in Copenhagen and is now in Sweden; I believe of all the German actors that he would be the best one to play the role of King Henry. I have been quite occupied with An Idealist these days, and believe that we could really get something out of this play (despite Hebbel!).⁵⁹ If only you would rewrite it and make it a lot shorter. What do you think?

I will be spending all summer here. It's a paradise, and if you take a vacation, I would advise you to come down. It's a couple of hours from Vienna, up in the mountains, and I can't imagine a better place to relax and work.

Sincerely, your devoted, Erwin Magnus"

Despite the fact that Payerbach is in a river valley named "Höllental" (Infernal), Magnus called his vacation place a paradise, and it probably was. One could still enjoy the summer vacation time; but the old Europe was breaking up, and it would be Magnus' last summer of freedom until the end of the Second World War. After the political changes in the spring of 1933, the Jews had become a persecuted people with no legal rights in Germany and unwanted in Austria. Several European countries had closed their borders to Jewish refugees in the thirties.

Vedersø, Ulfborg, Denmark, 7 May⁶⁰ 1932

Dear Erwin Magnus,

Many thanks for your greetings. I was very pleased. And you can believe that I would love to come down to see you in the mountains, to be able to sit in peace and work on the play that

---

⁵⁹ A reference to Friederich Hebbel's play *Herod and Mariamne* (1851) with the same theme.
⁶⁰ Munk answered Magnus' letter of 31 May 1932 on May 7th, so the date on one of the letters is incorrect.

I'm now grappling with, but unfortunately I have been so careless with my finances that there will be no vacation this year.

A week ago I put the last touches on a thorough revision and shortening of An Idealist. *I cannot see other than that the play must now have great chances to be accepted abroad. As soon as you give me the word that you are finished with* Cant, *I'll be sure to send you one of my four copies.*

Most sincerely
Kaj Munk

Munk had obviously revised *An Idealist*, and believed that the work would now have good chances for success abroad. Munk was certainly not troubled by modesty.

Chapter 3

Kaj Munk's Knight in the Mighty Realm

From the letters of the last half of 1932, with which this chapter deals, it can be seen that an almost friendly relationship developed between Kaj Munk and Magnus. These were working letters, sent between the author and the translator, and they show that Magnus had made an enormous effort with both the translation as well as the effort to have the works performed. It was right of Munk when he called him "my knight in the mighty realm." They worked intensely on *Cant* and *An Idealist,* and also got started on *The Word.* Magnus was by then finished with the translation of *Cant.*

Küb bei Payerbach a.d. Südbahn, Austria, June 8, 1932

Dear Kaj Munk

I am now finally finished, or at least to the extent that you can say that a work is finished, though it never really can be; and I of course will and shall continue to try to improve upon it. It was a job that gave me great joy, and that I was able to do with real enthusiasm. All of those fine touches that the play contains, your small salutes to Oehlenschläger* (about the elder tree, and then the neighbor wife's humorous little Morgiana reminiscence in the play's original form) that so pleased me, and I did my very best to get it all out again in German. I have furthermore translated both versions[61] of the play so that the theaters can choose between them, though I suspect that it will be the latter, which definitely supports the play better, rounds out the King's and Cromwell's psychology, and is more dramatic.

Before I was acquainted with that version, I felt there was a shortcoming with the play because Anne's imprisonment was not included. I now have only four copies of the play, and I will

---

* Adam Oehlenschläger (1779-1850), Danish poet and dramatist.

[61] Magnus refers to the changes that Munk made in the play for Axel Illum's provincial tour. The revised manuscript is printed in the 4th edition of *Cant.* Nyt Nordisk Forlag Arnold Busck, Copenhagen, 1932.

send them to the four publishers that are interested. As soon as I get one of them back, I will send it to you and ask you to read it through and write to me with any objections you have to my translation. Before the play gets sent to the theaters, I will go through it one more time. I have already written to Kortner, who at the present time is performing in Vienna, and who in several interviews just yesterday said something about a Danish play that he is interested in– I hope it is Cant.

Sincerely, your devoted
Erwin Magnus

The first of the salutes to Oehlenschläger mentioned in the letters, "the elder tree," occurs in the 4th act of *Aladdin*, where Aladdin's execution, which was averted, is being prepared:

Morgiana: Oh God! My son, shall we now be torn apart?
Aladdin: We'll soon be reunited.
Morgiana: Yes, soon. Farewell until then!
I have now, out behind the Mosque,
By the elder tree behind the old wall,
Where you oft as a boy did play,
Ordered two graves for us, me on the right,
And you on the left side of your father.[62]

In *Cant,* Munk used this salute in the 6th act right after the huntsman's song, where Anne Boleyn is seen sitting in the forest, meditating over her life.

You sweet flower, that winds yourself about,
Twisting boldly 'round the elder's stem,
Yes, I think you understand me. And if now I tore you
From your supporting and uplifting bed,
Then you would die. And that does make me fear.[63]

---

[62] *Aladdin*, op.cit. 4th act, pp. 140-141.
[63] Kaj Munk: *Cant.* NNF, 1st impression, 9 October 1931, 6th act, p. 65.

When writing "the neighbor wife's humorous little Morgiana reminiscence," Magnus was probably thinking about the 3rd act in Aladdin where Morgiana admonishes Aladdin, who wants to marry Princess Gulnare, explaining that equal children play best:

Haven't I told him, ten or twenty times?
Aladdin! Birds of a feather flock together;
A splotchy sow and scabbed boar get on
Best together. Dear son! Tell me, why put
A giant's head on a dwarf's body? [64]

A similar example from the animal kingdom is found in *Cant's* 5th Act, where Martha is afraid that Wolsey will have a hemorrhage if he happens to see the king and queen ride by and, therefore asks the neighbor wife to help her get him into the house:

The neighbor wife—
O Lord, do you believe it,
You mean, just from nervousness?
Yes, the power of memory is great,
A hemorrhage you say,
Well, once we had two sows,
Who were in the same stall, and then it happened,
Lightning struck and hit the one.
And just think, the next time there was thunder
The other fell down and died
With a great crash, though there was no lightning.
It must have been something of the like.[65]

With respect to form, maybe it's not that far between Munk and Oehlenschläger? Munk's enthusiasm for this poet of the golden age can be traced back to his boyhood when he took private lessons

---

[64] Aladdin, op.cit. 3rd act, p. 87.
[65] Kaj Munk, op.cit. 5th act, p.55. This text was changed in all following editions.

from the curate Oscar Geismar[66] in Brandstrup* and received, among other things, his first lessons in German. Instruction in the usual subjects bored them both; but when those were finished, they would start in on what really interested them– drama. Geismar would read aloud for the young pupil.

In his book- *About The Man Kaj Munk*- Geismar wrote: "Never before had Oehlenschläger been talked about and listened to with such a burning passion as in this classroom... For Kaj Munk this room became the gateway to a new and unforgettable world."

In return for those hours Munk would later dedicate his play *An Idealist* to Oscar Geismar.

Küb bei Payerbach a.d. Südbahn, Austria
June 23,1932

Dear Kaj Munk

I have in the meantime made a copy of Cant *so that I could send you one today. I am excited to hear what you think about my translation. I ask that you be quite open about it– I can deal with criticism, and I'm thankful for it. In the meantime I have only heard from one of the four publishers, Felix Bloch Erben,[67] who writes that they do not think chances in Germany are very good, but that Jannings is interested in the play, so they asked if they could send the manuscript to him. I wrote back, and said they should first tell me what his stipulations are. Otherwise it's too easy for a publisher to first send out a play and then take their chances without running any risk. I will tell you as soon as something positive happens. How is it going with* An Idealist? *It's an obvious role for Kortner (to whom I have also sent* Cant).

Sincerely, your devoted
Erwin Magnus

---

[66] Th.D. Oscar Geismar (1877-1950), pastor several places, last at Christianborg Castle 1931-1947, author and literary critic.
* Brandstrup, a small village close to Kaj Munk's boyhood home.
[67] German theatrical publisher

Munk had told Niels Nøjgaard what a wonderful feeling it was to hold the first galley for *An Idealist* in his hands. It must have been a similar experience for him to read *Cant* in German, and he was obviously satisfied with the translation.

Vedersø Vicarage, Ulfborg, June 28, 1932

Dear Erwin Magnus

I told myself at once to set all other work aside so that I could go through your translation of Cant. I thank you so much for it. It is rich in parts that have been squarely hit and retold beautifully. I noted a couple of misunderstandings: on page 8, heiraten– no: made him pure, this word pure is an adjective meaning born in wedlock, in other words to make Richmond the heir to the throne. Page 9, The appearance here tired His Grace, shouldn't it be Her Grace? But these are small things. Now I will hope with all my heart that you (and I) will be pleased by your toil and happy hand. However, we must, without reservation, arm ourselves with patience. Conditions for the theater are (also in Germany I understand) slow; and we must trust that there is no haste for the spirit. I enclose here the revised copy of An Idealist. It is the next to last copy that I have, so I would like to get it back sometime. Personally, as far as the foreign theater is concerned, I have greater faith in An Idealist than I have in Cant. It would make me happy if you could overcome the resistance and achieve a great victory with it.

With heartfelt thanks, and best greetings. Your devoted
Kaj Munk

Playbook for Erwin Magnus' translation of Cant 1932
Reproduced by permission of Gustav Kiepenheuer Publisher
Author's archive

As seen in the following letter, the suggestions by Kaj Munk, so capable in German, were followed.[68]

---

[68] In 2002 Paul Gerhard Schoenborn found a copy of the German edition of *Cant*. The playbook had been in the Gustav Kiepenheuer Archive in Berlin since 1932. The frontispiece: *Cant*, theater play by Kaj Munk, the only authorized translation from the Danish, by Erwin Magnus. Archival copy. Gustav Kiepenheuer Stage Management G.m.b.H. Berlin, Charlottenburg 2, Kantstrasse 10. A copy of the playbook has been available for the writing of this book.

He called them small things, just to be diplomatic, but he was definitely not interested in having any mistakes find their way into his play.[69]

Küb bei Payerbach a.d. Südbahn, Austria
July 4, 1932

Dear Kaj Munk

Many thanks for your friendly letter of June 28th. I am very happy that you are pleased with my translation. I will correct the mistakes that you found as soon as I get a copy back. It would probably be best for now if you could send back your copy, as that one contains many corrections from the first manuscript, and the other two copies have been sent to the actor Kortner, and to the Burg Theater, so it is hard to know when I'll get them back.

I think that An Idealist is a magnificent play in its present form. There is just one thing that I would ask you to consider: right now the play concentrates much more on the relationship between Herod and Mariamne, and that increases its similarity to Hebbel's drama, in particular at the end, except that in Hebbel's play Maria and the infant Jesus do not appear but rather the Three Wise Men. For that reason I'm not sure if it isn't best, anyway, to keep those last two acts, although in a rather shortened version. I would ask you to make your own comparison between Hebbel's Herod and Mariamne and An Idealist. Otherwise, I'll soon get started on the translation.

I am now in negotiation with several publishers concerning Cant, but I can hardly think that it will be possible to get an advance, as times are ten times harder in Germany than in Denmark, and the publishers are afraid (or pretend that they are) that there will be a prohibition against foreign plays in

---

[69] Magnus changed "heiraten" to "legitimierten": "...the fact is this, I have Richmond, Wolsey– a son. Now if one way or another we could make him legitimate...."

In Rolf Lehfeldt's translation of *Cant* in the book: Kaj Munk, Plays, South Schleswig League, ATE Publisher, Münster, 2003, p.215, the same phrase was given another translation: "...look, it's this way, I have Richmond, Wolsey– a son. If we somehow could make him lawfully begotten...."

*Germany, similar to the new Film law, which of course is quite out of the question ***

The ordinary conditions are of course that the publisher gets 20% of performances in Germany and 1/3 of German performances abroad (with German theaters in Austria, Switzerland, Czechoslovakia, etc.). Please let me know if I may write a contract with the publisher that I think will be the best one for us. Only larger and well-known publishers are being considered: Ullstein, Kiepenheuer, Felix Bloch Erben, and Drei Masken Verlag.

I am very interested in hearing about your new play! Sincerely, your devoted

Erwin Magnus

The new play that Magnus wanted to hear more about was *The Word*. Magnus did not yet know the play's title, but two months before its premiere, on September 2, 1932, he knew that Munk had something going on in the theater.

Küb bei Payerbach a.d. Südbahn, Austria

July 14, 1932

Dear Kaj Munk

A well-known German actress visited me yesterday and I read part of An Idealist *for her, including the ending of the play's first version. She was very moved by it, and that reinforces my hope that you will retain the last two acts as they originally were; I am also afraid that the play is now rather short– the performance should last 2 to 2 1/2 hours, not more, but not less either.**

(* In 1934 the Reich Film Law was enacted, instituting rigid censorship requiring that all films be "German" in character, and that directors and actors be of Aryan descent. The German film industry was nationalized in 1937 and was placed under the Minister of Propaganda, Joseph Goebbels.)

I have already started on the translation and have finished the first act. It would be good if you could send me a list of players, which the German theaters absolutely require when a manuscript is presented, as it would be difficult for me to make one because I don't know how the individual characters should be described (for example, Menahem).

The actress mentioned had also seen Cant *performed in Stockholm[70] and had a strong impression of the play, even though she does not understand Swedish. Which version of the play was performed there? She asked for a copy, but I couldn't give her one, as I don't have a single copy left. Now there are three publishers interested in the play. Today I got a letter from Ullstein: 'With respect to Cant, you can expect an answer in the next few days. The play contains, without doubt, considerable qualities.' (a.t.) I heard at one time that you had written a kind of introduction to the play that was printed in the Royal Theater's program pamphlet. Could you send me a copy?*

Sincerely, Erwin Magnus
*Better 2 1/2 than 2 for a play of this magnitude!

When *An Idealist* was again performed at the Royal Theater in 1938, it was in a revised and shortened version. Niels Nøjgaard suggests that Munk made these changes in 1932.[71] They might be the same changes that are mentioned in the two letters above, and in Munk's letter of May 7, 1932 quoted earlier.

The introduction in the Royal Theater's program pamphlet that Magnus requested a copy of has the heading: "The word *Cant.*" In the text, Munk assumes that there were some who disliked having an English title for a Danish play. Maybe it's because they don't know what the word means? Therefore, he used a page to explain

---

[70] *Cant* had its premiere at Dramaten in Stockholm on March 5th, 1932. Harald Mogensen: *Kaj Munk at the Theater.* NNF 1953, p. 31.
[71] Kaj Munk: *Commemorative Edition, Pilate and other Plays.* NNF 1949, p. 224.

that the word "cant" actually means hypocrisy and excused himself by saying that he could not find a title in Danish.[72]

Vedersø, Ulfborg
July 20, 1932

Dear Erwin Magnus

Thanks for the two letters. Travel, and then several days of illness, has kept me from answering you before. I am still a bit weak.

I am thankful for the great interest you have shown for my work. You will have your reward for it!

I enclose here your own manuscript, with thanks, and one of my many changes to An Idealist. Go ahead and make agreements with a German company if you can do it on advantageous terms.

Sincerely
Kaj Munk

It's a fine declaration of confidence that Munk gives to Magnus, who he had never met: the authority to make an agreement with a German publisher as long as he can do it on advantageous terms! It could have turned into a good business for them both.

Küb bei Payerbach a.d. Südbahn, Austria
July 21, 1932

Dear Kaj Munk

It will please you to read Arcadia Publishing's evaluation of Cant, *which they sent to me today:*

'It is a play of unusual magnitude, strict, not immediately inviting, but often spellbinding in the grandeur of the spiritual landscape and in its linguistic form. I believe that the play should be performed in Germany, and that it at least deserves a respectable original performance. The two main roles of Henry

---

[72] "The word Cant." The Royal Theater's program pamphlet. October 1931.

VIII and Anne Boleyn will certainly be of some interest for great actors.' (a.t.)

I therefore ask you to soon tell me if I may sign a contract with the theatrical publisher that I think best suited and that will offer us the best conditions.

As for An Idealist, I'm now finished with 7 acts. I couldn't sleep a whole night because I was so agitated, so enthusiastic.

I hope to hear from you soon.
Sincerely, your devoted
Erwin Magnus

Such a statement from a well-known publisher like Arcadia had increased Munk's hopes for an early appearance on the German stage. Magnus' enthusiasm for *An Idealist* must have been pleasant reading as well.

Vedersø Vicarage, Ulfborg, July 25, 1932

Dear Erwin Magnus

Many thanks for your letter today. You are right, Arcadia's evaluation pleased me. Try now to get something concrete out of it. But, even more than Arcadias' evaluation, it is my acquaintanceship with you that pleases me, your interest for my work, your faith in it, and also your diligent and constant struggle for it!

I can't do otherwise than agree with you: Herod's greatness comes to full force only when we include the rather undramatic act in which he calls forth all of his spiritual forces and all of his abilities in all arenas, to ease his pain.

Sincerely, your devoted
Kaj Munk

Munk is both impressed and thankful for the effort that Magnus makes for his plays. The "undramatic act" mentioned in the letter is Act 9 in *An Idealist*, where Herod tries to repress his sorrow over Mariamne's execution, which he himself had ordered. The dates given for the previous and the following letters can be misleading; but the letters have been given in an order that reflects their contents.

Küb bei Payerbach a.d. Südbahn, Austria
July 25, 1932

Dear Kaj Munk

Thank you for your letter. I think that the present version of An Idealist *is excellent, and I will get started at once on the translation. It will please you to know that the director of the Hamburg Play House, Arnold Marlé,[73] to whom I had sent* Cant, *is very enthusiastic about the play. He has promised to do everything he can to have the play performed there.*

Among the publishers who have shown an interest for Cant *is Eugen Pohl & Co. of Copenhagen. He wrote me that he would like to obtain the rights for several countries, and I answered that he would have to approach you, and that I could only negotiate with him with respect to Germany. I did, however, send him the German manuscript, which he wanted to see, as he might be able to use it as a basis for negotiations with foreign countries. He has now written that he would very much like to have the play for Germany as well, but I don't know anything about his connections with the German theater. Therefore, I wrote to him that there could only be negotiations if he makes a large deposit as a guarantee. I still don't know who would be best to work with: Pohl, if he makes a large deposit, or Ullstein, who most likely won't pay anything in advance but probably has the best connections to all of the bigger German theaters. Do you know Pohl?*

Sincerely, your devoted
Erwin Magnus

Vedersø Vicarage, Ulfborg
July 27,1932

Dear Erwin Magnus

No, I don't know Pohl. However, I agree with you, that if Pohl instead of Ullstein shall have it, then it has to be a rather substantial deposit that gets paid to us in advance. Did I tell

---

[73] Arnold Marlé (1887-1970), Austrian-German actor. Emigrated in 1933 to Czechoslovakia, later to England. Married to Lilly Freud- Marlé. They were both Jews.

you that one evening some months ago I received a phone call
from a Mr. Strakosch[74] in Copenhagen? He told me that he had
succeeded in getting Jannings interested in Henry VIII. *Later*
on, this Strakosch asked me if you had the rights to negotiate
for the play in Germany or just the translation rights. I
answered: the latter. But as I haven't heard from the man
since, we can hardly wait for an answer from his publisher
(could it be Arcadia or which?), so we have to work on this
ourselves. Go ahead and feel free to make agreements
wherever you think it will serve our cause, but I find it to be
unquestionable that a guarantee deposit must be demanded
in all cases; otherwise they could simply diddle away
irresponsibly with the possibilities.

Sincerely, your devoted
Kaj Munk

The letter above clearly shows that there was competition not
only on the national level, but also on the European level, between
those who would help Munk (and themselves) move ahead.

The following is a peculiar letter. Is it a letter from Magnus
missing in the series? It is not clear which of Magnus' questions
that Munk is answering, but it is a dramatic description about how
Herod shall be presented.

Vedersø Vicarage, Ulfborg
July 28, 1932

Dear Erwin Magnus
That bit about Herod was not good!
Otherwise I love him. Yes, when I created him, those were
great days, really great. He was born in a blaze of passion.
Woman after woman snuck in to tempt me, but I held out
bravely. The world was in turmoil, the sores burned, and I
suffered! That is how you must portray him, no other way. I
have been sick today and can barely write. But you have to
know this. During that time I looked up at the stars and prayed

---

[74] Carl Strakosch A/S, Theatrical agent, Copenhagen. Representative for
the Drei Masken Verlag (Three Masks Publisher) in Denmark. Mentioned
in Magnus' first letter to Munk, 17 October 1931.

and prayed, and it helped me. Now I am lying here in bed, staring out of the window. Magnus, it isn't easy to create, but a bird comes and tells me everything I need to know. Now do what you can, and write to me.

Sincerely, your devoted
Kaj Munk

The conditions in Germany were now catastrophic. Six million people were out of work. There was fighting in the streets, where the Nazis fought against the communists and the social democrats. Political murders had become part of everyday life. The time of the Weimar Republic was ebbing out. On July 13, 1932 there was an election for parliament in Germany. The Nazis got 37.4 % of the votes, giving them 230 seats in the parliament, thereby becoming Germany's biggest party.

The scene was now set for a European drama that in cruelty and length would far surpass the plays in the theater. The Third Reich was about to take center stage!

Vedersø Vicarage, Ulfborg
September 10, 1932

Dear Erwin Magnus

Thank you for your beautiful translation of An Idealist. *I have had time to examine a few parts, even though work is overwhelming me almost to the breaking point. Unfortunately, the play is marred by the last two acts lack of concentration. Don't you think they should be shortened even more wherever you find it fitting?*

At the same time I am sending you my last play, [75] which might also be my best. However, it is so typically Danish that a translation is hopeless; then it would have to be a pure re-creation, where the Grundtvigish character, which is so purely national, is recreated in whatever character would be similar in Germany.

Sincerely, your devoted
Kaj Munk

---

[75] Kaj Munk: *Ordet* (*The Word*)

(Magnus received this letter after he had written the following one)

Although Munk thought that a translation of *The Word* was nearly impossible, that did not stop Magnus from getting started on it.

Küb bei Payerbach a.d. Südbahn, Austria
September 11, 1932

Dear Kaj Munk

You are probably wondering why it is taking so long to achieve results in Germany. The situation is that the two publishers that I have concentrated my negotiations with, Arcadia Publishers (Ullstein) and Kiepenheuer, are both very cautious and reticent in regards to taking on a play, and in particular when it is a new author for Germany. They are furthermore very timid when it comes to "historical" plays. On the other hand, it can be an advantage when one of these publishers does offer a play, as their cautiousness is well known, and serves as a kind of guarantee for the theaters.

I had sent the translation of An Idealist *to Arcadia Publishers, but they didn't think much of it. It turned out that Hebbel does in fact stand in the way as far as Germany is concerned.*

I wrote to the publisher that I had read in Politiken *that you have now written a play that deals with a modern subject,[76] and I then received two postcards, which I enclose here, together with my letter concerning* An Idealist *(I ask you to please send them back).*

It would be best now if you would send me your new play as soon as possible (assuming that you have confidence in me, and believe that I am working in the most effective manner for you in Germany), and I'll translate the play at once.

I will probably travel to Vienna on October 1st, where I intend to remain for some time so that I can negotiate personally with the Burg Theater and Reinhardt about Cant *and* An Idealist, *and possibly already about the new play. Theaters in Germany are in no hurry when it comes to*

---

[76] Ibid.

accepting new plays, and I think it is always best to negotiate in person. I haven't yet heard anything definitive from Hamburg either, though in this case I have not done anything to hasten the decision as it would be much better if we could have the premiere performance in Vienna or Berlin.

Does your new play have a feminine role, a "Vamp-like" character? I am a very good friend of Maria Eis,[77] who is engaged with the Burg Theater for just such roles, and I know (the director told me) that they are looking for plays with a role for her.

I hope to hear from you soon, and remain most sincerely, your devoted
Erwin Magnus

The new play that Erwin is talking about is *The Word*, and there is no *Vamp-like* role in it. *The Word* had its premiere performance at the Betty Nansen Theater on September 2nd, 1932. The play was a success for Munk as well as Betty Nansen. For the latter it was also a badly needed financial success. On the same day *The Word* came out in book form. By the end of the year 12,000 copies had been printed.

Vedersø Vicarage, Ulfborg
September 14, 1932

Dear Magnus

That was an interesting collection of letters that you sent to me. Looking at the evaluation of An Idealist, *I had to laugh out loud. It's a shame for you, who have worked so faithfully and enthusiastically, if we don't get anything out of it. I hope you received the new play; but it will be difficult to adapt, while a good deal must be deleted in Act II, and a little in Act I.[78]*

I'll hear from you at some time
Sincerely, your devoted
Kaj Munk

---

[77] Austrian actress
[78] In which Grundtvig is much talked about.

Küb bei Payerbach a.d. Südbahn, Austria
September 15, 1932

Dear Kaj Munk

Thanks for the new play that you sent to me, and best of luck with it! It is a great and true work of poetry. I have read it, and was deeply moved. The impression that it made on me was very strong, as I had written a play about twenty years ago about the Danish Evangelicals.[79] In that play as well there was one who awoke from the dead, in a struggle against God, but only to bear witness to God, and then to die again. The play was accepted in Aalborg, but the director (Svend Wedel)[80] did not dare perform it, as he was afraid of a theater scandal. If you ever have the time, I would like you to read it.

It is unfortunately true when you write that the play, in its present form, could hardly be performed in Germany, where the public doesn't even know who Grundtvig is. But I'll think it over, and try to see if there is some way to rewrite it to suit a German background. I will discuss this with counselor Beth in Vienna, professor with the Protestant Theological Faculty, whose name you might know.

Even if we don't see any chances for having the play performed in Germany, I will still translate it just to show Arcadia Publishers that you are the great poet for whom they can and must make an effort.

I do personally consider you to be the greatest living Scandinavian dramatist, and maybe the greatest dramatist that Denmark has ever had. For that reason I do not regret the rather large job that I have had with Cant *and* An Idealist, *and that I will also have with* The Word, *even if we don't get any actual profit from the latter. Maybe not even* An Idealist *or even* Cant, *which I am sure I can have performed in the German theater, will bring us any great riches.*

---

[79] It has not been possible to find the title or the manuscript to the play mentioned here.

[80] Svend Wedel (1878.1953), actor and theater manager. Leader of the Aalborg Theater 1915-1920.

However, I do ask you for your word, that between you and me there will always be a relationship of trust, as for example that which exists between Shaw and his German translator, Trebitsch, and that which has existed between Strindberg and his translator Schering: that the German translator is now and will always be the poet's representative and spokesperson in Germany, so that for me it will become a life's work to establish you in Germany, as it also was for Schering and Trebitsch with respect to Strindberg and Shaw.

I will now send An Idealist *to Arnold Marlé in Hamburg. If he likes the play, and can arrange a performance there, then he would be the best one to make whatever cuts he might find are necessary.*

Sincerely, your devoted
Erwin Magnus

Magnus, who had a broad knowledge of European drama, was not reluctant to call Munk: "... maybe the greatest dramatist that Denmark has ever had." A similar contemporary understanding of Munk was given by Henning Kehler[81] in an article in *Berlingske Tidende**, where he reviewed several of Munk's plays. About *The Word* he wrote: "...It is a tragicomedy that ends as a mystery. One might try to criticize it by calling it a folk comedy, but then just let them try to write that kind of folk comedy.

But they just can't. It's not so agonizing that farmer Mikkel Borgen's son can't have tailor Peter's daughter, but it is humorous that even tailor Peter considers the alliance to be a huge mistake. The showdown between him and Mikkel Borgen in Act II, however, is not folk comedy, but cultural comedy in the best sense. Such dramatic poetry has not been written in Danish since Holberg** wrote the comedy *Erasmus Montanus.*"[82]

---

* Berlingske Tidende, a large Danish newspaper, Denmark's oldest, founded in 1749

[81] Henning Kehler (1891-1979), MA, journalist, critic, and dramatist.

** Ludvig Holberg, Danish author and dramatist (1684-1754).

[82] "Kaj Munk". Articles by Henning Kehler, I-II, *Berlingske Tidende* 13th and 15th of September 1932.

Vedersø Vicarage, Ulfborg
October 2, 1932

Dear Erwin Magnus

Thanks for your recent beautiful heartfelt letter. It is going great with The Word *at Betty Nansen's, and they're counting on a continuation until Christmas. That of course is Fata Morgana optimism. Oh, so sad, that the adaptation to German is so difficult.*

Yes, dear Magnus, I have been happy with our cooperation so far. I think that you exercise both finesse and care and act with full faith in reaching our goals. I wish for you much joy for being my knight in the mighty realm.

Most sincerely, your devoted
Kaj Munk

All that about the "mighty realm" sounded great, but within a few months Germany became "The Third Reich," a police state where not just political opponents but all who disagreed with the Nazis, were persecuted. This included German citizens of Jewish descent, which meant that Magnus could no longer live in his own country.

Vienna IX, Strudlhofgasse 13
October 7, 1932
c/o Mrs. Rositta David

Dear Kaj Munk

Many thanks for your friendly letter, which came right at that moment today when I had just finished the translation of the last two acts in The Word, *which I then sent to Arcadia Publishers.*

I agreed today with "Neues Wiener Tageblatt" to write an article about you. For that reason I want to learn a little more about Grundtvig's followers and the evangelicals. Do you know of any book in German about this that I might be able to find here in the national library, or do you have a shorter article about the subject that you could lend to me for a while?

I have unfortunately not seen any Danish magazines for a couple of weeks, but I saw from your letter that The Word *is already being performed at the Betty Nansen Theater and has had great success, which you and I had both expected. That makes me very happy, and I send my heartfelt congratulations. Could you perhaps send me the most important reviews?*

Warmest regards, your devoted
Erwin Magnus

Vedersø Vicarage, Ulfborg
October 16, 1932

Dear Erwin Magnus

Many thanks for your last letter. Herewith, I am sending you some clippings about The Word.

Now I have to tell you that I have had to give up. I could no longer deal with all of the business related complications. I have joined the Danish Dramatists' League, at Tietgensgade 30, Copenhagen V, to which you must in the future address all negotiations concerning business affairs.

However, of course I will still be happy, personally, to receive letters from you about what is happening with me abroad.

Sincerely, your devoted
Kaj Munk

[The following was written on the back of the page]

No, I really don't have any articles about Grundtvigism or evangelicals. But, dear Magnus, I have a friend, Th.D. Nøjgaard, Udby, Holbæk, Denmark, who you can most likely get some information from; if you write to him say that I have referred you to him. He is practical and clear.

KM

The Danish Dramatists' League wrote in a letter to Munk on January 4, 1933 that because he had completed a contract with Erwin Magnus on the translation and presentation of his plays to the German stage and publishers, the Danish Dramatists' League could do no more than-

"... sit quietly and wait for Magnus to do his duty. I would advise you to do the same, and in the future not to sign any contracts, as I honestly think that you have been quite unlucky so far, but anyhow, good New Year to you and yours.

Signed Lemkow"[83]

On October 25, 1932, the conservative *Dagens Nyheder**, in an editorial with the heading "Hitler in Decline," predicted that in the coming election for parliament in Germany, Hitler would lose several seats. The editorial also included several quotations from Hitler's speeches:

For that reason Hitler couldn't say anything more unfortunate than when recently, in a campaign speech, he said: 'We will see, however, if there is not some decent way to come to power.' In a decent way? For the storm troopers of the Third Reich, this prescription is just as embarrassing and as unacceptable as the final reply, by which Kaj Munk, in his miracle play [The Word] holds the door open for a natural explanation.

To mention Munk in this editorial seems out of place. The editorial writer otherwise gave a good introduction into the chaotic political situation in Germany, and he furthermore did not believe that Hitler had any political future:

From him [Hitler] and his movement, the industrial and financial magnates are now dropping away, those who had seen in Hitler the fighter and the destroyer of the Marxist politicians, as well as the unions, and who, without any thought, accepted the revolutionary madness to the extent that

---

Dagens Nyheder (Daily News), conservative Danish newspaper (1868-1961).

[83] Victor Lemkow (1882-1954), director for the Danish Dramatists' League. KMF Archive.

they saw Hitler as a naive fool. In reality they were correct in both of their calculations.

First of all, Hitler had paralyzed and destroyed the Social Democrats for years to come. Moreover, as it turned out, there really wasn't any danger with the revolutionary Hitler... large-scale industry's money paid to Hitler was not a bad investment. But now it is enough. Now it would be more natural, and at least without risk, to put them in von Papen's[84] campaign coffers.

Three months later Hitler became the Reich Chancellor and von Papen his deputy.

The *Dagens Nyheder's* editorial writer considered Hitler to be a useful idiot, whom one had no reason to fear. At the same time a certain conservative enthusiasm for Hitler's victory over the Social Democrats can be sensed in the article.

In an answer to the article above, Munk asked briefly, in the same newspaper on October 27, 1932, if one should not leave that kind of "expose" to *Politiken*. *Politiken's* editorial board, which is described by Kaj Munk as "stultifying," included editor Svend Borberg,[85] one of Munk's harshest critics. It certainly did not suit Munk to be named in that article.

And with the election of parliament that is mentioned here, on November 6, 1932, the Nazis received fewer votes than in the election in July, but with 196 seats in the parliament remained Germany's strongest party. The three largest parties– the Nazis, the Communists, and the Social Democrats– could no longer work together. The political chaos in Germany continued for a couple of months longer.

---

[84] Franz von Papen (1879-1969), politician with the liberal centrists party, Reich chancellor June to November 1932, Hitler's vice chancellor 1933-1934.

[85] Svend Borberg (1888-1947), Danish dramatist, journalist, and critic.

Chapter 4

The New Germany 1933

The prospect of imminent political upheaval in Germany had not discouraged the energetic Magnus, but that he continued to live in Austria was a sign that he had suspicions about what could happen in Germany. His wife Margarete Magnus, son Michael, and daughter from his first marriage Inge Magnus, continued to live in Berlin. The last Christmas in the crumbling Weimar Republic was approaching. On December 22, 1932 Magnus was in Austria, where he wrote a short Christmas greeting to Munk:

Author Kaj Munk
Merry Christmas
Erwin Magnus

After the start of the New Year Magnus received a letter from Kiepenheuer with good news that he at once sent on to Vedersø.

Vienna IX, Liechteneinstr. 119
January 2, 1933

Dear Kaj Munk
Even though I am not supposed to send you business related messages, I think you will be happy to know that I received a letter today from Kiepenheuer in which he writes as follows: 'Today we have the pleasure to inform you that Emil Jannings, to whom we had sent the book, has sent us an enthusiastic telegram and asked us to reserve the play (i.e. Cant) *for him in Berlin and Vienna. He's coming to Berlin on Tuesday, and has already made Hilpert aware of the play for the Volksbühne.'[86]*
(a.t.)

---

[86] Volksbühne, a famous theater in Berlin, originally founded by the labor movement's league, sometime around 1890.

Sending you the most heartfelt wishes for a good 1933
I remain your devoted
Erwin Magnus

Magnus sent Munk "the most heartfelt wishes for a good 1933," and for Munk, as far as the theater goes, it did become a good year. In the years 1932 and 1933 his plays *Cant* and *The Word* were together performed 669 times in Scandinavia.[87] Munk was known in all of Scandinavia, and with Magnus' help would become just as well known in the German speaking areas of Europe. The fact that Emil Jannings, Germany's most famous actor, was so interested in *Cant* that he asked for sole rights to the play in two capital cities, would facilitate negotiations with the theaters there.

Vedersø vicarage, Ulfborg.
New Year 1933

Dear Erwin Magnus

It's been such a long time since I'd gotten a sign of life from you; and therefore the two that finally came were especially welcome. The Christmas greeting I return with a hearty 'Happy New Year,' and your postcard yesterday filled me with great delight; I can hardly tell you what an experience I expect if it all really takes place, such is my respect and admiration for Jannings.

I thank you, dear Magnus, for all the good that we have shared so far, and I hope that the future will hold much joy for us to share.

Your devoted
Kaj Munk

The future did hold a lot, but it wasn't pure pleasure. For Magnus and his Jewish companions, 1933 did not turn out to be a good year. After a month of political negotiations, on January 30, 1933, the president of the Reich, Paul von Hindenburg, appointed Adolf Hitler as Reich Chancellor. With the new chancellor came the

---

[87] Harald Mogensen, *Kaj Munk paa Teatret* (*Kaj Munk at The Theater*). NNF 1953, p.8

beginning of 12 years of cruel persecution and death for, among others, Germany's 500,000 Jews. That fateful appointment that would lead to the Second World War, leaving, at its end, chaotic conditions not only in Europe, but also in other parts of the world.

In the next letter Magnus wrote, among other things, about his good connections with the Playhouse in Hamburg where his brother-in-law, Arnold Marlé, was stage director. This good connection didn't last long. Marlé was a Jew and had to leave the theater a couple of months later.

> *Vienna IX, Liechtensteinstr. 119*
> *February 11, 1933*

Dear Kaj Munk

I would have written to you long ago, if only there had been anything positive to say, but, unfortunately, there is still nothing. The theater's mill grinds slowly; and although there are many expressions of recognition from some of the larger theaters, they are all still waiting. Hamburg, for example, where I have especially good connections and where Peter Freuchen's[88] play Osakrak[89] *has just been a great success, has written that they think* Cant *is excellent, but that they cannot stage such a large play this year. As the Playhouse in Hamburg is the only theater in Hamburg that can put on such a large stage performance they feel that they can easily wait until next year before they decide. The German Folk Theater in Vienna will probably conclude a contract as soon as they have made arrangements with Jannings, but he is doing a film abroad at this time. I have in the meantime been able to get the Burg Theater interested in* An Idealist, *and the director has promised that he would read it himself. I am almost finished with* The Word– *it is that play that we might begin with in Germany.*

---

[88] Peter Freuchen (1886-1957), Danish polar explorer and author.

[89] Peter Freuchen's play, *Osakrak,* based on the novel *Great Hunter (Storfanger),* was translated into German by Erwin Magnus, who had translated several of Freuchen's books into German.

Right now I'm reading old Flavius Josephus,[90] inspired by your An Idealist *and Feuchtwanger's* Jewish War *(have you read the book?). I think it's full of Biblical drama that would be just something for you. For example, I think "Saul" is a character that is crying out for dramatization. If you look behind the scenes and use your imagination, then you will discover quite another Saul than the one the Bible talks about. It is the brave and naive man that Samuel tries to exploit as an obedient tool. When Samuel finds out that Saul has a will of his own and is not as bloodthirsty as he thought, he starts scheming, and sets David,* a young guy glowing with artifice, against him. Saul's suspicion of David is completely justified, and he is not so dumb that he doesn't see what's going on. His own children, his daughter, who is married to David, and his son Jonathan, are taking part in the scheme against their father, who in the end is deposed by the priest, who represents the always-victorious church. (I don't know if you, as a man of the church, will approve of this interpretation?)*

Do you have anything new in the works?

I hope to hear from you again soon. Sincerely, your devoted Erwin Magnus

*It is that David who would later send Uriah to his death.

(Handwritten note added).

This letter was a direct invitation to dramatize the Biblical stories about David and Saul. And that's what Munk did; on June 7, 1933 he sent a play to Professor Hans Brix[91] with a note: "Dear Professor Hans Brix. Is this junk any good?"[92] The play was *The Chosen* (*De Udvalgte*), about David and Bathsheba.

In his reference to *The Chosen* Niels Nøjgaard wrote: "If he found inspiration in his travels is hard to say, but he was soon at work on a great new play with religious content. [*The Chosen*]"[93]

---

[90] Flavius Josephus (approx. 38-100), Jewish historian.

[91] PhD Hans Brix (1870-1961), Danish literature historian, literary censor at the Royal Theater.

[92] Hans Brix, *Hurtig svandt den lyse Sommer* (*Swiftly Paled the Shining Summer*) WST 1946, p.136

[93] Niels Nøjgaard, op.cit., p.247.

The travels mentioned were Munk's theater trips to London and Berlin in the spring of 1933. According to Niels Nøjgaard, Munk started work on a play about Saul in November 1933.[94]

Even though Munk often used Biblical themes, he had written in his memoirs that he had only had a vague idea that the purpose of his life was that he should dramatize the great figures from the Bible.[95] Therefore, it is remarkable that just four months after Magnus had suggested that he write a play about David that he would be finished with *The Chosen* and in November would begin on *King Saul*, which would remain unfinished. Munk, of course, knew the characters and themes in the play in advance, but perhaps the letter from Magnus had induced him to take up his pen.

Munk delivered *The Chosen* to the Royal Theater in the summer of 1933, where it was at once accepted and put on the playbill. It had its premiere on November 9, 1933.

The well-known Swedish painter professor Isaac Grünewald (1889-1946) made the sensational decorations in *The Chosen.* [96] Grünewald was of Jewish descent, and it sounded like a form of Scandinavian anti-Semitism when his critics called his art degenerate and primitive.[97]

The Chosen was not a success. It received generally negative press and was only played 22 times at the Royal Theater. After its theater premiere the noted critic Svend Borberg, among others, wrote that Calderon had treated the subject of David and Bathsheba much better.[98]

The day after its premiere, *The Chosen* came out in book form, and Borberg again compared it with Calderon's David play[99] that had been staged two years earlier in Copenhagen by a Jewish

---

[94] Niels Nøjgaard, op.cit., p.258.

[95] Kaj Munk: *Foraaret saa sagte kommer -Erindringer* p. 240.

[96] Kirsten Jacobsen, *Johannes Poulsen som iscenesætter (Johannes Poulsen as producer).* Rhodos Publisher 1990, p. 139 and pp. 168-169.

[97] Introduction to the exhibition, Sigrid Hjertén and Isaac Grünewald. Arken, Museum of Modern Art 2002.

[98] Pedro Calderon de la Barca (1600-1681), Spanish dramatist.

[99] Svend Borberg, "*De Udvalgte*– Kaj Munks nye Skuespil virkede kedeligt og tomt" (*The Chosen*–Kaj Munk's new play was boring and vacuous). *Politiken*, 10 November 1933.

theater ensemble.[100] Borberg wrote at the end, "Munk's work always reminds you so much of the work of others."[101]

A. Drewsen Christensen devoted a whole chapter of his book to the genesis of *The Chosen,* which he experienced at close hand with Munk, and he does not mention anything about any influence from other persons or other plays.[102] No mention of Calderon's play has been found in Munk's texts.

The dramatist and critic Carl Gandrup[103] wrote an article in *Forum* about the approaching theater season. In it he continued Borberg's insinuation that Munk always "borrowed" from others:

Great expectations are quite naturally held for pastor Kaj Munk's Old Testament drama about King David and Bathsheba. It's called The Chosen. *His first drama, about Herod and Mariamne (called* An Idealist*), was a great disappointment for both the theater and its actors. This delightful subject was, after all, treated so much better and lovelier by Friedrich Hebbel. His first big success was with* Cant *(Henry VIII and Anna Boleyn), a very tactless extract of Francis Hackett's* great monograph.*

About *The Word,* he thought: "The play's inner format was actually quite small, although the questions asked were significant."[104]

---

*Francis Hackett (1883-1962), Irish author and critic. Wrote a biography of Henry VIII in 1929, and of Anne Boleyn in 1939.

[100] The play mentioned here is Calderon's *Absalom's Locks,* played by the Habima players under the title *King David's Throne.* (Absalom, King David's son, see the Old Testament, II Samuel, chapter 18).

[101] Svend Borberg, "Bavl og Savl" (Twaddle and Drool). *Politiken* 11 November 1933.

[102] A. Drewsen Christensen: *Kaj Munk paa Tomandshaand* (*Kaj Munk, One on One*). Poul Branner Publisher 1947, pp. 61-75.

[103] Carl Gandrup (1880-1936), Danish dramatist and critic.

[104] Carl Gandrup, "Gyldne og kongelige løfter for sæsonen der kommer" (Golden and Royal Promises for the Coming Season). *Forum, Magazine for the Theater,* August 1933, p. 12.

After the premiere of *The Chosen,* Gandrup wrote a review in *The Social Democrat* with the heading: "God's Words from Vedersø." He found absolutely nothing useful in the play.[105] Munk had the review sent to him and then wrote to Gandrup that "it had gone into the stove and up in flames, so what should he do now?"

Gandrup answered in a new article:

Whether you bother to read my articles, or prefer to use them as fuel for your stove, or for another intimate hygienic purpose, is of absolutely no importance to me. I did not, after all, write it to amuse or annoy you but simply to express my resentment that so many of our best artists from the national stage have had to waste time and energy on this terribly boring and sexually charged product of speculation from your hand. Your most respectful, Carl Gandrup.[106]

In a "rejoinder" in *Forum,* Gandrup praised Borberg's review of *The Chosen:*

The power and daring, the well analyzed clarity and brilliant stylistic art whereby he [Borberg] recently told the truth– the real truth– about the impudent and unappetizing little Munk from Vedersø and his extremely boring, sexually laden mess, that most of all reminds one of an insane opera, will force us to stand, with hat in hand, the next time we meet S.B. [Svend Borberg] in a Roman bath! A better and more fitting theater review has not been written in the Danish language since Aaron's almond rod blossomed.[107]

In the following year, 1934, Carl Gandrup wrote the play *It Is Never Enough* about the persecution of Jews in Germany. It will be

---

[105] Carl Gandrup, "Guds Ord fra Vedersø" (The Word of God from Vedersø), *Social Democrat,* feature article 2-December 1933.

[106] Carl Gandrup, "Lille muntert Efterspil" (A Merry Little Sequel), *Social Democrat,* feature article 22 December1933.

[107] "Hr. Carl Gandrups Duplik "(Mr. Carl Gandrup's Rejoinder) *Forum, Magazine for the Theater,* December 1933, pp. 9-13.

discussed at greater length in the chapter about Munk's play, *He Sits at the Melting Pot,* on the same subject.

I don't know how Svend Borberg and Gandrup got on with each other, but in their views on Munk and his dramas they had found common ground. The four articles by Carl Gandrup, from which quotations have been given here, are all from 1933, the year in which Munk found real acceptance in the Danish theater world. Borberg and Gandrup were both playwrights. Munk, who was in demand in theaters in Denmark and all of Scandinavia, was also a competitor. On the question of whether or not he felt wronged by the criticism, Munk said in an interview at the time:

> *There can be critics who have disreputable motives, and there can be political viewpoints or personal grudges mixed into an opinion. For example, Svend Borberg has always been on my back.*[108]

Borberg grumbled about that statement the next day in *Politiken.*[109] On the same day Munk had a "disclaimer" in the *Berlingske Evening* edition:

> *I have been told that a theater reviewer in a local morning paper had complained that I had mentioned him by name in an interview in the* Berlingske Evening *edition as one who was constantly hounding me. This mistake must be politely denounced. For the first, such a statement would not be in agreement with the facts, and furthermore the writings by the reviewer in question about me and my plays have become so totally irrelevant to me that I no longer waste my time on them, or him.*[110]

---

[108] "I Dag er jeg 30 Gange klogere end i Gaar" (Today I am 30 times wiser than yesterday), says Kaj Munk in an interview in Berlingske Tidende, 10 November 1933.

[109] Svend Borberg, "Twaddle and Drool", review of Kaj Munk's play *The Chosen*, which was published in book form by NNF 1933, *Politiken* 11 November 1933.

[110] "Svar til Hr. Borberg fra Kaj Munk" (An answer to Mr. Borberg from Kaj Munk) *Berlingske Evening* edition, 11 November 1933.

The intellectual elite of Denmark used a brutal language at the time. In an article about critics and their reviews, Rikke Rottensten referred to the harsh criticism of Munk's play, *An Idealist*, from 1928, and wrote: "Such a deadly blow could easily have written Munk out of Danish theater history even before he had gotten into it if he had been weaker in spirit and mental fortitude or if those in the theater had been." The article closes with a warning:

Even with the benefit of hindsight one cannot say that the reviewers were completely wrong about what they saw that evening at the Royal Theater, but they can be criticized for one thing: their tone. There are living people behind all art and that should be in the consciousness of every reviewer when he sits down to work. They should, as reviewers, never be afraid to have an opinion of something, for then they would become meaningless; but they should be aware of their tone. Theater reviewers in particular! For each evening a group of actors has to deliver to a new public the play that the reviewers have murdered.[111]

On February 27, the Reichstag building in Berlin was set ablaze, supposedly the work of the Dutch communist Marinus van der Lubbe. The National Socialists (Nazis) used this episode as fuel for propaganda against the KPD (the communist party in Germany). The KPD, together with the social democrats, would soon be eliminated with the help of the new law enacted on March 31, 1933, "The Enabling Law." This law gave Hitler the power to rule without authorization by the parliament. Nazi rule had become a reality.

The new times in Germany could also be felt in the world of the theater as can be seen in the remarks by Magnus in the following letter, where he writes about " The new direction of the German Theater." Here, as everywhere else, the national socialists had installed the party faithful in the leadership; but even Kiepenheuer's belief that, "for the time being," it would be

---

[111] "Tænk på tonen" (Watch your tone) Rikke Rottensten, *Kristeligt Dagblad* 28 June 2005.

impossible to stage a play with Jewish content, gives an impression of the turbulent conditions in Germany. Nobody realized that "for the time being" would stretch out over 12 years.

Vienna I. Bartensteingasse 13

Pension Rathaus

March 1, 1933

Dear Kaj Munk

I moved to the address above today, and the first letter that I received here was– I take it as a good omen– the happy message that the German Theater's new management in Berlin is very interested in Cant *and that they are now negotiating with Jannings. However, Jannings feels that a large role for him is missing in the play's second act. Can and will you write it for him? I beg you to answer me at once! I believe that if you can grant Jannings' wish, then the matter will be settled.*

I finished the translation of The Word *the day before yesterday, and I believe that I have found the right adaptation for Germany, as everything that was about Grundtvig has been deleted, and it is now about the differences between the Lutherans and the pietists. I had thought about sending my translation to you at once, but then a letter came yesterday from a man in Budapest who is interested in your plays. He represents one of the large theaters in New York– I unfortunately cannot say which one now, as his letter is packed away in one of my suitcases.*

So I sent him Cant *and* The Word *(which I consider to be especially well suited for America). I did not have a copy of* An Idealist, *but I wrote to him about the play.*

Kiepenheuer, by the way, is very enthusiastic about An Idealist, *and there are several who have read the play who think it's better than* Cant. *Kiepenheuer just thinks that it will be impossible to stage any play with Jewish content (!) in Germany at this time! However, I hope that I will be able to have it staged here at the Burg Theater.*

When will we get something new from you? Don't be impatient because it is taking so long in Germany; if I am not mistaken, it took a good ten years before Shaw's translator, Trebitsch, was able to get him established in Germany. You

know that I have faith in you, and that faith will give me the
strength to convince the German theater.

So, please write soon to your devoted
Erwin Magnus

Making changes to his original plays was, as mentioned earlier, not something that Munk relished.

Munk was on a "theater trip" in February and March of 1933, traveling over London and Paris and ending in Berlin, where he wrote to Magnus:

Christl. Hospiz, Mittelstrasse 5-6, Berlin NW. 7
March 16, 1933

My dear champion

Thanks for your letter, which I have just received. I have in fact been in London and Paris, not to sell my plays as some believe, as I don't lift a finger for that– I have not spoken with anyone – but to see what's being done in the world's theaters; and they are not making anything there that's better than I can make, and for that reason I'm not making anything.

First I want to congratulate you with your Hamburgian Freuchen success, and I was very happy that it went so well. And it pleases and excites me that you have managed to recreate The Word, *as there must have been some rewriting, as translation would not have been enough. How great and joyful it would be for both of us if we could travel together in the big wide world with just that play.*

You write: 'don't be impatient.' No, just be at ease. You are a man who I have faith in and that is enough for me. I am not that eager about having my plays set up. As long as I can get them written! That is the main thing for me.

As far as Cant *and Jannings are concerned, I have just one answer: The actor must learn that the plays are written for their own sake and not for his, that he is there for the play's sake and not for his own.*

I did once undertake to make revisions in a finished play; in fact it was Cant– *and I would never do that again.*[112] *Jannings should be happy and thankful to have a good play to perform in again after that junk his previous endeavors were about; for example Nero in 'Quo Vadis.'*

If Jannings will do me the honor and pleasure (and himself the favor), together with other talented artists, to play Cant *as it is, then I am happy. However, if it has to be, then I can also be happy without it.*

With many, many good greetings, your devoted
Kaj Munk

That his colleague and Falster* resident Peter Freuchen's play had been a success in Hamburg pleased Munk.

Munk had faith in Magnus' ability to recreate *The Word;* and he wished that they both "could travel together in the big wide world with just that play," *Cant,* written with his heart's blood, a play with roots in his experiences as a child and youth on Lolland*, where several of the play's characters originated.[113] It was primarily *The Word* that Kaj Munk wanted to succeed. And the style in the well-formulated, and ironically quite self-appreciative, last paragraph was typical Munk.

The numerous performances of *Cant* and *The Word* in Denmark and the other Nordic countries had been effective in attracting theatrical publishers. Even to the extent that Kiepenheuer had sent the manager of their theater publisher to Munk's hotel in Berlin to speak with him. Munk was not there, but Julius Berstl left the following letter:

---

* Lolland and Falster, two large islands in south eastern Denmark.

[112] Munk had, however, changed the manuscript of *An Idealist.* Possibly in consideration of the translation.

[113] *Understrømmen, En bog om Lolland og Falster (Undercurrents, A Book about Lolland and Falster)* Bent Vinn Nielsen and Gorm Rasmussen (ed.), Gyldendal 2006, p.126.

Christl. Hospiz, Mittelstrasse 5-6, Berlin NW. 7
March 18, 1933

Honorable pastor!

I have just heard through Mr. Erwin Magnus that you are in Berlin. Unfortunately I did not get to meet you here at the Hospiz. It would please me if you could visit us at the publisher's office (Charlottenburg, Kantstr. 10, close to the train station by the zoo). Among the publishers managers, on Monday you can meet Dr. Landshoff, and on Tuesday me as well. I would be grateful if you could call us on the phone in advance, and inform us of your visit.

With best regards
Julius Berstl (a.t.)

A short time after writing this letter, Julius Berstl and Dr. Fritz Landshoff, who were both Jews, had to leave Germany.[114] Dr. Fritz Landshoff, who was a leading figure in the German publishing business, became a manager at a publishing house in Holland after 1933. After WWII he received an honorary doctorate at the Free University in Berlin.

The letter is dated March 18, 1933. Two days later the chief of police in Munich, Heinrich Himmler, started Germany's first concentration camp in Dachau. It was established in a former explosives factory.

During the stay in Berlin mentioned above, Kaj Munk wrote the article "The New Germany," which was printed in *Jyllands-Posten* on March 26, 1933. Munk describes the enthusiasm felt in Germany after the National Socialists, and thereby Hitler, had taken power.

There were flaming words in all the newspapers about Germany's reconstruction, words ringing out about the rise of the Fatherland from every loudspeaker, and there are a lot of loudspeakers in Germany now!

---

[114] A letter from business manager Dr. Maria Müller-Sommer. Gustav Kiepenheuer Theater Publisher Ltd., 23 June 2004, with information about Julius Berstl and Fritz Landshoff.

There was talk everywhere about the new times for the German people. Munk went on to write that people were enchanted by the "barker in the coachman's seat, by his powerful lungs, and constant broadside balladry." But what had he accomplished other than whipping up a hatred for Jews, communists, and social democrats? And what if it's all true? If the Jew's thriftiness and the socialist's "accommodating" ideals of equality were preparing the way for communism, and if it could not be stopped in any other way than with Hitler's help, then Munk preferred Hitler to the communists. Munk was not at all dismissive of the "new" taking place in Germany, but he was careful and closed with: "For now the future has the word. Berlin. The Parliament's opening day, March 1933 [March 21, 1933 in Garnison's Church in Potsdam]."

The next day, March 27, *Berlingske Tidende* printed an article by Munk: "Germany and Hauptmann von Köpenick." Munk was thinking back to June of 1931, when he saw *Der Hauptmann von Köpenick (The Captain of Köpenick)* at the German Theater in Berlin. Munk was pondering over the current situation in the country and found that the play was just as relevant to the new Germany. Carl Zuckmayer's play was about a poor shoemaker who rented a captain's uniform, took charge of a random squad of soldiers in the street, and with their help emptied the safe at the city hall in Köpenick. It was a humoresque over the respect for uniforms in Germany at the time (The idea for the play came from a real event.* in Berlin in 1906). Munk believed that it could have had a preventative effect if it had been played in 1913-1914 before WWI.

---

*On October 16, 1906, a German impostor named Wilhelm Voigt, masquerading as a Prussian military officer in a stolen uniform, went to the local army barracks in the Berlin district of Koepenick, stopped four grenadiers and a sergeant on their way back to barracks, and told them to come with him. Indoctrinated to obey officers without question, they followed. He dismissed the commanding sergeant to report to his superiors and later commandeered 6 more grenadiers from a shooting range. Then he took the soldiers to the Köpenick city hall and told them to cover all exits. He had the town secretary Rosenkranz and mayor Georg Langerhans arrested for suspicion of crooked bookkeeping and confiscated 4000 marks and 70 pfennigs.

In his book *Munk*, Per Stig Møller sets forth a similar idea that an American film, based on *He Sits at the Melting Pot*, "could have opened the world's eyes" to the persecution of Jews in Germany. There had been negotiations between the film company MGM and Munk in 1938-39, but nothing came of them.[115]

Both Møller's and Munk's thoughts are appealing, though it is doubtful that a play in 1913, or a film shortly before WWII, could have had any influence over the course of politics in Europe.

In Hitler's Germany you could no longer perform a play that ridiculed uniforms. "Where is the Captain of Köpenick now? I don't dare write the answer for fear that *Berlingske Tidende* might be 'put on leave.' But in short, uniforms are again in control in Zuckmayer's Germany," wrote Kaj Munk. He recommends having a very brave theater manager stage the play in Germany in 1933, and then one would see "to what extent we have become 'Uniforms'."* Munk had noticed the enormous number of uniformed people in Germany and understood the danger of so much regimentation, which is always the objective of uniforms. Munk believed that when Germany's present crisis was over, the Germans would remember *The Captain of Köpenick* and learn its lesson when they "...build up their great and vibrant future."

As in the two previous articles, it was the same theater trip that Kaj Munk wrote about in "A Little News from the World's Theaters" in *Berlingske Tidende* on April 12, 1933. It was again an article with a mixture of theater and politics. Munk was a bit disappointed with the theater performances in London, among others a Shakespearean play. When he arrived on the continent in Berlin and saw the play *Much Ado About Nothing* by William Shakespeare, he thought that the play had been performed better in Berlin.

---

[115] Per Stig Møller: *Munk*. Gyldendal 2000, p. 213.

* In the Danish text Munk indirectly references Henrik Ibsen's play *Ghosts* (*Gengangere*), which could also be translated as "zombies." Here, "uniform" represents empty uniforms, as it seemed that they had become more important than the people inside them, which is what *The Captain of Köpenick* is all about.

Munk continued to discuss the theater in Berlin, including the German Theater, where they were playing Hugo von Hofmannsthal; *Greater Theater of the World* (Das Grosse Welttheater).[116]

Munk was more worried about what was happening in real life, which he described as "The Great Theater of the World." Things were happening fast:

> *Bank closures in New York, a revolt in Greece, earthquakes in Japan, and war in China. And in the intimate theaters: Einstein in Exile, Reinhardt banished, rats Murdered, and Hitler kicking the Jews (who, as usual, duck and sneak away behind the curtain and sit down quietly on the money bags), while the Deutsch Mark turns pale and gets sick.*

Even in Copenhagen a grotesque "play" was performed: A Danish association obeyed a request from a foreign envoy– not very sensible of the association or of the envoy.

The reason that Munk wrote about Einstein, Reinhardt, and the Jews, who Hitler was kicking around, was the so-called Jewish boycott on April 1, 1933. It was the first action planned against the Jews after the Nazis took power. The Nazi press wrote that this "was just a general rehearsal,"[117] and they were right. Throughout the thirties, the Nazis continued taking all civil rights away from the Jews. By the afternoon of April 1, 1933 newspapers were already reporting on the civil unrest in Germany. *Lollands Tidende* (a provincial newspaper from the island of Lolland) printed a telegram from Berlin saying that action against the Jews had begun in full force by 10 a.m. Nazi storm troopers [SA] drove around the city and encouraged people to participate in the campaign against Jewish businesses. On the same day the streetcars and trains were decorated with flags, but that was because of Bismarck's birthday.

Munk's unfortunate remark about the Jews who "snuck out and sat down on the money bags" also had some consequences. In a

---

[116] Hugo von Hofmannsthal (1874-1929), Austrian dramatist.
[117] Frederich V. Grunfeld, *Die deutsche Tragödie, Adolf Hitler und das Deutsche Reich 1918-1945 in Bildern,* Hoffman and Campe Publisher 1975, p. 174 (*The German Tragedy, Adolf Hitler and the German Reich 1918-1945 in Pictures*).

short article, author Julius Magnussen reproached Munk with harsh words for having achieved a quick laugh at the expense of the German Jews.[118] In an equally short answer, and with even harsher words, Munk answered that he had, in the article, touched upon "the possibility of a connection between the faltering Mark and Germany's persecution of the Jews. My view on this [persecution of Jews] appeared in the same article, where I spoke with indignation about The Society of 1916."[119] The correct name of the society mentioned was *The Company of 1916*.[120]

The events surrounding *The Company of 1916*, which Munk called "a grotesque," is a story that, for several reasons, should be told here.

It is about the relationship between Germany and Denmark just two months after Hitler had taken power and about the relationship to the Jews from both German and Danish sides. The story's central person, Lilly Freud-Marlé,[121] was Erwin Magnus' sister-in-law.

---

[118] "A Question for Kaj Munk", Julius Magnussen, *Berlingske Evening* edition, 15 April 1933.

[119] "An Answer", Kaj Munk, *Berlingske Evening* edition, 18 April 1933.

[120] Carl Roos, *Indhøstningens Tid, Livserindringer* Bind 2 (*The Time to Harvest, Memoirs*, Volume 2) G.E.C. Gads Publishing, Copenhagen 1961, On page 140 Carl Roos writes about *The Company of 1916*, of which he was foreman from 1931 until 1933: "An association which was founded during WWI to counter the very common hatred for everything German. The association's program: to work for a reciprocal knowledge between the two peoples and thus to foster a sympathetic understanding".

[121] Lilly Freud-Marlé (1888-1970), Austrian actress, married to the above-mentioned actor Arnold Marlé. Lilly Freud-Marlé's sister, Margarete Freud, was married to Erwin Magnus. The two sisters were Sigmund Freud's nieces. Information from the Freud family tree, made available by the Sigmund Freud Private Foundation, Vienna. See the biographies.

Under the heading "The German Recitalist at the University," a small notice was printed in *Berlingske Tidende* on April 4th, 1933:

> *Last night the well-known German recitalist, Lilly Freud-Marlé, spoke about Rainer Maria Rilke.*[122] *After a warm introduction by professor Carl Roos,*[123] *the lady held the interested listeners spellbound by telling them a little about the life of the strange poet. With her clear bright voice she occasionally recited one of Rilke's more accessible poems, told about his relationship to J.P.Jacobsen* and Copenhagen, and vividly recounted her own meeting with the poet.*

As foreman for *The Company of 1916*, Professor Carl Roos had also arranged a Rilke evening with Lilly Freud-Marlé at *The Company* on April 7. This arrangement was cancelled on April 5. The next day, April 6, *Berlingske Evening* edition ran an article with a partial explanation of the story. Under the heading "Disruption on the Board of *The Company of 1916*, the paper wrote that Roos had received a message from *The Company's* secretary that the recital must be cancelled due to a demand from "outside". Roos then demanded that a board meeting be held, which occurred on April 1. He demanded a vote on whether or not *The Company* should be independent or if external forces working on behalf of a certain cause should control it. The majority voted to cancel the evening with Lilly Freud-Marlé, and Roos resigned his post as foreman. Board members Ph.D. Torben Krogh and D.Tech Holger Schmidt also resigned.

---

*   J.P.Jakobsen (Jens Peter Jakobsen) Danish author (1847-1885).

[122] Rainer Maria Rilke (1875-1926), Austrian poet.

[123] Professor Carl Roos (1884-1962), Danish philologist, PhD, professor in German at the University of Copenhagen. The year before, in April 1932, Roos had arranged a Goethe evening with Lilly Freud-Marlé in recital. (Letters from Roos to Lilly Freud-Marlé, 15,24,28 of February 1932. The Royal Library, Carl Roos 2574 I,B,1).

Board member Julius Bomholt,[124] a Member of Parliament, was not present, and could not be contacted. Roos spoke about the cancellation to the newspaper saying, "I regret it for the sake of *The Company*, and I regret it because it can give the impression that in Denmark we allow ourselves to be influenced by anti-Semitic movements in Germany."

Lilly Freud-Marlé (1888-1970)
Michael Freud-Magnus, Private Archive

In the article "The Commotion in The Company of 1916" in *Berlingske Tidende* on April 7, a declaration by the company's

---

[124] Julius Bomholt (1896-1969), B.D., Minister of Culture, author.

four remaining board members concerning the cancellation of the Lilly Freud-Marlé recital and the ensuing unrest on the board was discussed. The German envoy[125] had, through *The Company's* secretary, directed a friendly request to *The Company's* foreman[126] that in the interest of *The Company* the planned lecture be cancelled. The declaration also stated "It seems to us quite an unreasonable idea that a Danish-German society should not be on speaking terms with the German government's representative in the country." They wanted peace and quiet about *The Company*, and no sensationalism, the declaration said, and further "... that *The Company's* eighth board member, member of parliament Julius Bomholt, had also resigned on April 6th."[127]

The episode surrounding this cancellation clearly shows how much influence the German envoy had, as well as the cheek to dictate that a certain artist could not perform in a neutral neighbor country. However, German anti-Semitism seemed to be acceptable

---

[125] Dr. Herbert Samuel Siegfried Baron von Richthofen, Germany's envoy to Denmark from 1930 until 1936.

[126] In his memoirs, Roos writes that the German envoy, through *The Company's* secretary, had informed him that he would consider it to be a "an unfriendly behavior toward him personally," if the play was not cancelled. Carl Roos: *Indhøstningens Tid. Livserindringer* Bind 2, G.E.C. Gads Publishing, Copenhagen 1961, p. 142.

[127] In the article " Not without Ulterior Motives" in *Berlingske Tidende*, 13 February 2000, Per Stig Møller discussed the affair around "The Company of 1916." He wrote "On the board of directors were, among others, the Social Democratic Member of Parliament and Minister of Culture Julius Bomholt," and later in the same article, "Bomholt had not participated in the decision of the board...but he refrained from following Carl Roos in resigning from the board", which would have been difficult, as he was not present at the time. On page 233 in the book *Munk*, which was published on October 24, 2000, Per Stig Møller again wrote about "The Company of 1916," and about Bomholt's role in the affair: "Board member Julius Bomholt had not been present during the vote but did not resign his position in protest against it." However, it appears from the newspaper article quoted here about the declaration sent out by the board, that Bomholt had resigned from the board of "The Company of 1916" on April 6, i.e., a few days after the board meeting referred to. Bomholt's resignation must therefore be seen as a protest against the infamous decision.

some places in Denmark. Shortly before Lilly Freud-Marlé travelled to Denmark, her husband, Arnold Marlé, as mentioned earlier, had been dismissed from his job as theater director and actor at the Hamburg Playhouse due to his Jewish heritage.

The frequent discussions of Jewish persecution motivated engineer Poul Wilde to write a long article in *Jyllands-Posten* on April 23, 1933: "God's Green Pastures and the German Hatred of Jews – a prayer to Pastor Kaj Munk." The title is from the play *The Green Pastures* by Marc Connelly,[128] in which God is portrayed as an old Negro. The play caused quite a stir in religious circles, and the article in *Jyllands-Posten* was written as a question to Munk about why Christians considered it blasphemous to portray God as a Negro but apparently could quietly resign themselves to the German treatment of the Jews. Poul Wilde also wrote about:

> *How a Danish society allowed itself to be threatened by the German legation in Copenhagen and cancelled a quite apolitical performance by a Jewish actress. I cannot say that my heart swelled with national pride when I read that.*

On April 25 Munk answered in *Jyllands-Posten*, and the answer had the same heading as the question: "God's Green Pastures and the German Hatred of Jews – Parish Pastor Kaj Munk answers". Munk wrote that the opposition to *God's Green Pastures* was cowardly and hypocritical. He wrote that it doesn't cost the Christians anything at all to just stand in the square and indignantly demonstrate against a play, but in the case of something much more important, such as Hitler's persecution of the Jews, where the price might be a lot higher, then they stay nice and quiet. Munk also believed that there should be protests:

> *Something I will never understand is this Hitlerish bullying as a way to deal with the Jews... to take away all possibilities*

---

128 Marc Connelly (1890-1980), American dramatist and journalist. *The Green Pastures (Guds grønne Enge)* was performed in Copenhagen in 1933.

for them to make a living, and to prohibit them from traveling.
This behavior should call forth a heartfelt Christian protest.

But "Why the Christians?" he asked. There are, after all, many others who also do not have the same view of the Jews as the Nazis, including those who were proud of Einstein and Reinhardt. Where were they– the politicians, the scientists, the artists, journalists, doctors, and pastors? Munk looked for the intelligentsia in Germany. They couldn't all be in jail! Munk wrote that what was happening with the Jews in the neighbor country was a disgrace. He also mentioned *The Company of 1916*: "It is not easy to think of the four board members in *The Company* without contempt."

A powerful reaction to Munk's article came from a German actor. In the book *I Would Wish You Life (Livet gad jeg ønske jer)* by pastor Svend Aage Nielsen,[129] a letter dated July 7, 1933 from Munk to Ingeborg and Ebbe Rasmussen[130] is reprinted. In the letter, Munk expresses gratitude for their hospitality during his stay in Berlin in March of 1933:

> *It was so nice that you were both there when I was! We had such a grand time together. If I could just come again, but now it's all over. Fred Koester[131] wrote in an open letter to me in Jyllands-Posten, that if I were to show my face in Germany, my skin would be pulled off, up over my ears, and if I anyhow showed up at his door in Charlottenlund, I would get a taste of the whip. My articles, he says, are forwarded to Hitler, and any play by me would be repressed in Germany. Thanks for the kindness!*

It must have been Munk's statement about the "Hitlerish bullying" of the Jews that had stirred Fred Koester's anger. Munk mentioned in the letter that Koester had written an open letter in

---

[129] Livet gad jeg ønske jer. Erindringer om, taler af og breve fra Kaj Munk (I Would Wish You Life. Memories of, Speeches by, and Letters from Kaj Munk). Ed. Svend Aage Nielsen. Poul Kristensen's Publishing 1984, p. 62.

[130] Ebbe Kjeld Rasmussen (1901-1959), professor of physics at the University of Copenhagen. Attended high school in Nykøbing Falster together with Kaj Munk. Studied during the year 1933 at the Physical-Technical Institute in Berlin.

[131] Fred Koester, German actor, lived for a time in Denmark.

Jyllands-Posten. It has not been possible to find that letter, which makes reconstruction of this incident difficult. According to a handwritten note on Koester's letter quoted below, it appears that he had written an answer to Munk's article ("God's Green Pastures and the German Hatred of Jews"), and sent it to *Jyllands-Posten*. They allowed Munk to read it, and asked if he wanted to have it printed in the paper. He did not want it printed but had them send the following letter to Koester:

Vedersø vicarage, Ulfborg
May 16, 1933

Mr. Fred Koester
I have received your abusive words.

If you continue to give me similar insights into modern German culture I will hand the case documents over to the Danish police and see if we can have you deported from a country whose hospitality you seem to abuse.

Kaj Munk[132]

(Koester had presumably returned Munk's letter to the editor at *Jyllands-Posten*).

The next day Munk received a letter from the editor at *Jyllands-Posten*:

Aarhus
May 17, 1933

Dear Pastor Kaj Munk
I think it will amuse you to read the enclosed product of the German actor. At a newspaper's editorial office you come across all kinds of things, but I can't remember ever having seen anything like this. The letter should probably be kept for the right occasion.

Sincerely, Your devoted
H. Hansen.[133]

---

[132] KMF
[133] KMF

Enclosed was Koester's harsh letter to Munk, given here in an abbreviated form.

Fred Koester Copenhagen
May 16, 1933

"Through Jyllands-Posten, *Aarhus"*

To one Kaj Munk

In answer to his tactless letter which I received through you.

I did not want to receive an answer from this person. Whoever insults my Fatherland, as you do, in speech and writing, deserves the dog whip.

Your obvious clumsy stupidity, that you set great store on Germany, is seen in your open letter [Munk's article], which in the meantime is in good hands in Germany.

In it one can read not only the opposite, but also that you, with insipid phrases, shamefully insult the German people and their present government.

Maybe sometime you'll be pulled down off the pulpit. In Germany you'd get quite a different treatment.

I can quite understand that you don't want to have my answer in the newspaper:

1. Because you would disgrace yourself completely with the readers.

2. Because my answer (article) would open the Danish eyes for how the Marxist crimes had completely ruined Germany, in cooperation with the Jewish pest.

3. Because my article fully documents the truth about Germany's honor and greatness.

I will, through the National Socialist Authors League and Reich's Minister Dr. Goebbels, with the help of documentation, make sure that if you ever have a play or book in Germany, which I can hardly believe, that through this action it will be destroyed. Maybe the Jews have bought something from you? And for that reason you rant and rage about Germany.

After such behavior one could take you for a Jew.
Signed. Fred Koester."[134] (a.t.)

In the letter, Fred Koester actually called Munk a frightened coward, and threatened him with corporal punishment, which, in National Socialist jargon was commonly used towards opponents. Together with the uniforms, they had also acquired the uniformed military's method to crush people by using raw and brutal language. Perhaps language at the time was harsher than it is now. Some of Munk's critics in the thirties also used language, as related above, that was not always polite in their reviews. Koester wrote that Munk deserved the dog whip, which had an almost symbolic meaning for the Nazis. Hitler was often photographed with a dog whip in his hand, a symbol of power, until his "stylists" recommended against it in the early thirties.[135] In a newspaper article under the heading "Nazi Terror," we are told about a German city where the Jews, two at a time, were taken away and beaten:

"The Nazis went around the town with loaded revolvers in one hand, and a dog whip in the other. It was impossible to buy a whip in the town because the Nazis had bought them all up."[136] Both whipping and beating were now legal in Nazis Germany. The inflated nationalism, as seen in Koester's letter, was very common in Germany at the time. Anti-Semitism was also clearly expressed in his letter. That Magnus, a German Jew, had already translated three plays by Munk was probably not known to Koester

While the quarrels between Koester and Munk were taking place, more serious things were happening in Germany. On March 10 the *auto-da-fé* flamed up across all of Germany, when the Nazis burned "un-German literature" in bonfires. These included the works of Thomas and Heinrich Mann, Sigmund Freud, Karl Marx, Erich Kästner, Erich Maria Remarque, Carl von Ossietzky, Arnold and Stefan Zweig, Arthur Schnitzler,

---

[134] KMF

[135] Wolfgang Benz: *Geschichte des Dritten Reiches* (*History of the Third Reich*). Publisher C.H. Beck, Munich, 2000, p. 196.

[136] "Nazi Terror", Lollands Tidende, 8 April 1933.

Lion Feuchtwanger, Kurt Tucholsky, as well as many others. Simultaneously their books were taken off the shelves in the bookstores and libraries. These authors were also the targets of hatred, both for what they had written and for many because of their Jewish extraction. Heinrich Heine, a German poet with Jewish heritage, had written many years earlier: "It is just a rehearsal; there, where they burn books, they will eventually burn people."[137] (a.t.)

[137] Frederich V. Grunfeld: op.cit. p. 247.

Chapter 5

The Hitler Plague - spring 1934

In the election for parliament in November 1933, Hitler received 92% of the votes. That could be felt in the Germany that Munk and his wife Lise experienced on a trip down through Europe and on to Egypt and Israel in the spring of 1934. During that trip Munk wrote 20 travel letters, 18 of which were printed in *Jyllands-Posten*, one in *Berlingske Evening* edition, and one in *Dagens Nyheder*.

In one of the letters, "Theater in the Third Reich,"[138] Munk deals in depth with conditions for the theater in Germany at the time. He remarked that the new masters in Germany understood the power of the stage for political agitation, entertainment, and propaganda at the same time. The very low ticket prices in Germany were, in Munk's opinion, actually good thing in comparison to conditions in Copenhagen, where the government subsidized theater demanded 8 kroner* for a ticket. Munk continued that it would probably not prevent the Danes from calling Goebbels and his colleagues "barbarians." Munk enthusiastically discussed everything that was happening at the theater in Flensborg and compared it with conditions in Denmark. Danish theater people should not go home and lie down, but get up and do something. The letter finishes with a mention of the play *Alle gegen Einen, Einer für Alle (All against One, One for All)*, which he had seen in Flensborg. In the play's program brochure Munk read that new rules for writing theater reviews had been declared: *Guidelines for Critics in the New Germany (Richtlinien der Kritik im neuen Deutschland)*.[139] He would quote from these *Guidelines* in his travel letters.

Didn't Munk feel the regimentation in all of this? Yes, and it appears from the following that he had an eye for these defects: "But it still seems that the Hitlerish leadership, despite all the good-will, has been more commanding than inspiring."

---

* About $1.00 US in 1922, equivalent to $70.80 US in 2010, based on nominal GDP per capita. An expensive ticket!

[138] *Berlingske Evening*, 24 February 1934.

[139] Stadt-Theater Flensburg, Program, schedule 1933-1934. KMF

The next travel letter, "Through Hitler's Germany," appeared in Jyllands-Posten on February 25, 1934. In the article Munk wrote about conditions in Germany with the usual mixture of both enthusiasm and scepticism:

> However, there is unity and order in the Reich. Just think about what there was when Hitler came to power. Oh yes, certainly, unity and order, concentration camps, refugees, lay-offs, and arrests. Well, that's a necessary part of it. And it's better than sniper murders and street fighting as a permanent institution, and the eternal, barren, and filthy squabbling.

But even if they had managed to get rid of democracy in Germany, he could sense a certain dissatisfaction with many things: that the party made Hitler out to be a god, that the Nazis worshipped Odin, and that there was talk about abolishing marriage. He was sure that Hitler was above that; that it was his "inflamed disciples" who were to blame for these excesses. They should quiet down, he wrote.

Munk wrote as well about foreign politics. Did Germany and Hitler want peace with the world, and with France, asked Munk, and he continued:

> We'll trust you, Comrade Hitler when you guarantee it. We don't dare do otherwise for the sake of Europe. But have you thought about– but no, you probably don't know it– a poem by one of your own countrymen who was also great– about a sorcerer who could conjure great spirits up from his bag. When it went wrong, he couldn't get them back in, and they took away his power? Or could your peace treaty with Poland be the Word that proves you have the power over them?

The example from Goethe's *Der Zauberlehrling (The Sorcerer's Apprentice)* was well chosen and very fitting. That the "spirits" would finally, years later, be put back into the bag, was in large part due to the democracy that Munk, in the thirties, was opposed to. It was too late when he realized that democracy could be a weapon against dictatorship, as well as what was happening in Germany. However, in 1934 he was not yet ready to dismiss Nazism. He asked: "National Socialism, what is that? Do you [Hitler] know yourself?" Then Kaj Munk referred back to Feuchtwanger's novel *Success*, which dealt with National Socialism in the twenties:

> *Ten years ago Lion Feuchtwanger wrote his great novel* Success *about the Germany of the time. In it, he said that if anyone asked the new party's leader what his plans were when he eventually took control of the government, he would point to a drawer, and say: It's all in there. That morning, when they arrested him, they broke open the drawer. It was empty.*

Munk continued, "Now the great author is sitting somewhere in exile, while the ridiculed leader is sitting on the chair over the Reich. I wonder which of the two has the best seat?"

After taking power Hitler asked the German people for four years to build up what others had torn down. About a year later Munk wrote:

> *One of the four years has now passed. You look at this 'leader,' this nimble, manly, vigorous character, this face, glowing with a lack of intelligence.[140] Did you do him an injustice, Feuchtwanger? You can't judge a leader by his mustache. There might not have been any plans in his drawer, but they could well have been in his head: that's where such things are often best kept.*

The collected travel letters were published in September 1934 in book form, *Vedersø-Jerusalem and Back*.[141] The book's closing chapter, "Denmark," had not been published before and probably shouldn't have been then. Here Munk's aversion to democracy and democratic politicians was expressed with great arrogance.

---

[140] Munk's description of The Fuhrer's "face, glowing with a lack of intelligence" is presumably an ironic reference to Lion Feuchtwanger's unflattering portrait of Rupert Kutzner [Hitler] in the novel *Success*. Munk thought that Lion Feuchtwanger had misjudged Hitler.

[141] Kaj Munk, *Vedersø–Jerusalem Retur* (*Vedersø-Jerusalem and Back*) NNF 1934.

He wrote about how poorly the democratic parties and their politicians had dealt with their challenges after WWI: "For Hitler it was sickening. He saw how they lied, these talkative con artists; lied to themselves and lied to others." Hitler drove out parliamentarianism with the help of parliamentarianism, so what were the offended democrats so upset over Munk asked. After all, the German people had elected him.

Munk used one-and-a-half pages to give his view of the execution of SA chief Ernst Röhm,[142] who had been accused of planning a revolt against Hitler. He believed that the sympathy that Hitler and Nazi Germany had gained in various countries had been lost with the execution of Röhm. Munk continued:

> But history's lofty muses bent down over him and spread the royal cape of greatness and loneliness over the shoulders they so far had bestowed so little dignity upon.
>
> The black hours of despair and action in the chalk white face's night made him– quite regardless of whether or not his fate will belong to victory, fiasco, or murder– into a great man, a Herod who would sacrifice his wife, or a Christiern II* who would not shy away from the name of tyranny on Stockholm's bloody square, one of the few who, during all the ages that the Earth had orbited that remote planet we call the sun, would dare to live out that purity of heart which is to will one thing.

In the real event this "purity of heart" didn't just cost Röhm his life, but also an additional 200 randomly chosen people who were murdered. A head of state in one of Europe's largest countries allowed, in 1934, so many people to die without a trial. Were there no protestors? Yes, there were, and Munk named them as well:

> But all of the small, insignificant politicians in Europe simply whined in dismay and indignation. What did they understand about the great things happening in the world? How much did Hitler have to give to overcome himself and

---

[142] Ernst Röhm (1887-1934) SA Chief of Staff.
* Archaic spelling of Christian II, king of Denmark, 1513-1523.

make the bloody sacrifice? He did it for Germany's sake. He acted with strength and wisdom; he acted in a Christian manner, and greatly. With determination and forethought he took up that frightening word, 'Responsibility,' which is just an unknown word in parliamentary countries. In the beginning was the Word, but then parliamentarianism came along with nonsense as the guiding principle. New men are now bringing the Word to life. Long live the loner who sacrifices himself for the many; he, who knows what he will and dares what he knows. Long live the man in the house!

Many believed that times were tough, and they could be dark, Munk admitted; but in the darkness he saw the light shine forth:

For many right-thinking people dictatorship's victories around the world in recent years is just the fulfillment of impossible hopes. Parliamentarianism's freedom, with its right to publically piss on each other, is something we will gladly do without.

Kaj Munk's prior scepticism of Hitler and Nazism was brushed aside; but if one thought that Munk bowed down dutifully for the strong men, then they were mistaken. He was one of them! In the following it appears as if Munk is looking for himself:

Denmark, my fatherland, don't you understand it? Not yet? The man will come to you, too. He, who will lift you up out of the materialistic struggle, the quest for relief, and the jovial Icouldcarelessedness. He will lift you up and gather you about an idea, a belief in spirit, an understanding. That life is so precious– for the individual, as for a people– that no terror is too deep to wade through to have gotten it as a gift and to turn it into a calling.

Both with and without a calling, and with or without blame, in the coming years many would come to wade through a sea of terror.

Munk finishes the chapter by writing about Jesus, who had said:

I give you my peace. That peace is not simply a feeling of security, an accommodation to life, or a pact with homemade guarantees, but rather an eternal unrest, a readiness to fight for that, which at any given moment, is given to you to believe in, an instinct, that only under the Sign of the Cross can there be victory.[143]

When Kaj Munk writes that we shall fight for that which, at any given moment, we are given to have faith in, then it is not a constant faith but a faith dependent on the moment. This sensible attitude makes it possible to change one's viewpoint, something that Munk would later have use for in his changing attitude toward Hitler and Mussolini.

Three weeks before *Vedersø-Jerusalem and Back* was published, Munk again received, after a lull, letters from Erwin Magnus, who had already had bad experiences with Hitler and Nazism:

> *Erwin Magnus*
> *c/o Peter Freuchen, Enehøje pr. Nakskov*
> *August 27, 1934*

> *Dear Kaj Munk*

> *It's been a long time since you've heard from me, but there hasn't been much to say. I was very fortunate to be in Austria when the Hitler Plague broke out,[144] which meant financial ruin for my entire family, me included, so I have had to work hard just to stay alive during all this time. I arrived in Denmark two months ago, via Poland. In the beginning I spent several weeks in Copenhagen, then a while in Middelfart, and now I'm staying with my friend Peter Freuchen. Next week I'll be back in Copenhagen where I intend to stay.*

> *I have so far, unfortunately, not been able to achieve anything with your play. An Idealist, with its Jewish theme, is of course quite impossible in Germany at this time (and this applies to an even higher degree to your play about David,*

---

[143] Kaj Munk, op.cit., pp. 143-151.
[144] Hitler's take over of power, spring of 1933, and the following Jewish boycott.

102

which I read with admiration). Jannings was for a time very interested in Cant,[145] *but then another play about Henry VIII by an Austrian writer came along, and ruined our chances in Vienna for the time being. Then the English film came out.[146] When Jannings saw it, he said that he would no longer play Henry VIII!* The Word *is still at Kiepenheuer Publishers, but I haven't heard from them in a long time.*

I have not at all given up hope to see you performed in Germany (or Austria), and at any rate would like to see your Hamlet adaptation. Starting next week you can reach me at Steen Hasselbalch's address: Copenhagen, Boldhusgade 2.

I read one day in Politiken *that you were in Copenhagen and would give a lecture at the Palace Theater; but when I went to visit you, I heard that you had not come but had instead just sent your lecture. I hope that you will soon come over so that we can meet.*

Sincerely, your devoted
Erwin Magnus

The contents of Magnus' letter were not in accord with Munk's view of conditions in Hitler's Germany, which is plainly apparent from his answer:

Vedersø Præstegaard 1934 – 30/8

Dear Erwin Magnus

Thank you for your letter. It is not looking very good for our collaboration. I understand quite well your view of Hitler. It could hardly be otherwise, but my view is the exact opposite. Under these conditions I fear that a conversation between us is more likely to separate us than bring us closer.

Sincerely, your devoted
Kaj Munk

---

[145] Letter from Magnus to Munk, 27 July 1932.
[146] The film mentioned here must be *The Private Life of Henry VIII* (1933) with Charles Laughton as Henry VIII.

When one considers the fact that during the previous three years Magnus had worked energetically, and without pay, first with the translation of the three plays, and then through several attempts to have them performed, Kaj Munk's refusal to have a conversation with him does seem extremely rude. After having praised Hitler and Nazism in the last chapter of his travel book, it was not pleasant for Kaj Munk to see his German translator use an expression like "the Hitler Plague" about what was happening in Germany. Furthermore, Magnus had fled. In Munk's view that was wrong. One should stay and fight for one's cause, as he himself would later do.

It would be understandable if their relationship had ended at this time after Munk's very unsympathetic letter. Munk's following letters were also very brief, but Magnus' letters to Munk continued in the same friendly tone.

In 1946, when Magnus handed over the 21 letters that he had received from Munk to Captain Ove Marcussen,[147] he kept, at the request of his son, a copy of that particular letter.

Magnus' family and friends wondered why he had not remained in Germany. That was the attitude of many German Jews to the conditions in Germany at the time, which is incomprehensible to us today. They felt secure. Their people had been integrated into the country for generations. They were represented in all levels of society, and many were highly decorated for their service in WWI. Many German Jews believed until late in the thirties, just like Kaj Munk, that the persecution of the Jews taking place at the time was a passing phenomenon.

Magnus' mother-in-law Maria Freud was murdered, at age 80, in the Treblinka concentration camp's gas chamber together with two sisters. A third sister died the same year in Theresienstadt.[148]

---

[147] Ove Marcussen, Kaj Munk collector. The collection is held at the Royal Library.
[148] Information from the Freud family tree, made available by the Sigmund Freud Private Fund, Vienna.

Vederø Pgd   1934 - 30/8

Kære Hr. Erwin Magnus,

Tak for Deres Brev. Det er ikke lyst ud
for vort Samarbejde. Jeg forstaar
saa udmærket Deres Syn paa Hitler,
det kan næppe være andet; men min
Indstilling er en stikmodsat. Under
disse Forhold frygter jeg, at en Samtale
mellem os vilde mere skille end nærme.

Med venlig Hilsen.
            Deres hengivne
                Kaj Munk.

Kaj Munk's letter to Erwin Magnus of 30 August 1934
Document collection, Royal Library

In Denmark people had had the opportunity for some time to read about conditions in the new Germany. Nazi propaganda, also written by Danish authors, was in good supply; but there were also books published about persecution and torture. As early as 1934, Fremad in Copenhagen published a book with the title: *Oranienburg, The First Authentic Report from the Concentration Camp at Oranienburg, by Gerhart Seger, Refugee.*

Gerhart Seger was a journalist and had been a member of the German parliament through four election periods, representing the SPD, The Social Democratic Party of Germany. On June 14, 1933, barely a half year after Hitler had taken power, he was transferred from the prison located in Dessau to the concentration camp at Oranienburg north of Berlin. He escaped five months later and reached safety in Prague. In the spring of 1934 he finished his book about his prison experience in Oranienburg. The German concentration camps had not yet developed into the death camps that they would later become, but Gerhart Seger and the others inmates experienced a degrading and cruel treatment. Several of his fellow inmates died after having been tortured during questioning. The book's significance was supported by the foreword written by the well-known author Heinrich Mann.[149]

A young Norwegian journalist, Ragnar Vold,[150] who had resided in Germany during the fall of the Weimar Republic and Hitler's take over of power, described the new Germany in the book: *Germany on the March– Why?– From Where?– To Where?* The book was published in Danish in September 1934. In the preface the author wrote that he did not consider it his job to pass sentence on National Socialism or to glorify it, but would allow the reader to make that judgment.

However, the 282 pages of the work make up a very informative and urgent warning against National Socialism and its very nature. The book did not become a bestseller.[151]

If the Danes of that time were not aware of what was happening openly in their great neighbor country to the south, then they

---

[149] Heinrich Mann (1871-1950), German author with Jewish heritage. Emigrated to the USA in 1933.

[150] Ragnar Vold, Norwegian journalist and author.

[151] Ragnar Vold, *Tyskland marcherer– hvorfor? – hvorfra?– hvorhen? (Germany on the March – Why? – From Where? – To Where?)* NNF 1934.

themselves were to blame. The documentation was on the shelves at the bookstores, and in the libraries.

Munk wrote the play *Mrs. Koltschak (Fru Koltschak)* in the spring of 1934. The democratic Prime Minister Mrs. Koltschak is a feminine Stauning type*, a socially inclined pacifist. Her son, who has become a communist, burns down the parliament building in an attempt to start a revolt against his mother! The foreign minister exploits the ensuing commotion to take power. He stops the revolt, brings peace and order to the country, and becomes its dictator.

The dictator, originally an indebted baron, condemns Mrs. Koltschak and her son to death.[152] It is obviously a play based on the current events in Germany, where the parliament building was destroyed by fire in 1933, supposedly started by communists. Mrs. Koltschak was never printed and has never been performed.

---

* Thorvald Stauning (1873-1942) Prime Minister 1924-1926 and 1929-1942.
[152] Niels Nøjgaard, op.cit. p. 266.

Chapter 6

"The Word" in Schwerin

Magnus was now living in Denmark as a refugee and without many opportunities. Friends and business acquaintances helped him. Among others, the writer Karin Michaëlis gave him some financial assistance.[153] Magnus continued to work for several authors, including Munk and Freuchen. Despite the conditions in Germany, in September Magnus received good news from Kiepenheuer Publishers, which he passed on to Kaj Munk:

> *Copenhagen, September 18, 1934*
> *Pension City, Christian IX's Gade 7*
>
> *Dear Kaj Munk*
>
> *To my great sorrow I heard that you had been in an auto accident, but I hope you will soon be well again. As a little consolation I can inform you that just today I received the news that* The Word *has been accepted at the Staatstheater in Schwerin; opening night will be before 30 November this year.*
>
> *Wishing the best for a speedy recovery, and best regards. Your devoted*
>
> *Erwin Magnus*

The accident mentioned here occurred during a car trip when Munk had a puppy as a passenger. The puppy distracted Munk so much while he was driving that the car ended up running into a telephone pole. The resulting head-slam into the windshield changed Munk's handsome eagle nose into a so-called saddle nose. The aftermath of the collision, together with several freezing hunting trips, resulted in Munk being sick all autumn. The puppy got by with no injury.

---

[153] Steffen Steffensen, *Escaping Nazism (På flugt fra nazismen). German-speaking Emigrants in Denmark after 1933.* C.A. Reitzel Publisher, Copenhagen 1986, p. 46. Karin Michaëlis (1872-1950) made an enormous effort to help, in particular, German, ethnic, and political refugees.

The most important thing in the short letter was, however, the news that *The Word* would be performed in Schwerin.

> *Vedersø vicarage*
> *September 26, 1934*
>
> *My dear Erwin Magnus*
> *Yes, that really was something of a consolation. I hope that events in Schwerin will be the beginning of a good time for you and me in Germany.*
> *With three cheers for the future. Your devoted*
> *Kaj Munk*

Magnus had worked long and hard with Munk's works, and finally a play would be performed in a theater in Germany; but Munk's optimistic hopes for a good time for them both in Germany would not be fulfilled.

> *Copenhagen, September 25, 1934*
> *Pension City, Christian IX Gade 7*
>
> *Dear Kaj Munk*
> *Kiepenheuer informs me that opening night for your play* The Word *in Schwerin is set for November 23, in the setting of a "Nordic Week," probably as a representative for Denmark. Furthermore, Kiepenheuer is now negotiating with Deutsches Theater in Prague, where my brother-in-law Arnold Marlé, previously in Hamburg, is now working. I just spoke with Lemkow[154] yesterday, and we are both afraid that it will not be possible to transfer money from Germany to here. We believe, in any case, it would be easier if the contract with Kiepenheuer, which is now in my name, could be transferred over to you, as you are a foreigner and could probably get help from the Danish consulate. Therefore, I ask you to please inform me at once if I should write to Kiepenheuer and ask them to rewrite the contract for you.*

---

[154] Danish Dramatists' League.

I hope that you have recovered from the results of your auto accident.

With best regards, Your devoted
Erwin Magnus

Erwin was a well-known person in Germany. The German authorities knew he was a Jew and where he lived, but might not at the time have been able to prevent a bank transfer to him. But they could have caused delays. It was probably for that reason that Magnus wanted Munk to take over the contract.

Vedersø Vicarage
September 27, 1934

Dear Erwin Magnus,
I think that arrangement is excellent.
Sincerely, your devoted
Kaj Munk

The talkative Munk had become very brief. Nowhere in these letters are there any questions to Magnus about his family, his health, or his life as a refugee.

Copenhagen, October 6, 1934
Pension City, Christian IX Gade 7

Dear Kaj Munk

Enclosed is the new contract that Kiepenheuer sent to me today; it is exactly like the old one, except that it is in your name. I ask that you sign it and send it back to me, or else directly to Gustav Kiepenheuer Theater Publisher Ltd., Berlin–Charlottenburg, Kantstr. 10. He will then send you the carbon copy. In addition I ask that you sign the enclosed Beitrittserklärung (declaration of acceptance), without which no play can be performed in Germany. It doesn't cost anything except the percentage, which is deducted from the commission.

Sincerely, your devoted
Erwin Magnus

Many things were difficult and unpleasant in the new Germany, and the grip on the Jews was constantly being tightened. Magnus had previously translated Jack London into German, 35 volumes, a few of which were to come out in a new edition at Büchergilde Gutenberg (which was once owned by the book printers union, now taken over by the Nazis). They set as a requirement that the name of the translator, Erwin Magnus, be deleted from the new edition.[155]

> *Copenhagen, December 6, 1934*
> *Pension City, Christian IX Gade 7*
>
> *Dear Kaj Munk*
>
> *The premiere of* The Word, *which should have been about 14 days ago, has been postponed. I wrote to the publisher and asked for an explanation and have just received a copy of the letter that the Staatstheater in Schwerin had written to Kiepenheuer: Concerning the performance of the play* In the Beginning was The Word *by Kaj Munk, it was necessary to negotiate with the relevant authorities. These negotiations are now finished, and we ask that you postpone the date for the premiere performance until March 31, 1935, as the play cannot be rushed into a schedule that must be planned out well in advance. You will understand our position when you realize that even the leader of a theater must comply with the relevant authorities. In this case we are grateful that there even were negotiations, and that a quick decision was reached. We ask for your speedy confirmation. (a.t.)*
>
> *In response, Kiepenheuer replied that the new deadline seemed to him to be rather late, and he suggested that the play be performed no later than February 28, 1935.*
>
> *Sincerely, your devoted*
> *Erwin Magnus*

---

[155] Letter from Magnus to Peter Freuchen, 28 September 1934, The Royal Library.

The difficult negotiations concerning the performance of *The Word* were undoubtedly also due to the Jewish heritage of the translator.

Vedersø, December 8, 1934

Dear Erwin Magnus

Yes, this is awfully annoying. Probably nothing will come of any of it, but it's worse for Germany.

A very merry Christmas, your devoted
Kaj Munk

Kaj Munk was ready to give up the whole business with *The Word* in Schwerin. The self-deprecating remark, that it was actually worse for Germany, showed that Munk still had a sense of humor. This is the last letter from Munk to Magnus that was available during the work on this book.

Munk had a lot of other things in the works. The Royal Theater had asked him to write a prologue to Holberg's 250th birthday. *Late Evening outside the Royal Theater* was performed on December 3, 1934. It was in the form of a conversation between Holberg and Oehlenschläger. And at the end of the prologue Oehlenschläger offers a tribute to Holberg:

Holberg, our father! — It was, after all, you, who with the acuity of genius saw gold where others saw only impoverished dust, you saw Danish words and thought in the art of the stage. You lifted Jeppe up and put him in the Baron's bed, you made him worthy to be there. That Denmark, that today's generation stands upon, you laid the foundation for. You were Scandinavia's and your ages' Hitler; but in a purely Danish way. You made us aware of our essential selves, but not through drills and orders, no, you laughed your wisdom into our hearts; you smiled courage to us and let us grow with your spirit's warmth. Therefore we salute you.

Although Munk immediately tried to soften that a bit by writing about a Hitler "in a Danish way," it is still a strange comparison, especially when one thinks about the "foundations" that Hitler had laid by 1934. Munk often had something that itched in his texts.

Readers and the public had to be kept awake, and in this case he used Hitler's name to do it.

There were other views of Hitler in 1934, and Munk and the Royal Theater had each their own. To Munk's annoyance the Royal Theater edited the prologue. For that reason he had the *Berlingske Tidende* print the original text in the Sunday supplement on December 9, 1934. What had the Royal Theater done to annoy Munk so much?

Poster from the performance of The Word at the Staatstheater Schwerin, 16 February 1935, City Archive Schwerin

Five minor lines between Oehlenschläger and the actor Olaf Poulsen were probably not the reason, but they had deleted the sentence: "You were Scandinavia's and your ages' Hitler, but in a purely Danish way."[156] They had removed Munk's "itch," but it could still be read in *Berlingske Tidende*.

After the annoyance with the prologue Munk received a welcome message. A date had been set for the premiere of *The Word* in Schwerin. During the last days of January the posters declared that *In the Beginning was the Word*, a Nordic play in four acts by Kaj Munk, would have its premiere performance at the Staatstheater in Schwerin on Friday, February 1, 1935.[157]

According to Magnus' letter to Munk of September 25, 1934, the play was originally programmed in connection with a Nordic Week.

These Nordic Weeks were held several places in Germany, arranged by the Nordic Society, a cultural organization that was started in the twenties and taken over by the National Socialists after 1933. The Nordic Society's mission then became to create connections between Hitler's Germany and Scandinavia in the cultural arena.[158]

Comments on *The Word* in Staatstheater Schwerin's program brochure:

> *In the Beginning was The Word*
> *A play by Kaj Munk*
>
> *In the series of Scandinavian dramas that the Staatstheater is performing this season, thereby emphasizing and promoting the cultural solidarity between Germany and its Nordic neighbors, belongs the play* In the Beginning was The Word *by the Dane Kaj Munk. One can hardly imagine another play*

---

[156] "The theater's corrections to the performance on 3 December. The scene is a late evening outside the Royal Theater" Manuscript's page 3, The Royal Theater's archive.

[157] Copy of the theater poster. KMF

[158] Hans Bay-Petersen, *A Friendly Invitation. The Royal Theater's Guest Performance in Nazi Germany in the Thirties.* Multivers Copenhagen 2003, p.24.

where the Nordic essence is more clearly portrayed than in this play. The subject reminds one a bit of Bjørnson's dramatic play Beyond Powers (Over Evne). *Here, too, religious questions are asked, pondered, debated, and turned end for end; different sects, each with the belief that they alone have the power of salvation, stand face to face. Even here there is the question of whether or not a miracle will play the lead role. Faith, that has the apparent power to make the impossible possible, resonates throughout the play as a guiding thread.*

Faith still has the power, as in the time of Jesus, to take life back out of the grasp of death; and in this way the miracle is made real, carried forth by a child's faith. The child's mother has just died; the dead is awakened unto life. Was it a miracle? The doctor says absolutely not. The pastor has serious doubts. Those who want to see a miracle in this will see one. For those who think otherwise there will be a natural explanation. This struggle of the soul, this conflict for and against each other, is consummated in a dramatic clash between the residents of a Scandinavian farmhouse, all good people, though possessing somewhat of a strange character. Perhaps it's a special characteristic of the Nordic type, that in the hearts of all these people, no matter how different they are, and even if they sometimes appear to repel each other, a good and pure heart is beating. Each of them tries, in their own way, to find God, even if it does happen in such a confusing manner. It is, above all, a poem that glorifies the omnipotence of faith. For that reason it is especially relevant to us Germans and our new era; because it was faith, faith in Germany and its leader, that made our new progress possible. "In the Beginning there was Faith" could be an equally good title for this play H."[159] *(a.t.)*

The article in the program brochure was a tribute to the racially pure Aryan, in this case the Nordic people. The article's author could not imagine a more Nordic play than *The Word*. He wrote about the Nordic farmhouse, with its good people, in whom, as the special characteristic of the Nordic type, beats a good and pure heart. The "Nordic type" was a concept in Nazi Germany, and in

---

[159] Mecklenburgisches Staatstheater Schwerin. NS Kulturgemeinde. Program brochure. Schwerin 1935. City Archives, Schwerin.

the schools there were display posters with "German racial features" showing how the Germanic races should appear. One of the six types shown was called "Nordic."[160] In the last lines of the brochure the play's story about the power of faith gets mixed up with the German people's faith in Hitler and the accompanying Nazi takeover in Germany.

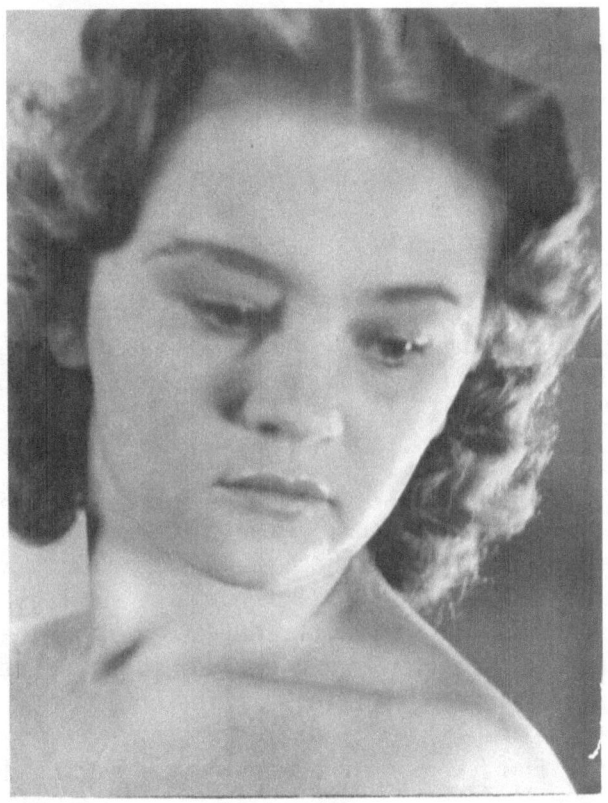

Marga Heiden (1921-) played in 1935 as the 14 year old Little Inger in "The Word" in Schwerin. In the Danish edition Little Inger is only five years old, so Magnus must have changed a lot in the play.
Photo Niese, Schwerin, Marga Heiden's Archive

---

[160] Frederich V. Grunfeld, op.cit.pp. 238-239.

The article was a another classic example of how the National Socialists used all available means for agitation. Two years after taking power Nazi ideology had spread everywhere, including the theater. To think that Munk's play The Word could be used in that connection!

There are three reviews of the premiere in Schwerin. Here are three short excerpts:

Under the by-line Dr. ul., the *Niederdeutscher Beobachter* (February 3, 1935) wrote,

> *It was a play full of emotion and keen thinking, and seen as drama a handsome testimonial to technical ability... the most beautiful scene is where Johannes talks with little Maren about the joy of having a mother in heaven, though this is contradicted by life. Yet the joy of having a mother on Earth is greater... the theatergoers will have something to think about concerning the poet's idea and intention with the play, and to have gotten that far is already a win for the author.*

In the Rostocker Anzeiger (February 3, 1935) the reviewer (W.T.) ranges far: Kierkegaard, Grundtvig, the religious climate in Scandinavia, and Bjørnson, whose play *Beyond Powers* is compared with *The Word*. "One asks himself, where is Munk going with all these prayers, the discussions, and the sacred rituals that he brings to the stage." The reviewer was also indignant over the last act where Inger is called back to life and thought that it seemed offensive. After having praised the actors in a few lines, the review ends with, "The friendly applause in the beginning dropped off sharply later."

In the *Mecklenbürgische Zeitung* (3 February 1935) the critic (F.z.) wrote that in the program brochure's strong emphasis on the Nordic in the play is a hint that the German public is unable to understand the Nordic culture, but that is not true "...because we feel through blood and spirit strongly tied to the Nordic." Among other things in the comprehensive review it is stated that a very conscious dramatic technique was employed, and that it did not fail in its effect on the audience. However, the reviewer continued, "The powerful scenes with the family gathered around the coffin seemed more repulsive than gripping." Finally it is mentioned that there were several curtain calls.

The references in the program brochure, and the first review, show that there is some sympathy for the play and its characters and content, whereas the other two reviewers are more occupied with describing their own knowledge of religion and theater in Scandinavian.

The extensive discussion in the program brochure, and the last review of the Nordic, the Germanic, and the noble peasant fit in well with the Nazi "Blood and Earth" (Blut und Boden) ideology of the German/Germanic people's close bond to the homeland. In the reviews there is a trace of arrogance with respect to Christianity, and it is not mentioned either in the program or the reviews that the play's author was a pastor. Theologians were not popular in Nazi circles. In a later letter Magnus called these reviews idiotic.[161]

Staatstheater Schwerin
Photo Oliver Demeyere
Staatstheater Schwerin–Archive

---

[161] Letter from Erwin Magnus to Kaj Munk, 8 April 1935.

The Nazis had accomplished a lot during the two years they had been in power. Three months earlier one could read the following about persecution of the Jews in Germany in an article in *Forum*: "After just one-and-a-half years of National Socialist governance, the theaters had become racially pure."[162] The author wrote that approximately 2000 actors and employees of Jewish heritage had now been removed from the German theaters.

In the theater programs, in the reviews, and on the posters, one would look in vain for the translator's name. The name Erwin Magnus had been consciously erased in Germany.

In the Beginning Was The Word was performed in Schwerin in 1935 on the 1, 8, 16, and the 19 of February, and as a guest performance at the Stadttheater zu Wismar on February 4.[163] The performances in Schwerin and Wismar were the only ones outside of Scandinavia during Munk's life. Except for the correspondence with Magnus, Kaj Munk had apparently not mentioned or written about these German performances of *The Word*.

---

[162] Dr. Max Hochdorf, "German Comedians–German Emigrants". *Forum, Magazine for the theater,* November 1934, p.3.
[163] According to information from the City Archive in Schwerin.

Chapter 7

It's a Painful Joy to be a Jew

The title of this chapter is a quote from the last available letter from Magnus to Munk. The quotation can be seen as a common denominator for Europe's Jews in this and the following years. The year was 1935, and Munk was busy with premiere performances, film, reviews, and newspaper articles, while Erwin Magnus, after the performance in Schwerin, continued trying to get the royalties transferred from Germany.

> *Copenhagen, April 3, 1935*
> *Pension City. Christian IX Gade 7*
>
> *Dear Kaj Munk*
> *Kiepenheuer asked me to send you the enclosed by-laws and forms from the German Authors' League (Verband deutscher Bühnenschriftsteller), which you are requested to fill out and return directly to the league. Don't write anything about me being your translator– as you have probably read, it is now completely illegal for Jews to write in Germany, and I am now working together with a Dane.*
> *I hope you soon get a statement and money from Schwerin, and I would be grateful if you would then send me my half at once. I can't get more than 10 Marks a month, and am therefore quite broke.*
> *Sincerely, your devoted*
> *Erwin Magnus*

Erwin Magnus was fighting a tough battle to continue to get his translation work sold in Germany. In a letter to Peter Freuchen on January 15, 1935 he wrote, among other things, "I don't know if I will still be allowed to work as a translator in Germany; but even if there should be problems I can always find a front man who I can pay something for the use of his name."

According to the above mentioned letter to Kaj Munk, Magnus was now working together with a Dane. It has not been possible to find out who this Danish front man was. It must have been humiliating for Magnus to write about his financial situation and at the same time ask Munk not to mention his name to the theater in Schwerin.

Copenhagen, April 8, 1935
Pension City. Christian IX's Gade 7

Dear Kaj Munk

Thank you for your letter! I think you should sign the Verband deutscher Bühnenschriftsteller's papers. You, as a foreigner, do not enter into any obligation by doing so; and I believe it is a requirement for us to be able to get our money. It probably won't be much that we'll get from Schwerin, but in these times a little is always better than nothing. I haven't heard anything from Schwerin, except for a couple of reviews that were so idiotic that I at once threw them in the wastebasket.[164]

In 1916– I had just been sent home from the war– I wrote a play with a Buddhist theme that I am now re-working and translating into Danish (in verse).[165] Would you be interested in reading it?

Wouldn't it be an interesting subject: What would happen to Jesus if he came to Germany today?

Sincerely, your devoted, Erwin Magnus

The letter from Munk that Magnus is thanking him for has not been found. Its contents might have explained why their correspondence ended.

Magnus again asks Munk to sign the papers for the German Authors' League. Was Munk reluctant to sign them? Did this letter from Magnus have any influence on Munk's play *He Sits at the Melting-Pot*? In that play Jesus comes to Germany in the form of a picture on several potsherds found in Palestine. *The Melting-Pot*, which Munk wrote in 1938, is about the National Socialists'

---

[164] Magnus must have taken them out of the wastebasket again, as he later turned them over to Ove Marcussen. Letter from Michael Freud-Magnus, 2003.

[165] It has not been possible to find the manuscript to the play mentioned.

persecution of the Jews, which in the same year resulted in the raw and brutal Crystal Night on November 9, 1938.

On May 29, 1935, Munk sent a postal certificate for 78.84 Danish crowns to Erwin Magnus in Copenhagen. That must have been the royalty from Schwerin. The amount seems ridiculously small today, but in 1935 a factory seamstress in Copenhagen would have had to work 100 hours, over two weeks, to earn a similar amount.

On September 14, 1935 Kaj Munk's play *Love* had its premiere at The Royal Theater, and in that connection Magnus wrote to Munk.

Copenhagen, September 13, 1935
Pension City. Christian IX's Gade 7

Dear Kaj Munk

I am hereby sending you my heartfelt wishes for the premiere tonight. I hope it will be the great success that your talents deserve. You should no longer feel bound to me as a translator as it is now illegal to perform plays in Germany that are written or translated by Jews. It is a painful joy to be a Jew and probably always has been.

Sincerely, your devoted, Erwin Magnus

This touching letter sounds like a farewell. It has not been possible to find any more letters from the correspondence between Magnus and Munk. Almost all of the letters from Magnus to Munk were typewritten, but this last letter was written by hand.

Why the connection between them was now broken is not known. Whatever the reason, it was certainly not because Magnus had stopped working. He returned to Copenhagen in 1945, where he would continue to translate until his death in 1947. His correspondence with Peter Freuchen, which continued until May of 1946, shows that Magnus continued to translate and sell Scandinavian authors to the German-speaking countries after 1935.

In the same year, March 8, 1935, Munk had a premiere at the Betty Nansen Theater with a very controversial play, *Shakespeare's Hamlet*, recast by Kaj Munk. The play is a vehement but timely confrontation with democracy in Denmark. At the same time it is a call for a "politically strong man," and a warning about what could happen (Germany– National Socialism?) if Denmark did not act.

Probably the last letter from Erwin Magnus to Kaj Munk
13 September 1935
KMF Archive

In Kaj Munk's recast of *Hamlet*, Hamlet's father is the good and just democrat. He is deposed by his brother, Claudius, who becomes a sly and corrupt prime minister, backed by his equally incompetent minister Polonius. Shakespeare's young Norwegian prince, Fortinbras, has been recast by Munk into a young Nazi leader (Fritz Clausen*?), who at the play's end sets off with 40,000 men from Jutland to Copenhagen to depose the incompetent regime. Hamlet, the man with great abilities who does nothing for his country, is killed at the end, shot with a revolver. In the last lines Hamlet speaks, he gives his support to Fortinbras, saying, "I am dying, Horatio, but I hear the people choosing Fortinbras, and so do I. He shall sit in Father's chair, the one that I was never fit for. Tell him that in death I give him my vote."[166]

In an article written at the same time, Munk wrote about his intentions with *Hamlet*:

My thoughts were about the fate of my country, this country that we simultaneously love, are tired of, and fear for. I fought for a new character, one who could create a new spirit or at least renew the old one– a hero, man or woman, who could lead us away from this age that is without spirit, without Danish spirit, an Absalon** for today. I yearned to write a play that could wake us up from this national hibernation, to speak as Grundtvig, and to inspire that single individual that must be found somewhere among us, to tackle the great work for which he only needs the call and inspiration to fulfill.

But it wouldn't work for me. Those models that I would have tried to bring home from abroad were useless on Danish soil. Hitler? B+ in Germany, impossible here. Mussolini? A- in Italy, impossible here. Were they all impossible here?

Suddenly a thought occurred to me– then let the play be based on impossibility. Let it be a great tragedy. Tell the story about one who wanted to act but couldn't, because of the

* Fritz Clausen (1893-1947) leader of Denmark's National Socialist Workers' Party (DNSAP) 1933-1944.
** Absalon (1128-1201), Danish Archbishop.
[166] *Shakespeare's Hamlet recast by Kaj Munk*. NNF 1938, p.89.

people, because it is Danish, because of himself, because he was Danish [Hamlet].[167]

In reference to the quotation above, Svend Erichsen[168] wrote:

> *This can never be Danish. Fritz Clausen, as we know, is far from being a Danish Fuehrer type. He is more like a Schleswigian Hitler imitation but without the political stature of his role model. One gets the impression that this recasting of Hamlet is really a showdown that Munk had with himself. He wanted to see his own soul in Hamlet's character– and thus, unfortunately, revealed his own impotence. He wanted to set himself up as the dictator over Danish intellectual life but collapses and hands the sword over to another.*[169]

Despite the bad reviews, on April 14, 1935 the Betty Nansen Theater ran an announcement in the *Politiken* that *Hamlet* would be performed for the third from the last time, and that to date there had been 18,500 "enthusiastic audience members."

In *Hamlet*, Munk was still looking for a "strong" man or woman who could save Denmark. At the same time he was uneasy about the border with that Germany that was now being run by a "strong" man, as can be seen from a newspaper article that Munk wrote about Denmark's increasing dependence on England:

> *Of course, it's always a little comforting, that if it all goes wrong, then it's the British ideal of freedom, and not the hunger for territorial expansion, that our course is set for. We could probably use a Danish Hitler here but absolutely not the*

---

[167] "Kaj Munk speaks with Shakespeare". *Forum, Magazine for the Theater*, March 1935, p.7.

[168] Svend Erichsen (1903-1984), Danish theater and literary critic, editor of *Forum, Magazine for the Theater*, 1934-1941.

[169] Svend Erichsen, "Kaj Munk's Nazi Hamlet". *Forum, Magazine for the Theater*, March 1935, p.16.

German one. *The border to the south has perhaps never been as cherished by the Danes as in this last score of years.*[170]

Five years after the premiere of Munk's *Hamlet* it would not be Fortinbras with his 40,000 men marching through south Jutland towards Copenhagen. It would be Nazi led German troops.

In an article in *Jyllands-Posten* on September 1, 1935 with the headline "Two Dictatorships, Two Assaults," Kaj Munk wrote about Italy's war of conquest against Abyssinia, that it was a serious case but no different than other places in Africa where other European countries had taken colonies for themselves:

Why does Mussolini do it? Because he has an ideal: Italy. And those who take their ideals seriously ask only about that, and nothing else. They don't ask about human life, and they don't ask about justice. Isn't justice an ideal as well? It of course must be for the supporters of the League of Nations. Then let them show their ideals in action as Mussolini shows his!

Munk also suggested that Foreign Minister P.Munch[171] and other offended European knights travel to Addis Ababa to fight against the fascists. In the last third of the article Munk is occupied with conditions in Germany:

Another injustice, less observed but at least just as deserving of observation, is taking place in Europe, and that is the treatment of the Jews in Germany. In comparison to the Abyssinians, the Jews of Naziland are a helpless people; they hardly know themselves that they are Jews.

Concerning Germany's reasons for a showdown with the Jews, he continued:

---

[170] Kaj Munk, "Denmark – English or Scandinavian". *Jyllands-Posten*, 19 May 1935.
[171] Peter Munch (1870-1948), PhD, Danish Foreign Minister 1929-1940.

They have only themselves to blame. And let's just admit it. They [the Jews] have played this instrument during Germany's period of decline, so the new rebuilt realm felt that they had to be put in their place. There was hardly any reason to protest against that. But when this 'putting in place' seems to be endless, and takes a form that seems to require that the instruments of torture in the museum at Nurnberg must be taken out into the street and used again, then one would wish that the world's Christian countries would make a serious attempt to agree on one thing: use all means possible to make Germany realize that it is either in a state of revolution, or outside of civilization, as long as gross injustices and raw assaults are tolerated by the authorities.

This appeal did not get much of a reaction in the Christian countries. Munk thought that if there wasn't room for the Jews in Germany, then they would have to leave and that the Reich should show its strength by letting them take their money with them:

That Hitler, who toppled The Social Democrats, smashed communism...and lifted out of the gutter a great, strong, united, and shining Germany, is that the same man who doesn't know what to do in this religious conflict and cannot stop the convulsive persecution of a helpless people?

In a review of Chief Rabbi M. Friediger's book on Palestine, *The Land of Reconstruction* (*Landet der genopbygges*), Munk returned to the German persecution of the Jews, which he believed to be God's punishment of the Jews:

Of course the Chief Rabbi is proud of his people, and of course he has reason to be. Of course God is being good to his favorite child when he sometimes cuts a switch out of the world's tree and whips him with it. With the help of this whip he can create, from the loathsome and skeptical, hedonistic upper class Jew in Berlin's drawing rooms, a hero, a martyr, a believer, who will sacrifice himself for that which he previously denied– who, instead of discussing silk stockings in nightclubs, digs a hallowed ditch in the mountain under Palestine's unbearable sun. We do not doubt it; this reconstruction also strengthens us in our fearful and bleeding hearts by, on rare occasions like right now, clearly letting us see how God can put Satan in traces before His carriage.[172]

These were some very arrogant words about the German Jews, followed by a comparison of Hitler's Germany to Satan harnessed in the traces of God's carriage. Was Munk, with God's help, looking for an excuse for the persecution of the Jews? Can one also include those actors that Munk idolized, many of whom were well off, as belonging to the "hedonistic upper class Jews"? With regard to digging ditches, the Germans put many Jews to work with pickaxe and shovel, but not in a hallowed cause.

On April 5, 1936, Kaj Munk's play *The Victory* (*Sejren*), with the subtitle *A Play About The World Today*, had its premiere performance at the Norwegian Theater in Oslo. The play is about Mussolini's attack on Abyssinia. After *Hamlet*, this was another politically relevant play.

In Denmark, the Betty Nansen Theater and the Dagmar Theater, among others, would not perform the play. If this was due to its quality or the hot political subject, is not known. Munk had sent the play to a reading by Dr. Normann, who was the state's censor* for all private theaters. The following statement could be read in an article in *Berlingske Tidende*:

Concerning the play, the censor, Dr. Normann, had among other things said that it probably would not be forbidden, but that it should, in any case, be changed in several parts. What do you say to Dr. Normann's statement, we asked Kaj Munk last night? That's news to me, was the answer from Vedersø. In

---

*Theater censorship existed in Denmark from 1853 to 1954. The Royal Theater had a separate censor.

[172] Kaj Munk, "Hvor bor de hjemløse" (Where Do the Homeless Live?) *Dagens Nyheder* 25 February 1936.

fact I recently received a letter from him in which he categorically forbids performance of the play here at home.[173]

At the premier in Oslo, Kaj Munk spoke to the stage before the play began. In an article one reads, "The author remained in the audience throughout the performance, and in between the acts he amused himself in a lively fashion with the well-known people present. In the first row one noted the Italian envoy and press secretary." Obviously, Italy was keeping an eye on Munk. There were 33 performances in Norway.

The day after the premiere in Oslo *The Victory* came out in book form from Nyt Nordisk Publishing Arnold Busck. With small changes to the text, *The Victory* had its premiere on August 31, 1937 at the Folk Theater in Copenhagen. Both before and after the premiere the Italian Legation, through the Danish Foreign Ministry, had small changes made to the play. Among other things, the Fascist hymn was cut out. The censor had also required that the chancellor not be played with a "Mussolini mask." Had he received a request from the minister?[174]

The critic Svend Erichsen wrote in September 1937 in *Forum* that *The Victory* was the best play Munk had written since *An Idealist*, and continued,

> *From earlier works and articles we know that Munk is sympathetic towards dictatorships, both as an ideology and as a form of government..*
>
> *So one would think that when he gives fascism a dramatic portrayal in a play, then the propaganda would be clearly seen. However, strangely enough,* The Victory– *the drama about a dictator– seems much less fascist in its character than, for example, the Hamlet recasting that ended in pure agitation. Believe me, if there is any country where* The Victory *cannot be played, then it's Italy. And therefore not in Germany either!*

---

[173] "Vilde Kaj Munks kasserede Stykke have bragt Danmark i fare?" (Would Kaj Munk's rejected play have put Denmark in danger?) *Berlingske Tidende* 14 March 1936.

[174] Niels Nøjgaard, op.cit. p. 287.

Alexi, the dictator in *The Victory*, is a good and humane person, a hero, who due to circumstances is changed into a war crazy despot willing to sacrifice everything, including his own family, for the sake of the Fatherland. Concerning this transformation of the dictator, Svend Erichsen wrote: "If, in this transformation, you see Kaj Munk's dictator as a hero, a coward, or a cynic; or if you feel sympathy or antipathy toward him, will depend on your own personal human and political disposition. A democratic nature, at any rate, would not feel attracted to this "hero." Sven Erichsen finishes with: "*The Victory* was Kaj Munk's. A dramatic triumph that we have not experienced on the Danish stage in a long time."

Ole Palsbo also attended the premiere and wrote about the play:

> *It was a shrill and dissonant chord, a strangely divided evening, but still a strong and interesting one. Few living dramatists have so many sound, keen, and valuable things to say. It's in the periphery that the rogue and the joker romp about. The core is undamaged. The play's most basic idea, as it is portrayed in the figure of the chancellor, is done to perfection. The line is unbroken. It is a human depiction, a role, a motley presentation, a worldview, a minor comedy, a revue and a double murder– but not a boring start to the season!*[175]

The Victory ran 60 times at the Folk Theater.

The Victory had its premiere in Sweden on February 14, 1939 at the New Theater (Nya Teatern) in Stockholm. The Italian legation in Sweden complained about certain things in the play. The legation thought, among several other things, that the name Ethiopia should be changed to "Negro Land," and they were not happy that the chancellor looked so much like Mussolini. The theater's director, Sandro Malmquist, said that was correct, but that the actor Niels Ekstam, who played the main role had, from nature's hand, a hopeless resemblance to Mussolini.[176]

---

[175] *Sejren (The Victory)* at the Folk Theater. Ole Palsbo, *Nationaltidende*, September 1, 1937.

[176] "Mussolini's Answer to Kaj Munk!", a Danish newspaper article without a date or place.

Dark Clouds were forming across Europe. A storm was imminent; and on July 9, 1936, in a letter to Peter Freuchen, Erwin Magnus wrote:

> *I am presently at work on a play that I expect a great deal from; and, I have to earn money, especially so that I can get my son up here.*[177] *I got a letter from him today, in which he writes: 'Unfortunately I have to tell you that there is a strong anti-Semitism directed towards us in school. Try to arrange it so that I can get away from here.' (a.t.) Isn't it terrible that an eleven-year-old child has to write that way?*
>
> *Sincere greetings to you and your wife, and to Gelsted,*[178]
> *Your devoted*
> *Erwin Magnus"*

Not everything new in Germany received Munk's sympathy. In a review of Gustav Frenssen's book,[179] *My Homeland-Faith (Der Glaube der Nordmark)*, Munk wondered why the Christian faith that the Germanic people had practiced for 1500 years was suddenly wrong, almost criminal, and not at all suitable for the noble Aryan mind. Pastor Frenssen practiced something he called "The Universal," and insisted that Jesus was not a Jew. As in other articles from that time, Munk also touched upon the Nazis' racial theories and persecution of the Jews. He suggests that the German Jews might have gone too far during the period of decline [after WWI], and that therefore Germany had the right to punish them but at the same time warned against going too far.

In connection with the Nazis' talk about sub-humans and super-humans, he also expressed nervousness with respect to the Germans' belief that they are a kind of super-human:

---

[177] Michael Freud-Magnus (1924-2010)
[178] Otto Gelsted (1888-1968), journalist, poet, and frequent visitor to Peter Freuchen on his island Enehøje in Nakskov Fjord.
[179] Gustav Frenssen (1863-1945), German pastor and writer.

This idea should hopefully not enter the people's blood and remain there; because then Hitler isn't Hitler, but just an Old Prussian, one of those who told the south Jutlanders that it was a joy for the dumb Danes to be incorporated into German culture.

It was this spirit, Munk believed, that led to the Versailles Peace Treaty; and if it once again became ingrained in the German people, it would lead to a new Versailles. "We sense it. We sense it. It is this spirit, the spirit from Hell, that, with the help of God, and without him even suspecting it, speaks through little Frenssen's mouth when he appoints 'The Universal' to be the German National God."

Here Munk clearly saw what could happen in Germany, but then why had it taken him so long to realize that the above-mentioned German "spirit" had been ingrained in the Third Reich since 1933? The review of Frenssen's book ends with the statement that it's not Hitler who is to blame for the troubles in Germany, but rather his supporters:

It's hard, hard, hard to be the Fuehrer. He has to deal with the stress of winter, a lack of raw materials, fight with the Communists and Marxists, and be a friend with the Hail-Generals and fallen priests who see it as their mission to out-Hitler Hitler.[180]

This article, together with several earlier articles about Luther and the celebration of the 400th anniversary of the introduction of the Reformation in Denmark, received critical mention in the Schleswig-Holstein *Landeszeitung*. It provoked a complaint from Germany to the Foreign Office, and then a letter to Munk from Bishop S.M. Westergaard in Ribe,* which Munk immediately answered in an angry letter. Here's a single passage:

---

*Ribe, provincial town in southwest Jutland.
[180] Kaj Munk, "The Christian Hostile Germany", *Jyllands-Posten*, 29 November.

> *I was born a Petersen, and everything in me, so far that I know, is 'Nordic.' Now I'm told, through official conduit [through the Bishop] from Germany that the Munk spirit looks like Jewish pulp literature. This Germany, with Herr Streicher[181] in the lead, pleases itself with expressions that would be leniently described as privy greasing.[182]*

Munk was aware of Streicher's statements about the Jews in the newspapers and perhaps knew about publication from Streicher's press, *Der Stürmer*, of the illustrated children's book *The Toadstool (Der Giftpilz)*, which was intended to promote hatred of the Jews in German children.

Many in the 1930's, including Kaj Munk, expected that there would be a conflict in Europe, but there was a difference of opinion with respect to where the conflict would come from. *Vestlollands Avis* (*West-Lolland News*, conservative newspaper) wrote that it wasn't the relationship between Germany and France that was dangerous:

> *The danger lies in another place, and that place is in communism.... It's only now that it seems that events in France and Spain are starting to awaken a certain understanding for the cautionary voices which, for example at the National Socialist's Party meeting in Nurnberg last year, were so strongly expressed in the great speech by the Minister for Propaganda Goebbels in 'Communism Unmasked....' The Third Reich stands today as a bulwark against Bolshevism's attack on Western Europe, and it is for that reason that the hatred toward Hitler in Moscow's newspapers is as strong as it is.[183]*

As Germany grew in strength and influence, awareness grew in Denmark about what was taking place there. In 1937 there was a

---

[181] Julius Streicher (1885-1946), German district party leader (Gauleiter), publisher of the anti-Semitic magazine *Der Stürmer*.

[182] Kaj Munk: *Aldrig spørge om det nytter*, (Never ask if it's worth it) NNF 1958, pp. 204-206.

[183] "Foran Opgøret" (Before the Conflict) *Vestlollands Avis (West-Lolland News)*, 22 August 1936.

feature article in *Kristeligt Dagblad* (*The Christian Daily*) by the paper's editor at the time, Gunnar Helweg-Larsen, about the concentration camps in Sachsenburg (Sachsenhausen) north of Berlin, which he had visited together with 30 other journalists. The last section of Gunnar Helweg-Larsen's article is interesting reading:

> *Would one dare to hope, on this basis ("re-education" of the inmates) that the entire brutal system of force on which these camps are built is being dismantled? Hardly. A dictatorship needs concentration camps... and it's reasonable to expect that they will eventually be humanized... and there is reason to recognize the openness that was shown to the foreign journalists by allowing them to wander at will through such a camp. 'We have nothing to hide,' the camp leader said, whose persona was not only characterized by authority but also by humaneness. In a way he might be right. Barracks, workshops, kitchens, and sanitary installations– they were all very good. Moreover 'The System' should be judged on the basis of the bitter political struggle that was behind it.*[184]

That form of "popular education," with internment and concentration camps, is foreign to us and incompatible with our understanding of justice and humanness, wrote Helweg-Larsen. Then how should we understand his last sentence, how should "The System" be judged? Does the "bitter political struggle" give "The System" (the victor) the right to put the Jews, Communists, Social Democrats, and political opponents in concentration camps?

The fear of communism and the "Reds" in general, as in the editorial in *Vestlollands Avis*, surely had a great deal of influence on the political attitude of the Danes in the 1930's, and the antidote was, among others, National Socialism.

Munk wrote about Hitler's methods to get Germany on an even keel again: "That he had to use methods that can be criticized by

---

[184] Gunnar Helweg-Larsen: "Glædesløs Sang under jernhaard Tvang " (Sorrowful song under iron hard force) *Kristeligt Dagblad* 1937. Reprinted on 29 October 1999.

little people, who had never gotten their own hands dirty, was a necessity."[185]

This arrogant reference by Munk leads one to the slogan– "the ends justify the means."

---

[185] Kaj Munk, "The Christian Hostile Germany", Jyllands-Posten, 29 November 1936.

Chapter 8

He Sits at the Melting-Pot

An Idealist had its revival premiere at the Royal Theater on January 25, 1938. A few days later Munk returned home from a trip to France and Germany, and the *Nationaltidende* (*National Times*), among others, were ready to do an interview. They wanted to write about the new production of *An Idealist*, but Munk was tired and dismissive, and in answer to questions by the journalist about whether there was anything good going on in Paris or Berlin, he answered: "Good! – Yes, there are many good acts, but not in the theaters; I didn't go out to their plays, but rather more out in life. We Danes just don't know what life is." The journalist continued: "Suddenly he stands up and runs back and forth across the floor as if he would run away from himself. 'This Streicher,' he mumbles, 'this Streicher!' He stops in front of me, as if on command, and flashes his eyes in my face: 'This Hitler, he must not be the one we thought he was since he cannot get rid of this bandit' [Streicher]."

Munk said that he had not had much time for the theater as he had been writing a new play but wouldn't say what it was about. In response to the journalist who asked if it was a modern play, Munk answered,

> Do you know, there is a people in Germany, who with blood, screams, and tears must pay for each new step that the Third Reich ascends in greatness and admirable might. Do you know – oh, to be a poet of tragedy is loathsome: one sobs in despair over humanity's sorrows, but then exploits them as 'material.'[186]

For Munk, it was the subordinate Julius Streicher who was "the bandit," not the dictator Hitler. The "material" that Munk exploited was the German persecution of the Jews, and that material became the play *He Sits at the Melting-Pot*.

---

[186] "Nyt Skuespil af Kaj Munk" (New Play by Kaj Munk). Interview with Kaj Munk. *Nationaltidende* 31 January 1938.

On the same day, in *Politiken*, Kaj Munk was asked if Herod alluded to a contemporary person. To this he answered that modern dictators were driven by two emotions: love of the fatherland and hatred of other people.[187]

It was precisely the German dictator's hatred of another people, the Jews, which had for so long been apparent. Munk spoke about them as a people who, "with blood, screams, and tears" had to pay for Germany's progress. Since the "Jewish boycott" in 1933, conditions for Germans with Jewish heritage had become increasingly worse. For example, Jews could no longer be government officials. In 1935 marriage between Jews and Aryans was prohibited to protect German blood and German honor (The Nurnberg Laws).

This behavior toward a defenseless minority in Germany, this legislation, which took place completely in the open, aroused no great reaction in the democratic neighbor countries. Quite to the contrary, trade and cooperation continued almost as usual.

If Munk had remained in Berlin a while longer he would have witnessed the festivities in connection with the 5th anniversary of the National Socialists' takeover of power on January 30, 1933. Danish newspapers reported in detail from the festivities, and in the *National Times* one could read, among other things: "The word that in particular has dominated today on the 5th anniversary of the National Socialist regime, is the word 'power.'

There is of course no lack of topics for the 5th anniversary, as Germany's development since January 30, 1933 appears, after all, as an almost incomprehensible adventure." The article contained quotations from German newspapers, for example the *Berliner Börsenzeitung*: "We now have power, recognition, freedom, bread, honor, and work– and still the self-sufficient countries [those without territorial demands] deny us the necessary living space (*Lebensraum*). But we have time on our side...."

The *National Times* continued: "The struggle for living space will be Germany's struggle for the next five years." The article

---

[187] "I don't want applause on the way down from the pulpit" (Jeg ønsker ikke Haandklap paa Vej ned fra Prædikestolen). Interview with Kaj Munk, Politiken 31 January 1938.

ends with the following lines: "The rest of us can only hope that the regained power really will be used only in the service of peace."

Signed K-a.[188]

During this time Munk was on his triumphal journey in the theater world of Denmark and the Scandinavian countries. This quest to reach the heights of the theatrical world began in 1932-1933 and culminated in 1938-1939.

As mentioned, the Royal Theater presented a new and improved production of *An Idealist*, and that gave Munk redress for the fiasco with the first production in 1928. It was a success in the written reviews as well as on the stage. Svend Erichsen wrote this about the new production of *An Idealist*: "In the individual condensed characters that the play concentrates on, Kaj Munk captures one of the most pressing themes of our time– The dictator problem." Erichsen thought that the play in 1928 might have been confusing, but that Munk, through the plays *Cant*, *Love*, the *Hamlet* recasting, *In the Breakers*, and *The Victory*, had given us a key to an understanding of *An Idealist*:

And not least of all: The world's political developments during the last ten years have placed the play in the strongest cross currents of our time. The drama about the tyrant and the idealist Herod has become the drama about the European dictators. It was impossible to come to that conclusion in 1928, as then we only knew of Mussolini among the great European dictators. At the time he was considered more of a peculiarity than a phenomenon of the time.... There is an idolization of tyrants in his dramas, but in the last act the tyrant always bows down before God. The Edomite Herod, before his death, lays his royal robes over the Virgin Mary and the newborn royal child.... It is the pastor Kaj Munk's genuflection at the altar in Vedersø...The evening was a restoration of honor.... He

---

[188] "Hour after hour the ranks of torch bearers filed past Hitler's Palace last night", "Nazism's shining 5th Jubilee yesterday". *Nationaltidende* 31 January 1938, pp. 1-2.

[Munk] has, in his premiere play, a platform that can stand, even when one fears everything else is about to break.[189]

In the same issue of *Forum*, the well-known Swedish director and theatrical school leader Calle Flygare[190] suggested an exchange between the two countries: Olof Molander[191] should go to Copenhagen and stage Strindberg's *To Damascus*, and Svend Methling[192] should come to Stockholm, "... and stage our time's most important drama, *An Idealist*, by Kaj Munk."[193]

In those years one encountered Munk everywhere that drama and the theater were being discussed. He was probably the most talked about Dane in the late 1930's. He was seen, heard, and read.

In one article, where he discusses a statement made by Mr. Chamberlain, he writes: "Democracy can afford to make mistakes." It can afford it, Munk wrote, but;

The dictators cannot afford to make mistakes and in that Chamberlain is correct. But what an incentive to do the right thing this awareness is: You cannot afford a single loss! Both Hitler and Mussolini knew this, and have shown that they knew it. Then let us Danes get sick at hearing Hitler unroll this self-congratulatory record with massive demonstrations!

Munk realized, however, that not all of these miracles were created by Hitler alone, but that they were the result of technical developments and general progress in the world: "Even given that, it is impossible not to praise Hitler's leadership for wisdom upon

---

[189] Svend Erichsen: "A great work of drama, Kaj Munk's *An Idealist* at The Royal Theater". *Forum, Magazine for the Theater*, February 1938.

[190] Calle Flygare (1907-1972), Swedish actor, stage director, and author. Translated "The Melting-Pot" into Swedish, 1938-39.

[191] Olof Molander (1892-1966), Swedish actor, director, and theater manager.

[192] Svend Methling (1891-1977), Danish actor and director.

[193] Calle Flygare, "A Swede Looks at Danish Theater" *Forum, Magazine for the Theater*, February 1938.

wisdom, victory after victory. So far the same applies to the triumphator in Italy."[194]

Despite his admiration for Hitler's "wisdom," on January 24, 1938 Munk had finished a play about the rabid treatment of the German Jews. The play *He Sits at the Melting-Pot* was released in book form on April 8, 1938.[195] As mentioned, the play is about the German persecution of the Jews, which was beginning to assume grotesque proportions.

The play's protagonist is the archaeologist Professor Ernst Mensch, an obedient scientist who, while not interested in politics, accepts the new political climate, and thereby anti-Semitism.

During an archaeological dig in Palestine Mensch had found some potsherds from the time of Christ. Later, when Mensch and his secretary Annie Schmidt managed to put the shards together, they formed an image. The text under the image makes it clear that it was a picture of Jesus, a sensational discovery. Professor Mensch writes a letter to Hitler, and reports on the discovery of this unique image.

The subject of whether Jesus was Jewish or Aryan is part of the plot. The future Minister of Culture in the play, Professor Dorn, had "proven" in an article that Jesus was Aryan, not Jewish. Dorn, who had lost his wife, courts Annie Schmidt rather clumsily, unaware that in reality she is the Jewish singer Sara Levi. Besides having changed her identity and appearance, Sara Levi had helped her brother Dr. Helms obtain a position as a state director of libraries. Under the Nazi rule of the time, one could be sentenced to long prison terms for these acts. Mensch experiences anti-Semitism up close when the Jew, Dr. Helms, is exiled because he had falsified his "Aryan Certificate," and because he was engaged to a German woman. As mentioned earlier, such liaisons between Aryans and Jews were forbidden.

The play's religious figure, Bishop Beugel, is an honest and sympathetic Christian who reveres Hitler but rejects the Nazis' use of violence and their anti-Semitism. Bishop Beugel wanted the atheistic but honorable Mensch to be the Minister of Culture

---

[194] Kaj Munk, "Democracy Can Afford to Make Mistakes." *Jyllands-Posten* 13 March 1938.
[195] Kaj Munk, *Han Sidder ved Smeltediglen* (*He Sits at the Melting-Pot*) NNF 1938.

instead of the Nazi Dorn. That was something that Beugel should have stayed out of. He ended up in a concentration camp.[196]

In the play's 4th act, Mensch experiences serious problems. He tells his housekeeper Miss Schmidt that he loves her, and that love is reciprocated. However, when she admits that she is Jewish he throws her out, and then at once sends his housekeeper to bring her back. At the same time he receives a visit by Dorn, who reports that the Fuhrer is very interested in the image that Mensch had described to him, and that the Fuhrer himself would present Mensch with the German Prize, the highest order in the new Germany, on the following day.[197]

When Dorn realizes that the image that Mensch had shown him earlier is of Jesus, he persuades Mensch, for the sake of the Fatherland, not to make it public. The scientist Mensch is told not to reveal the truth.

In the last act in the assembly hall at the State University where the prize ceremony will be held, and where Adolph Hitler and the political upper class is present, Mensch asks Hitler: which is most important– the truth or the Fatherland? When Hitler says "The Fatherland," Mensch takes the potsherds bearing Jesus' image and throws them on the floor, smashing them, while at the same time shouting: "On the cross with him," a symbolic re-enactment of the crucifixion.

Then Mensch says that he will marry his secretary, the Jewess Sara Levi, which results in Dorn saying to him, "I will give you twelve hours." In other words, exile. Sara Levi and Mensch are then alone in the hall where Mensch, in the play's last line, says to Sara: "You will bear a son to me in my old age, Sara; he will be a good German, and a true man." The belief in the truth and a better future was something that Munk and Mensch had in common.

---

[196] Ibid., pp.51 ff., p. 66

[197] "Nazism's shining 5th Jubilee yesterday", Nationaltidende 31 January 1938, p.2. Here one can read that in connection with the 5th Jubilee, Hitler had instituted and awarded a new ribbon– "Treuedienst-Ehrenzeichen" (Loyal Service Award). There is probably some relation to the above mentioned "German Prize", which was called "The German Nobel Prize" the first time it was mentioned in *The Melting-Pot,* p.27.

The conditions in Germany at that time are reflected in the play with an almost German thoroughness, and in the characters the lines are sharply drawn. A character like the egoistic and boastful professor Dorn was easy to find among the top German Nazis in the thirties. The inspiration for the attractive Sara Levi goes back to 1933 when Munk visited Ingeborg and Ebbe Rasmussen in Berlin. Ebbe Rasmussen wrote later about this visit:

> *Munk stayed in Berlin for about a dozen days, and we had a great time. Together we studied Berlin's entertainment scene though, of course, mostly the theaters. Persecution of the Jews had not yet gained speed; so we saw both a Max Reinhardt play and Shakespeare's* Much Ado About Nothing, *with the adorable Grete Mosheim,[198] and we witnessed the delighted crowd follow her to her car after the performance. Only a few months later she had to leave the country because of her Jewish heritage. She was later to become Sara Levi in* He Sits at the Melting-Pot.[199]

Kaj Munk had delegated his own positions with respect to the many burning questions of the day to Bishop Beugel, and to Professor Mensch, in *The Melting-Pot*. And in particular, the professor's dilemma in choosing between the dictator and the truth is similar to Kaj Munk's own position in the thirties, and Bishop Beugel's Christian faith is obviously not far from Munk's. That the Christian message, and reverence for Christ, was important can be clearly seen in a letter of October 6, 1938 from Munk to the director of the Folk Theater, Thorvald Larsen, who at the time was at work on a new rehearsal of *The Melting-Pot* due to changes in the cast: "Remember now, dear friend, remember when you start again with rehearsals, that the image has the leading role– let them handle it gently, let them look at it

---

[198] Grete Mosheim (1905-1987), German actress, emigrated to the USA in 1933 where she performed at the "Deutches Theater New York". She returned to Berlin in 1952.

[199] *The Book about Kaj Munk*, WST 1946, chapter 8 "Automobile Adventures with Kaj Munk", Professor Ebbe Rasmussen, pp. 175-176.

with reverence, and let it be smashed to pieces on the stone floor– oh, how I dread this new performance."[200]

Grete Mosheim (1905-1987)
Author's Archive

---

[200] *Kaj Munk og Folketeatret (Kaj Munk and The Folk Theater)*. Letters from Kaj Munk to Thorvald Larsen, NNF 1957, p.39.

After Munk's play *The Melting-Pot* had been released in book form, Svend Erichsen reviewed it under the heading "Kaj Munk's Conversion." He wrote:

> He Sits at the Melting-Pot *is Kaj Munk's testament of conversion. There are thoughts and lines in it that knock over all of his earlier ideology.... Kaj Munk deserves thanks because he has had the courage to do it.... That hero worship in 1933-34 drove Munk into the clutches of Nazism is beyond doubt. He has often enough given an unambiguous expression of that – mostly in newspaper articles.... With his recent play he has, with one brutal act, torn himself loose from this embrace.*[201]

In a review in the *Berlingske Tidende*, Henning Kehler discussed parts of Munk's works, and wrote that with *Cant* and *The Word,* "he was hugely victorious as a Danish dramatic poet.... Not since Adam Oehlenschläger and H.C. Andersen has any Danish poet had a similar break-through." Henning Kehler continued that when Munk's dramatic genius unites with the gospel, he draws on inexhaustible sources of energy: "It is from this union of art and gospel that Munk's great plays emanate, including, and not least of all, *He Sits at the Melting-Pot.*" Henning Kehler was apparently not impressed by Munk's play *Hamlet.*

In the article there is a reference to Munk's *Hamlet*:

> In between [the plays mentioned] the Betty Nansen Theater staged Kaj Munk's parodic rewriting of Shakespeare's Hamlet. Kaj Munk has shown the good taste not to release this attempt in book form. In that way he has left behind a mission for the Kaj Munk Society, which, as one might suspect, will certainly be formed after– hopefully not for a long time– he dies.[202]

With respect to *Hamlet*, Henning Kehler was mistaken. The play was released in a private edition in December of the same year, but

---

[201] *Forum, Magazine for the Theater*, Spring Season 1938, pp.12-13.
[202] "Kaj Munk's new play: *He Sits at the Melting-Pot*", *Berlingske Tidende*, 11 April 1938.

his prediction of a Kaj Munk Society was fulfilled. It was founded on January 13, 1997.

On April 9, the day after *The Melting-Pot* came out, Munk read aloud for an audience in evening attire at the Student Union. Munk began by reading the hymn by Ingemann, from which he had found the title to the play: *The Great Master Cometh,* where in the first verse, third line, it is written: He sits at the Melting-Pot.[203]

Politiken wrote that in his introduction Munk had, among other things, recounted the accusations made against him in order to draw attention to his own person; but Munk said that the attention he received was only because he wrote better plays than others. The paper also praised Munk's recital of *The Melting-Pot*:

> *His work lives in him, glows through his countenance, and he can, with a glance, rivet his audience to their seats. Last night, and not in the least with the play's closing act, he produced an almost unheard of affect. Kaj Munk seemed to grow at the rostrum while he read.... The applause hailed, stormed, drummed, and rained down upon the poet when he finished speaking.*

Politiken's account ended with: "On the Second Day of Easter, *He Sits at the Melting-Pot* had its Scandinavian premiere at the Norwegian Theater. Up there they strike while the iron is hot. It is a consolation, however, that the iron is ours."[204]

Would the Royal Theater refuse to play the politically perilous play?[205] The theater had performed Gandrup's play *It Is Never Enough* (*Det er aldrig nok*), with the same theme, four years earlier. But whatever the reason, *The Melting-Pot* had its premiere performance on April 23, 1938 at the Norwegian Theater in Oslo, and it wasn't until August 27 that it was staged

---

[203] *Den Danske Salmebog* (*The Danish Hymnal*), 2003 edition, no. 612.

[204] "Kaj Munk Reads to the Students" (Kaj Munk læser for Studenterne), *Politiken*, 10 April 1938.

[205] Hans Bay-Petersen, *A Friendly Invitation. The Royal Theater's Guest Performances in Nazi Germany in the Thirties.* Multivers, Copenhagen 2003. Kaj Munk's correspondence with The Royal Theater's director Andreas Møller, and with The Folk Theater's director Thorvald Larsen, about *The Melting-Pot*, pp. 85-90.

at the Folk Theater in Copenhagen where it was performed 194 times. Shortly afterwards, Gerda Christophersen's Theater-tour took the play on the road and performed it 181 times in the provinces.[206]

Svend Erichsen's review of the Folk Theater's staging of *The Melting-Pot* has the title: "The Big and the Little World." The Big World was Munk's play, and the Little World was a play that was performed at the Royal Theater with the title *The Little World* (*Den Lille Verden*). Erichsen wrote:

> He Sits at the Melting-Pot *was a disappointment. It wasn't Kaj Munk's fault as the play is one of the most powerful he has written. During his recital at the Student Union last year, it struck like a bolt of lightning. Whether he wins on the stage or not depends on whether his interpreters are as great virtuosi as he is, and equally great artists. In this case they were not.*

He wrote furthermore that the "sermon" that Munk had given on Easter Saturday 1938 from the stage at the Royal Theater, in a performance in support of the construction of the Grundtvig Cathedral, was a good starting point for judging the Folk Theater's performance. Erichsen quoted from this speech:

> *In a time when the evil will that we call Satan has turned the Earth into Hell's front yard, we are assembled here tonight in the magnificent temple of Danish spiritual life. On this Earth Grundtvig lived out his stewardship for the good of the soul and the good of the people. He was as Christian as he was Danish. He spoke about the National and the Nordic in such a way that you could, in fear of insulting our neighbor to the south, catch yourself believing that he had borrowed his ideas from Hitler. At the same time Grundtvig proclaimed with all his power his love of freedom and his hatred of uniformity.*

We are building a new church for him, and some have mockingly said that we have no God to put in it. And we are not as poor as

---

[206] Harald Mogensen, *Kaj Munk at The Theater* (*Kaj Munk paa Teatret*). Nyt Nordisk Forlag Arnold Busck, Copenhagen 1953, pp.46-49.

those who have no God at all, nor as poor as those who must uplift a man to be their God.[207]

Svend Erichsen believed that this speech, when compared to *The Melting-Pot*, showed that Kaj Munk was against uniformity, for freedom, against racial persecution, for humanism, against the leader worship that turns a man into God, and for the God of Christianity. For that reason he finds it natural to call *The Melting-Pot* a testament of conversion. About the change in Kaj Munk's relationship to Nazism and Hitler, Erichsen wrote:

> *Kaj Munk had in a previous book given the Third Reich unconditional support.[208] It was his tendency to indulge in Hero worship that had led him to that. This phase in his development seems now to be behind him. He hasn't given up his admiration of Hitler; but on the other hand there are only tattered pieces left of his admiration for the system.*

Svend Erichsen is apparently happy with Munk's "conversion," and he ranges far and wide in his review. He mentions, among other things, that Munk had been criticized for using the ideas of others:

> *It's true that he does that. But that is not decisive for independence in a gifted mind. The only decisive thing is the way that the borrowed ideas are used. One can hardly say*

---

[207] Quotation from Kaj Munk, "For the Grundtvig Cathedral. A Speech on Easter Saturday in The Royal Theater", printed in *Jyllands-Posten* 17 April 1938. Re-printed in *Med Sol og Megen Glæde (With Sun and Lots of Joy)*, NNF 1942. Erichsen's quotation is comprised of sentences taken from different parts of the speech. The sentence about Grundtvig and Hitler appears in *Jyllands-Posten* as follows: "... then you could– in fear of insulting our great neighbor to the south– catch yourself believing that he [Grundtvig] had borrowed his ideas from Hitler". This sentence was left out of *With Sun and Lots of Joy*, which was published during the German occupation.

[208] Kaj Munk, *Vedersø-Jerusalem and Back*. NNF 1934.

there is any stolen property in The Melting-Pot. The plot that Munk had written is his own.[209]

Stolen property is a brutal expression, but the possibility that Kaj Munk had borrowed a couple ideas for *The Melting-Pot* from another Danish dramatist does exist.

Theater historian M.A. Hans Bay-Petersen[210] was, as far as I know, the first, in 2003, to draw attention to the existence of several parallels between *The Melting-Pot* and *It is Never Enough,*[211] written by the previously mentioned critic and dramatist Carl Gandrup. Gandrup's play was about the rapidly increasing anti-Semitism in Germany. *It is never Enough* had its premiere at the Royal Theater on October 3, 1934, almost four years before *The Melting-Pot,* which had its premiere at the Folk Theater on August 27, 1938. Despite bad reviews it was performed 17 times. The Royal Theater was, therefore, an early harbinger of what was then happening in Hitler's Germany.

Munk was well informed about what was happening in the theater, and was an avid theatergoer, so he had most likely seen or read Gandrup's play. Gandrup was a well-known person in the world of writers and the theater. His plays were performed in many theaters in Copenhagen and the provinces.

In the book edition of *It is never Enough*, Gandrup wrote very diplomatically in the list of characters: "The story takes place in a foreign country this year," but nobody was in doubt that it was the persecution of Jews in Germany and the associated problems that the book was about. The book was "Respectfully and with thankful friendship dedicated to Th. Stauning," and on the title page there was a visionary quotation by K. K. Steincke: "In the new dictatorships the state is a Moloch on whose altar any human creature can be sacrificed!"

---

[209] . Svend Erichsen, " The Big and the Little World." *Forum, Magazine for the Theater*, September 1938, pp. 6-9.

[210] Hans Bay-Petersen, A Friendly Invitation. The Royal Theater's Guest Performances in Nazi Germany in the Thirties. Multivers Copenhagen, 2003, pp.39-43.

[211] Carl Gandrup, *It is never Enough*. H. Hirschsprung's Publishing, Copenhagen 1934.

The play is about the power of the state and its anti-Semitism, in contrast to humanism and affection between people. The play's title suggests that no matter how much is given to the new dictators, it is never enough. When two Danish dramatists deal with the same subject within just a few years of each other, it is natural that there will be some similarities. However, there are a striking number of parallels between Gandrup and Munk's plays. It is tempting to make a short comparison between the characters and acts in *The Melting-Pot* and *It is Never Enough*.

The two male protagonists (Parelius in Gandrup, and Mensch in Munk) are both scientists, and they have, respectively, bronchitis and bad lungs. Parelius is married to a Jew, and Mensch wants to marry a Jew. They both experience short-lived anti-Semitic quandaries. The noble Michael da Costa is the intermediary between the state and Parelius. In *The Melting-Pot* it is the unsympathetic party-faithful Professor Dorn, who is the state's contact to Mensch. Parelius is offered a top position. Mensch is selected to receive "The German Prize." However, conditions are attached to both offers: Parelius must get a divorce from Jacobe, and Mensch must not make public the image that proves that Christ is a Jew. Parelius is imprisoned. Mensch and Sara Levi are exiled. In both plays there is talk about "dishonest" Jews. There is also talk about the gravity of the war (WWI). Parelius says to his wife, "I too have experienced a lot in my time; those four years at the front didn't leave one with a very exuberant spirit."[212] In *The Melting-Pot* Bishop Beugel says to Dorn, "In my younger days, my four years in the trenches– I was a serious man then. And just about lost my mind."[213]

The two main feminine roles also have much in common. They are both actresses. Jacobe is a Jew; and Sara is half Jewish. Both have rich uncles who support them. Both women experience being unwanted in their own country. Jacobe asks her husband, "The child we will have? Will that too be an impure progeny?"[214] In *The Melting-Pot*, Mensch wants Miss Schmidt to come to the university for the prize presentation, but she says: "You'll just

---

[212] Ibid. p.19.

[213] Kaj Munk, *Han sidder ved Smeltediglen*. NNF, p.50.

[214] Carl Gandrup, op.cit., p.15.

get unpleasantries from that if it comes out that I am impure. I don't dare, for your sake."[215]

It can make one wonder why none of Munk's otherwise persistent critics drew attention to the parallels between his and Gandrup's play concerning this contemporary subject. As far as I can see, *It is Never Enough* was never mentioned in the reviews in connection with *The Melting-Pot*, whereas several critics of Munk's earlier works were never in doubt as to where he had gotten his ideas.

Gandrup's *It is Never Enough* seems to be recognition of the reality of German anti-Semitism without being either for or against it. Munk's *The Melting-Pot* seems more like a warning. The nearly four years that had elapsed between the creation of the two plays meant that Munk now had knowledge of the extent of the brutality of the Jewish persecution that had developed in Germany between 1934 and 1938, and had been able to use that knowledge in his play. Newspapers had kept their readers informed on a daily basis about conditions in Germany, and that probably contributed to the success of *The Melting-Pot*. Carl Gandrup died in 1936 and, therefore, never saw Munk's play.

I believe that certain lines in Gandrup's play inspired Munk. Some of these similarities can, of course, be coincidental. However, regardless of where Munk found his inspiration, *The Melting-Pot* is exceptional drama. It was written in and for a certain time and about a subject that, unfortunately, is still relevant. It can be, and still is, performed.[216]

Henning Kehler wrote in 1932 about where dramatists found their ideas: "Great poets rarely, or never, invent the plot, the 'short story' that they dramatize. Holberg and Molière adapted material to their plays whenever they found something useful."

Kehler hoped that Munk would continue to use the entertaining historical biographies that he had, for example, used in *Cant*. "Then he will also in the future be a Royal son of

---

[215] Kaj Munk, op.cit, p.73.
[216] See appendix, section 1989-2007.

Danish poetry, called to awaken Danish dramatic poetry from its long slumber."[217]

---

[217] "Kaj Munk" Henning Kehler, *Berlingske Tidende* 15 September 1932.

Chapter 9

"The Melting-Pot" Reviewed in Paris

Despite the attempt by the authorities to keep them out, many German refugees did arrive in Denmark during the thirties. Among them were many Jews who thereby avoided prison, and possibly extermination, in Germany. One of the Jewish refugees, Professor Walter A. Berendsohn,[218] wrote to Munk:

Author, Pastor Kaj Munk
Vedersø
pr. Ulfborg, Jylland
18 November 1938
Dear Pastor!

Even though you have not yet answered my two letters, I have translated your play He Sits at the Melting-Pot *into German, under the German title 'Professor Mensch und das Christusbild.' I couldn't help it; it was an exciting job.*

I allowed myself some freedom when translating your wonderful dialogue into my mother tongue. The greatest freedom of course involved the blessing of the chamomile tea* and Sara Levi's little song. My problem there was that I didn't know the melody.

I have, furthermore, suggested several small changes in my translation. These start with the title. We don't know this lovely hymn by Ingemann in Germany, but I believe I have maintained the central plot of your play.

I have changed The Director of Libraries to Librarian because it's impossible in Germany for such a young man to be a director.

I have changed the name Miss Fürst to Miss Jung, because in Germany Fürst is recognized as a Jewish surname. As you call a doctor Dr. Hülfe and a professor Mensch, why not continue in

---

*Act III in He sits at The Melting-Pot.
[218] Walter A. Berendsohn (1884-1984). See biographies.

the same way and call the girl Miss Jung? She is, after all, very young, and doesn't understand anything at all.

Then Dorn's attack– he excuses himself– on the image of Jesus, which wasn't included at the Folk Theater. I have instead substituted a reference to the 'nose' in the image. Miss Schmidt speaks about it as a sign of royal heritage.

I have sent my translation to a friend in Lyngby near Copenhagen, and I plan on having some copies made. Maybe it's all for nothing. Maybe you have already given the translation rights to someone else, or all of the foreign transactions to an agent, Folmer Hansen, or another? But I won't whine or complain because I have had the pleasure of doing the work; and just to avoid further expenses, I would ask you to send me some advice at once. I include an envelope with my address and an international stamp.

If that is not the case then I would like to send a copy to you and ask for your authorization of my translation.

I am certain that this play could now, due to events in Germany, be a success worldwide, and in particular in England and the United States. I have spoken with several professionals who quickly became interested.

With deep respect
Yours faithfully
Walter A. Berendsohn

Bangor Hotel, 26 Bedford Place
London W.C.1

Why didn't Munk answer Berendsohn's letters? Due to reasons yet unknown, it appears that the cooperation with Erwin Magnus had by this time been brought to an end. Had Munk given the German translation rights to someone else?

Only two excerpts of Berendsohn's translation of *The Melting-Pot* have so far been found: most of Act 3, where the confrontation between Bishop Beugel and Professor Dorn takes place, and the part of Act 4 where Mensch finds out that he is to receive the "German Prize" and where Dorn convinces Mensch to turn over the image of Jesus to the Fuhrer.[219] This manuscript,[220] which is found in the Munk Archives, is comprised of 13 typewritten pages, with no dates or signatures, but with the following heading:

"Kay Munk, "Das Christusbild", a play in 5 acts.
Walter A. Berendsohn translated this play from the Danish in November of 1938 while the synagogues burned in Germany."

Walter A. Berendsohn (1884-1984)
Private Photo
City Historical Collection for Lyngby-Taarbæk Municipality

---

[219] Kaj Munk, *op.cit.*, pp. 43-54, and 64-68.
[220] KMF

It has so far not been possible to date this manuscript. Berendsohn, in his letter to Munk, suggests that he will have a friend make several copies of the translation. Kaj is spelled with a "y," whereas Berendsohn uses "j" everywhere else. Berendsohn's original title is shortened to *Das Christusbild,* and the statement that Berendsohn translated the play while the synagogues burned in Germany is formulated in a way that suggests that someone else might have written it. The Swedish theatrical publisher Arvid Englind[221] purchased Berendsohn's translation[222] in the spring of 1939, so the manuscript could be a copy of that, possibly proofread and edited by Englind's German dramatist Verner Arpe.[223]

In December of 1938, Walter Berendsohn wrote a review of *The Melting-Pot* in German. It is not known if he had tried to get his review in German or Austrian newspapers, but it ended up far from Denmark and the Folk Theater, in a German language newspaper in Paris. Experiencing the play on the stage and the work with the translation had given Berendsohn an insight into the play's details that made possible the multifaceted review that is given here in full:

> *"Professor Mensch and the Image of Jesus*
> *By Walter A. Berendsohn*
> *There has been a great deal of excitement in recent years about the Danish pastor and dramatist Kaj Munk. He is considered an excellent speaker, both in the pulpit and the lecture hall. Kaj Munk is a regular contributor to an ultra-conservative newspaper in Aarhus that is distributed in all of Jutland* [Jyllands-Posten]. *For over ten years he has written plays that are characterized by forceful scenes and excellent dialogue.*
>
> *The Jutlandic pastor is God-fearing, brash, witty, cheerful, and full of ideas. In recent years he has been occupied with contemporary questions. One play,* The Victory, *is a soulful analysis of the Italian dictator during the war in Abyssinia, whom he had simply given another name. In this way he delves fearlessly into current issues and speaks his mind without*

---

[221] Arvid Englind (1882-1972), Swedish theatrical publisher.
[222] *Forum, Magazine for the Theater,* March, 1939. News from abroad, p.12.
[223] Verner Arpe (1902-1979). See biographies.

hesitation. The Student Union in Copenhagen had elected him 'Poet of the Year.' [Honorary Artist]

The play that is being talked about here is He Sits at the Melting-Pot. The play's title is a line from a well-known hymn by B.S. Ingemann, which is about Jesus freeing and forgiving sinful souls. The play is about a professor in archaeology named Mensch who, through his excavations in Palestine, has achieved worldwide renown. Back home again he and his assistant Miss Anni Schmidt, have worked for four years on the potsherds they brought back. Among them they find pieces of an unusually beautiful portrait; and through an inscription on the last shard, it is revealed that the image is a contemporary one of the Savior. We are given an insight into the cooperation between these two and their ability to grasp the life revealed in the ancient artifacts. There have been rumors for a long time that the Fuhrer– the play takes place in The Third Reich– will award the German Prize (a substitute for the frowned upon Nobel Prize) to the famous researcher. Professor Mensch sees in him [Hitler] the Fatherland's savior from shame and degradation. For that reason the Fuhrer is the first to hear about the important discovery. There is no doubt now that the professor will get the prize. The Minister of Culture arrives on behalf of the Fuhrer to tell Mensch about the prize. However, there are strict conditions attached to the prize. The beautiful image leaves no doubt: Jesus Christ was a Jew. The Minister of Culture is one of the so-called 'German Christians' who will transform Christianity into a religion for those prepared to fight– for the warrior spirit. The German God– a Jew! That is impossible! He brutally forbids Professor Mensch from making this known to the German people. He demands to have the image handed over but in the end is content with a promise by Mensch not to do anything; and that the image will be given to the Fuhrer on the day the German Prize is awarded.

Within this main act a double act is interwoven. Miss Schmidt and her brother, university librarian Dr. Helm, both Jews, have used falsified papers and false Aryan Certificates to gain access into the world of science. Kaj Munk does not portray Judaism with much dignity. For most Jews such behavior would be beneath their dignity, but such cases probably do occur. At first the librarian is unmasked by the

157

Minister of Culture, fired, and imprisoned; however, he is shown mercy and released on the condition that he leaves Germany immediately. This torments his sister not just for his sake but also because she enjoys her work with Professor Mensch; and she loves him, this sensitive idealistic intellectual. She wants to be free, but he can no longer do without her and wants to make her his life's partner. Then she admits that she is a Jew. With harsh words he throws her out. However, the eyes in the image of Jesus will not give him peace, and he asks her to return. In compliance with his wishes, she reveals how she had transformed herself from the singer and actress Sara Levi to the assistant professor at the university, Anni Schmidt. He asks his long-time assistant to be at his side on the day the prize is awarded.

The short 5th act closes this tendentious play. The Minister of Culture gives a powerful German speech. Professor Mensch receives the prize from the Minister's hand. He asks the Fuhrer what his position is with respect to the truth. "My truth is Germany," the Fuhrer answers, "and if, on my path to this goal, another truth gets in my way, I will smash it." At that moment Professor Mensch throws the image of Jesus to the floor and smashes it. He sacrifices the newly found truth for the Fatherland, and then realizes that the image lives on even stronger in his heart and that he must make a sacrifice on the altar of mankind. His assistant, the Jewess Miss Sara Levi, who he can thank for half of his results, will be his wife. The Fuhrer storms out of the room, and everyone follows him. The Minister of Culture approaches them both and says: "I will give you twelve hours" (To leave Germany). Then he too leaves the room. Professor Mensch turns to his bride and says quietly: "You will bear me a son in my old age– he will be a good German, and a true man."

For the first time Kaj Munk had written an ideological drama. The play's direction is clear. As an admirer of dictators, who he considers to be great men, he leaves out any question of politics.

Not a word in this play is aimed at Adolf Hitler as the political leader of the German people. It is problematical whether a distinction between politics and religious conflict is possible, especially in this time of Jewish persecution in

Germany. Here, however, the religious questions are clearly illustrated, not just in short lines but also in the well-illustrated symbology of the archaeological discovery. This play has been performed more than 50 times for a full house at the Folk Theater in Copenhagen and at the same time in numerous places in the provinces by a traveling theater troupe.[224] It has recently premiered in Stockholm, and with great success. It will without doubt be performed on all the world's stages as soon as translations are available.[225] (a.t.)

At the end of this otherwise positive review Berendsohn points out that Munk has spared Hitler from criticism. In the play it is Professor Dorn, not Hitler, who represents the National Socialistic attitude toward the Jews. The idea that it is Hitler's staffers, who act incorrectly, occurs frequently with Munk. This can be seen in the quotation mentioned above (p.127) of January 31, 1938 in the *Nationaltidende* where he wondered why Hitler could not control the notorious Jew baiter Julius Streicher.

It is noteworthy that Munk's first translators, Magnus and Berendsohn, were both Jews, and especially that Berendsohn was the first to translate *The Melting-Pot* into German. A German refugee translates a Danish play about the persecution of Jews in the Germany of the time; the same conditions that would drastically change the course of his own life.

Berendsohn came to Denmark from Hamburg in July of 1933 where he had been professor at the university but had been dismissed for two reasons; that he was both a Jew and a Social Democrat. At the request of an acquaintance, Berendsohn applied for a teaching position at the University of Copenhagen. He later withdrew his application when he realized that it would not be

---

[224] The Gerda Christophersen Touring Company.
[225] Walter A Berendsohn: *Professor Mensch und das Christusbild, Parisian Daily* 11-12 The *Pariser Tageblatt* was a German language newspaper published in Paris 1933-1941. The paper's chief editor was the exiled German Georg Bernhard.

accepted.[226] Life in Denmark was not easy, at least not for Jewish emigrants from Germany.

---

[226] Steffen Steffensen, På flugt fra nazismen. Tysksprogede emigranter i Danmark efter 1933 (Escaping Nazism. German-speaking Emigrants in Denmark after 1933). C.A. Reitzels Forlag, Copenhagen 1986, p.255.

Chapter 10

"The Earth is burning"

Kaj Munk wrote the following in a preface to the program brochure for the Danish premiere of *The Melting-Pot* at the Folk Theater on August 27, 1938:

> *The Earth is burning. There are times in human history when one seems to forget that. Our time is not one of them. At least 7 days in every week we feel that we have been thrown into a crackling, seething bonfire.... Are they the flames of destruction that envelop us?*

The bonfires had been lit in Europe, and soon Kaj Munk had proof of his worst fears. It would mean annihilation for many. First the German Nazis burned books, and then they burned the synagogues.

On November 9, 1938, Germany, and in particular the German Jews, experienced what was called the "Crystal Night" (*Kristallnacht*). According to the Nazis it was a spontaneous demonstration, occurring ostensibly in response to a young Jew's assassination attempt on the German consul Ernst vom Rath in Paris. It was more likely a carefully planned act of terrorism by the Nazis, where the mistreatment and debasement of the Jews reached a previously unknown scale. Ninety-one Jews, mostly businessmen, were killed. About 30,000 Jews were temporarily arrested, and many were sent to the concentration camps in Dachau, Buchenwald, and Sachsenhausen.

In accordance with instructions from Göring,[227] the wealthy were allowed to buy their freedom, but at a very high price. Over 100 synagogues were set on fire and destroyed. About 7,500 Jewish businesses were completely demolished.

---

[227] Hermann Göring (1893-1946) National Socialist politician, Field Marshal.

When it eventually turned out that many of the properties that were destroyed were actually owned by Germans, and not by Jewish businessmen, the Jews were required to pay the damages. The Nazis even confiscated compensation payments from insurance companies.

In addition the Jews had to pay a "propitiatory sacrifice" of one billion Rigsmark.[228] Danish newspapers were well informed about this, and reported in detail on these excesses. But often with only muted condemnation.

The editorial printed in the *Jyllands-Posten* on November 15, 1938,[229] while not defending the Nazis' violent anti-Semitic acts, did to some degree express an understanding of the Germans' "animosity" towards the Jews. The editorial often highlighted the many proper and well-behaved Jews, both in Denmark and other places in Europe, while recounting in other sections on the unfortunate influence of certain Jews:

> *There are many Jews who have proven to be good Danish men... but there is also a striking number of Jews who, in a very unpleasant manner, have been prominent figures in swindle and, perhaps not least of all, even in the cases of unappetizing pornography and feticide that have occurred in recent years. Even in Danish business affairs some Jews have behaved in a manner that does not speak well for the profession.*

The editorial writer was aware that Germany was going to freeze out the Jews and that therefore the Jewish question had become a European question: "Europe, and the rest of the world, cannot watch silently while 750,000 people perish.... We can admit that Germany has a right to get rid of its Jews, but then we can also demand that it be carried out in a decent manner." The editorial was characterized by its confidence that a peaceful solution could be found to the current European problems concerning the Jews.

---

[228] Wolfgang Benz, op.cit. pp.143-148.

[229] Jødeforfølgelserne i Tyskland (The persecution of Jews in Germany), *Jyllands-Posten*, November 15, 1938.

On the same day, November 15, Erwin Magnus wrote in a letter to Peter Freuchen: "What do you think about all this taking place in Germany? And the world looks on, getting by with a few feeble responses which Germany does not care the least about." The next letter to Freuchen closes similarly with remarks about conditions in Germany: "It's all so horrible. These are not humans, they are devils!"[230]

The indignation that drove Munk to write *The Melting-Pot* was undiminished after the Crystal Night in Germany. His anger over the Germans' treatment of the Jews compelled him to ask Benito Mussolini for help. "An open letter to Mussolini" by Parish Pastor Kaj Munk was published in the *Jyllands-Posten* on November 17, 1938. In the letter Munk compares Mussolini to Caesar while heaping praise on the Italian dictator. Munk tries to come to terms with Mussolini's attack on Abyssinia, which he considers the only mistake he had made so far. By the middle of the letter he arrives at his real subject: the Jews. It is discouraging to him that a people like the Germans "...can disgrace themselves by mistreating the defenseless, and committing sacrilege." He thought Mussolini was too wise to mistreat a group of his own people; but by then Munk had heard "...that you have begun to change, and to behave like the Teutones' apprentice."

However, Munk doesn't believe that can be true, and he asks Mussolini to step up and set things right. "Do you have room in Abyssinia for the Jews... then give them a Goshen there![231] In the name of mercy, solve this problem for us." Munk also asks Mussolini to tell Hitler that he had disappointed "us" by choosing Goebbels instead of Schacht. Munk probably still believed that the excesses in Germany were because Hitler's staff had misled him.

By the expression "Teutones' apprentice," Munk referred to the fact that Italy had imitated Germany by introducing a law in 1938 "to protect the Italian race." In September of the same year the Italian cabinet announced that all Jews had to leave Italian territory

---

[230] Two letters from Erwin Magnus to Peter Freuchen, 15 & 20 November 1938, Peter Freuchen's archive at The Royal Library.

[231] The area in the northeast sector of the Nile Delta, where the Pharaohs gave the Jews land, and where they remained until the time of the Exodus. See Genesis, chapter 45-10.

within six months. The resistance of the military, and protests by the Catholic Church, insured that the law had no real affect.[232]

Was there room in Abyssinia for the Jews? After the Italian campaign in 1935-1936, using modern weapons of war, as well as mustard gas, there probably was. However, the idea of deporting 500,000 Europeans to Africa was not very sympathetic.

In the letter to Mussolini, Munk wrote that it now looked like the Jews would be eradicated by being driven to suicide. Could Munk reconcile himself with these conditions? No. He didn't know, but probably already suspected, where it was heading for the Jews in Germany and Italy. It was for that reason he saw the Abyssinian solution as an option.

In a follow-up article to the open letter, "Fault or no Fault-help them!" in the *Jyllands-Posten* on November 27, 1938, Munk explained why he felt justified in writing to the Italian dictator: "It would be hypocrisy to deny that, at the present time, I am– rightly or not– one of those in this country whose words are noted." He also mentioned that it would be of some influence if those men and women around the country "... whose words carried weight... would address Il Duce in the same way."

Kaj Munk's call for protest, printed in a Danish provincial newspaper, was probably not read by many people in other countries. That Kaj Munk did not address Hitler, but rather Mussolini, seems to indicate that Munk's otherwise unshakeable faith in the German dictator was beginning to crumble.

Munk was well aware that his words were noted. They carried weight. In this case he used that power to help the persecuted Jews, but his words would have had the same influence during the thirties when he was praising Hitler and Mussolini. He was aware that with an appeal to Mussolini he risked making a fool of himself, and that is what happened. His appeal was lambasted in a series of satirical verses and drawings.

However, one cannot deny that Munk both urgently and often drew attention to the inhumane conditions that the Jews

---

[232] Wolfgang Scheffler: *Persecution of the Jews in the Third Reich (Judenverfolgung im Dritten Reich)1933-1945*, Colloquium Publisher, Berlin 1960, p.45.

were subjected to in Germany, Italy, and later in occupied Denmark.

On Saturday, November 26, 1938, Kaj Munk's play *The Phoenix (Fugl Føniks)* had its premiere at the Student's Union.[233] It was a drama about the peace conference that led to the Treaty of Versailles in 1919, where the national leaders, President Woodrow Wilson of the USA, Prime Minister Lloyd George of England, and Prime Minister Georges Clemenceau of France, agreed upon the provisions for peace for Germany and the other vanquished nations after WWI– provisions that for Germany were so severe that they broke the Weimar Republic and paved the way for Hitler's rise to power. Twenty days before its premiere, *The Phoenix* had been read aloud by the actor Poul Reumert in the Odd Fellow Palæet as a benefit for the German Jews.

In 1938 Munk was being performed in all of Scandinavia. He was the most talked about and highest paid artist in Denmark. In a status article on New Year's Day 1938 with the title "The Annual Prize Cups," Ole Palsbo ranked the year's crop of plays and films. For him there was no doubt about who should receive the year's prize cups: Kaj Munk and Leni Riefenstahl.[234] Munk's dominance of Danish theater was enormous. In 1938 the public could attend no less than four of his plays in Copenhagen– *In The Breakers* (*I Brændingen*), *An Idealist, He Sits at the Melting-Pot*, and *The Dictatress* (*Diktatorinden*), and even hear the above-mentioned recital of *The Phoenix*. Palsbo wrote that the enormous interest for Munk had also increased the interest for the art of the theater: "Another thing is, that with the exception of Munk, there is undeniably little left to talk about." He did write about other dramatists, though for cinematic art only four films were taken into consideration by Palsbo, and in particular one of them: "The most outstanding of this year's films, and in the special genre of art film, was Leni Riefenstahl's first film on the Olympic Games, Olympia– Festival of Nations (Folkenes Fest/Fest der Völker)."

---

[233] Kaj Munk: *Fugl Føniks* (*The Phoenix*). NNF 1939.

[234] Leni Riefenstahl (1902-2003), German instructor, directed films for the National Socialist regime, including *Festival of Nations* and *Festival of Beauty* about the Olympics in Berlin in 1936. Wolfgang Benz, *Geschichte des Dritten Reiches*, pp.67-68.

At the end of the article he returned again to this film, and wrote that no one else could have given us "...anything even close to this tremendous, complete, and rounded impression of the mood of the Olympics, and revelations of beauty, characters, and events...." Like many others in Europe, Palsbo also fell for this fantastic film. The film was a very elegant tribute to Hitler, to Nazi Germany, and to the new "Aryan" man.[235]

In March of 1938 Kaj Munk received a government grant. He immediately gave the money to charity. Under the heading "A familiar quotation from Vedersø," a newspaper wrote that they had asked Munk how he felt when he was notified of this honor. Munk answered with his usual arrogance that he would quit his literary work: "I intend to live the rest of my life on the government's grant of honor!"[236] The grant was for 1,200 DKK. That same year Munk earned about 250,000 DKK,[237] according to Statistics Denmark equal to about 7 million DKK today.

A success like Munk's did not go unnoticed. It had, like so many things, more than one side. There was also the commercial side. Beside Erwin Magnus, there were many other translators and publishers trying to get the rights to Munk's work. One of the biggest publishers in Scandinavia, Theater Publisher Arvid Englind in Stockholm, had, as mentioned earlier, purchased Walter Berendsohn's German translation of *The Melting-Pot*. By May of 1938 Englind had written a contract with Munk for the sole and exclusive rights for his work worldwide with the exception of Denmark.[238]

In a letter to Munk, Englind's dramaturge Calle Flygare wrote that they had heard there was a chance that Munk's plays would be performed in Germany, except of course for *The Victory* and *The Melting-Pot*. With the assistance of their German born dramaturge Verner Arpe, the publisher had

---

[235] Ole Palsbo: "The Annual Prize Cups to Kaj Munk and Leni Riefenstahl," *Nationaltidende*, January 1, 1939.

[236] "A Familiar Quotation from Vedersø", unknown newspaper 1938.

[237] "Kaj Munks Sukces" (Kaj Munk's Success), *Lollands-Posten*, 26 January 1939.

[238] "Swedish publisher buys worldwide rights from Kaj Munk" *Lollands Tidende* 5 May 1938.

already begun to produce brochures for Germany and the German-speaking countries.[239]

In an interview, Englind said that all of Munk's plays were being translated into German, English, and French:

> *Norway has had its Ibsen, and Sweden its Strindberg. Now it's Denmark's turn on the world's stage, and the author's name is Munk. I even believe that his plays can be performed in Germany. Maybe not* The Melting-Pot, *but the others.[240]*

Such an effort for, and belief in, the German market in January of 1939! Was it optimism or naiveté? Englind Publishers had in fact received inquiries from German theaters.

The publisher's dramaturge Verner Arpe, in a letter to Munk written in German at the end of 1939, wrote that several German stage managers and theater managers had shown a strong interest for his work. Arpe also wrote: "...today we heard again from a very well-known theater manager in Berlin that he too would like to read your plays. But as you know, you are one of the authors who are difficult, or unwelcome, in Germany."[241] (a.t.)

Munk was still being promoted but without results. He had probably been blacklisted in Germany for a long time and, therefore, in the National Socialist controlled theater circles as well.

In 1945 Englind wrote in a jubilee article that in 1938:

> *I then made contact with ...Kaj Munk, the pastor with the sharp eyes for dramatic effects. It is easy to understand my satisfaction over being able to present him here in Scandinavia. The war hampered Munk in a double sense. As early as the autumn of 1939 his play would have been*

---

[239] Letter from Theater Publisher Arvid Englind Ltd. Stockholm to Kaj Munk, 9 January 1939. KMF Archive.

[240] "It's Denmark's Turn on the World Map" Newspaper article from 20 January 1939.

[241] Letter from Theater Publisher Arvid Englind Ltd. Stockholm to Kaj Munk, 2 October 1939. KMF Archive.

performed in London if Hitler had not attacked Poland at the time. Switzerland then became the first country outside of Scandinavia to draw attention to the Danish dramatist from the pulpit.[242]

The play that was performed in Switzerland was *Niels Ebbesen*. When Englind stated that Switzerland was the first place outside of Scandinavia that Munk had been performed, he obviously did not know that *The Word* had been performed in Schwerin in 1935.

Was it more profitable for Englind to have Munk's plays translated again, or was he simply unaware of the three plays that Magnus had already translated? In 2004, Christer Englind made available a list of the information contained in the publisher's archives concerning Munk's plays. It appears from that list that, besides *The Melting-Pot*, translated by Berendsohn, the above-mentioned dramaturge Verner Arpe had translated the plays *In the Breakers* and *The Dictatress* into German,[243] probably during the period 1938-1943 when he was employed by Arvid Englind.

With respect to the German translations of Kaj Munk's plays in the nineteen thirties, there remain several open questions. The correspondence between Magnus and Munk shows that Magnus had translated *Cant, An Idealist,* and *The Word.* All three translations had presumably been sent to the theater publisher Gustav Kiepenheuer in Berlin. As mentioned earlier, only one translation by Magnus has been found at Kiepenheuer: Munk's play *An Idealist.*

In response to an inquiry, Kiepenheuer Publishers said that in addition to *Cant,* they also have *The Word* (*Am Anfang war das Wort*) and *An Idealist* [244] in their archives.[245] The last two are marked as authorized translations from the Danish by Verner Arpe.

---

[242] Theater Publisher Arvid Englind Ltd. Stockholm, 1920-1945 (Jubilee brochure).

[243] Letter from Christer Englind. Theater Publisher Arvid Englind Ltd. Stockholm to Søren Daugbjerg 6 July 2004.

[244] A copy of the manuscript has been available for the work on this book.

[245] Letter from Dr. Maria Müller-Sommer. Gustav Kiepenheuer Theater Publisher (Bühnenvertrieb) Ltd., 23 June 2004.

The documents are undated. In Christer Englind's list there is no mention of Arpe having translated *The Word* or *An Idealist*.

In two of the letters quoted in this book– to Peter Freuchen on January 15, 1935, and to Munk on April 3, 1935, Magnus writes that he, as a Jew, could not get anything published in Germany, and for that reason might have to write under a pseudonym, or use a "front man." The idea of an agreement between Arpe and Magnus thus seems plausible. However, as it has not been possible to find any contact or correspondence between the two, and because Arpe, after immigrating to Sweden in 1938, was not in very high standing in Germany, it is unlikely that Magnus would have used his name in that connection. Why Arpe's translations of *The Word* and *An Idealist* are found at Kiepenheuer's is unknown.

In Knaur's Theater Guide (Schauspielführer), Arpe wrote in 1957 about Kaj Munk's plays and mentions, among others, *The Dictatress*, but strangely enough not *In the Breakers* or *The Word.*

Kaj Munk was often on the front pages as, for example, on January 20, 1939, when the *Berlingske Tidende* wrote:

> *Kaj Munk's* The Melting-Pot *cancelled in South Jutland after Mr. Steincke's intervention. The Attorney General K.K. Steincke told the newspaper: 'I find pastor Kaj Munk's play very interesting; but another thing is, that in particular in a border region, one should refrain from public performances of plays that can inflame nationalist passion,' a consideration that Steincke thought was natural to show '... towards those who are especially taken with the German viewpoint.'*

Although it was only a "suggestion" from the Attorney General, Gerda Christophersen followed it, and did not perform the play that evening, and cancelled other performances in South Jutland.

As mentioned earlier in this book, Carl Gandrup's play *It is never Enough* had a quotation from Steincke on the title page:

"In the new dictatorships the state is a Moloch on whose altar any human creature can be sacrificed!"*

The Attorney General's suggestion that *The Melting-Pot* not be performed had the result that this play, about the sacrifices of the Jews, became a Danish sacrifice on the German dictatorship's altar.

The Melting-Pot was criticized in several German newspapers as a malicious attack on the Fuhrer and on German politics, prompting Munk to answer in an article, "With cowardice nothing is achieved." Munk was indignant, and he refers to several lines in the play about "...the healthy, strong, and stern German people." Munk thought that he had shown a great understanding for Hitler and that the play was not an attack on Germany "... but a search-light into one of our time's dark sides of the German nature, a dark side that will, God willing, disappear when the sun rises...." With respect to that dark side we should be watchful and keep it in check until sunrise, Munk thought, and optimistically wrote: "In twenty years it will be played and loved in Germany."[246]

Austria was annexed by Germany in 1938, and few people took offence; they were, after all, Germans that were coming home. When German troops invaded Czechoslovakia in March of 1939, Munk commented in an article– "Europe on Fire." Munk called it a campaign for conquest, and was dumbfounded that Hitler had betrayed his own ideals of– "Germany for the Germans." The Czechs and the Slovaks were, after all, not Germans coming home to the empire. In Munk's opinion Hitler had made only one mistake so far and that was the treatment of the Jews. If there wasn't room for them in the empire, then a reasonable solution should have been found rather than to treat them in such a manner "...that thousands upon thousands have suffered unimaginably.... But Israel's suffering is small in comparison to what the honor of Germany has suffered from this treatment of a group of its own people."[247]

---

*Page 149

[246] Kaj Munk, "With cowardice nothing is achieved," *Jyllands-Posten*, January 29, 1939.

[247] Kaj Munk, "Europe on Fire," *Jyllands-Posten*, March 26, 1939 (Written during a stay in Paris).

When one thinks about what the German Jews had to endure in the years 1933-1939, which Kaj Munk also draws attention to, it seems arrogant of him– though the goal was to hit the Germans in their weakest spot– to compare their suffering to the disparagement inflicted on Germany's honor. A country's honor is dependent upon the people living in it and, in particular, on those in the government. Seen from the latter viewpoint, honor had been in short supply in the "Third Reich" already before 1939, the year in which Hitler announced the infamous Euthanasia Decree,* which led to the "mercy killing" of the mentally ill and handicapped.[248]

Shortly after Hitler's attack on Poland, September 1, 1939 – the beginning of World War II – Munk was ready with an article about the war: "Take up The Cross against the War." He was by now very disappointed in Hitler, who was not the "Dictator of Peace" that he had hoped for. The main theme of the article is the ugliness of war. Although war is hell, " God is also present there," and war as well brings out the "...comradeship beyond death, the self-destructive willingness to sacrifice, grand chivalry, and bravery reaching to Heaven...." There are differences between wars: "... acts so atrocious can be committed that those who have the power to act must declare: I cannot just stand by." It was a call to war against injustice. He also touched on the subject of the soldier's ability to think "...and to be aware of what he is getting into, which gives us some small hope that the next time... those soldiers who are to go to war will say no to the honor." A call from Munk to be a conscientious objector! And he finished in the same vein: "We are on the side of the innocent sufferers, those being massacred, and those who are forced to massacre."[249]

England and France declared war on Germany on September 3, 1939. The war incited Munk to call on the national leaders to spare Europe: "...don't burn down my village! Do you hear, you, who we elected as rulers because you promised us peace, find the way back, spare Europe's life!"

---

*Based on Hitler's secret memo of 1 September 1939, *Aktion T4.*

[248] Wolfgang Benz, op.cit., p.170.

[249] Kaj Munk, "Sæt Korset imod Krigen" (Take up The Cross against the War), *Jyllands-Posten*, 10 September 1939.

He was not very confident about the "Rulers" who he had admired earlier. And he was now afraid that the catastrophes that occurred during and after WWI would be repeated: "And shouldn't Germany, that has suffered so greatly and complained so bitterly over Versailles, be too wise and magnanimous to prepare the same fate of humiliation for another people?"[250] This would prove to be an undeserved idealization of that day's Germany and its leaders.

There was an ominous feeling in Europe, and the new Europe turned out to be very different from the one that Munk had envisaged. At Christmas in 1938 he wrote in a letter to Thorvald Larsen, the director of the Folk Theater: "And while we play *The Melting-Pot* a thousand times in Scandinavia, the persecutions grow. So impotent is the theater, and so meaningless the idea we serve."[251]

Kaj Munk had often talked about the power of the spoken and written word, but now he was discouraged. Had he really believed that *The Melting-Pot*, which was only performed in Scandinavia, would have any influence on the persecution of the Jews in Germany? However, the people of Scandinavia had, through the play, been made aware of the plight of the Jews. That had probably shaped their attitude, and thereby the willingness to help that was shown to the Jews during WWII.

William Michelsen[252] had written an introduction and commentary to an edition of *The Melting-Pot* that was published in 1960. He had access to the original manuscript from 1938, and wrote that it was dated: "Berlin, Monday morning, January 24, thirteen minutes into the new day." The play was written before the outbreak of war in Europe. Munk was shaken. He had taken out his copy of *The Melting-Pot*, and wrote under the words "The Potsherd Play," the original title on the cover:

---

[250] Kaj Munk, "Lad os tage fat!" (Let's Get Started!) *Jyllands-Posten*, 5 November 1939.

[251] *Kaj Munk and the Folk Theater*. Letters from Kaj Munk to Thorvald Larsen. Nyt Nordisk Forlag Arnold Busck, Copenhagen 1957, p.40.

[252] William Michelsen (1913-2001). See biographies.

Today, 1939– November 16, again I find the play about the image of Jesus on the potsherds that was composed in Paris and Berlin in January 1938. It is with reverence that I read it again, and with anguish over how it has turned out, that new day, spoken of on the last page, when the play closes.[253]

[253] Kaj Munk: Han sidder ved Smeltediglen (He Sits at the Melting-Pot). With an introduction by William Michelsen,NNF 1960,p.55

Chapter 11

The Second World War

On November 28, 1939, Finland was attacked by the Soviet Union. The war had now moved into Scandinavian territory. Denmark could retain its status as a neutral country, but neutrality was not an option for Munk; you were either for it or against it. There was no middle ground. Munk was not the only one who felt that way. In a sermon on New Year's Day of 1940, K.E. Løgstrup spoke about how everyone agreed in wishing for a new year with peace and the right to live in a free Denmark. However, peace could only be bought with neutrality, and that included the right to have an opinion. Løgstrup thought that neutrality could end up meaning that we wouldn't dare to say either yes or no. As an example he used a current subject:

> Let's take the Jewish question. We can't be bothered to say no, an unambiguous no, to persecution of the Jews, and only no! So then we differentiate between the 'justified' and the 'unjustified' in the persecution of the Jews. We have become too afraid, too neutral, too cowardly, too 'scientific' to bother to be unilateral, to take a stand, to bother to discriminate between right and wrong, between evil and truth.[254]

Løgstrup believed that with that attitude we would end up being unable to hear or understand the gospel.

K.E. Løgstrup was not very enthusiastic about Kaj Munk at this time, but with respect to "spinelessness" they were in agreement, which can be seen in a sermon that Munk gave a month later: "The Day Has Come" (Dagen er inde).

In that sermon he discussed the war in Finland, and the Christian's duty to fight against evil and injustice:

---

[254] K.E. Løgstrup, *Sermons from Sandager-Holevad* (*Prædikener fra Sandager-Holevad*). A selection by Elsebeth Diderichsen and Ole Jensen. Gyldendal 1995.

If women and children are threatened by wild animals then it is unchristian to just sit and be a spectator...that's why Christianity is a religion for heroes; that's why the flag of Christ always flies in the front line of the fight against hatred and lies.

The heroic struggle of the Finns made an impression on him. "If it has ever been the case that a people is fighting for truth and justice, then it is certainly here." At the end of the sermon he blessed the Danish volunteers who had gone to Finland. Munk also expressed his dismay over the fact that "...a Christian civilization like Germany" could have a treaty of friendship with the Soviet Union.[255] I don't believe that it was ironic when Munk called Germany a "Christian civilization." It could hardly have been called that in 1939, but Munk had not yet given up hope for a new and better Germany, after Hitler had gotten over his beginner problems.

On April ninth, 1940, Denmark was attacked and occupied by Germany. Later Munk recounted how he had experienced the 9th of April. "It was a morning when the spirits of Hell screamed in the air above us. Then we understood that our independence was lost."[256]

One month later Munk wrote an article— "While We Wait,"[257] about the Danes who sat by in the shelters and waited while the war raged outside. He thought that there should have been stronger protests "...by us, who saw where it was headed," an apparent allusion to the fate of the partially demilitarized and defenceless Denmark.

Among Munk's many speeches, the one which even to this day is the most talked about and discussed was given at Ollerup Sports College where he had been invited to speak by the school's principal, Niels Bukh. Munk destroyed the original manuscript,

---

[255] Kaj Munk, "Dagen er inde" (The Day Has Come). *Jyllands-Posten*, 28 January 1940.

[256] Kaj Munk's speech at Arnborg, 24 August 1941 (Tale i Arnborg). "Public meeting overshadowed by the occupation's brutal reality." Memorial publication for the 60th anniversary of Denmark's liberation. Skarrild 2005. Edited by Arne Mosgaard.

[257] Kaj Munk, "Mens vi venter" (While We Wait) *Nationaltidende*, 7 May 1940.

but there are two surviving accounts of the speech. The first one was printed in the *Svendborg News* (*Svendborg Avis*) on July 29, 1940, written under the self-censorship imposed by the German occupation. The other account was written by Dean Richard Fauerskov Laursen, who was parish pastor at the time in Fjelsted-Harndrup on Funen (Fyn). It is Fauerskov Laursen's account that is used in the following.

Laursen's account of the speech is given in full in Bjarne Nielsen Brovst's book *Kaj Munk, The War and The Murder* (*Kaj Munk, krigen og mordet*). Talking about the German occupation, Munk said: "Where people can come in, they can also go out, as long as the door doesn't jam." He also commented on Hitler's efforts for Germany and the German people: "He is one of the greatest figures in world history.... It is Hitler who made them [the German people] what they are today. And he has advanced not as a coarse general, but from the start with the word, the living word...."

Munk also expressed his disappointment over surrendering almost without a fight on April 9; and he believed that Germany, in its attack on Denmark, had betrayed the idea of the dictatorship. Munk and Hitler had different conceptions about the "idea" of dictatorship. Hitler's idea from the beginning was to gain the necessary living space and agricultural area for the German people through a war of conquest,[258] and the food producing Denmark was favourably positioned. For Munk, the "idea" of dictatorship should not be represented by a brutal attacker but by a noble and just Christian dictator. Munk's confidence that Hitler could have developed into such a moral person continued to crumble. At the end of the Ollerup speech he urged propriety and aloofness towards the Germans.[259]

Munk's description of Hitler, who triumphed with the help of "the living word," is confirmed by what is written in *Mein Kampf*, Hitler's political manifesto. In it Adolf Hitler wrote that in the beginning, as a political speaker, he would take along a stack of leaflets to meetings; but it turned out that the spoken word was

---

[258] Adolf Hitler, Mein Kampf. Zentralverlag der NSDAP 1941, pp. 152-153.
[259] Bjarne Nielsen Brovst, *Kaj Munk, krigen og mordet* (*Kaj Munk, The War and The Murder*), Centrum 1993, pp. 49-53.

far more important.[260] In the Danish translation, Hitler's words are given as follows: "But the emphasis was on the living word; and in fact, that is the only thing that can bring about great revolutions."[261]*

On August 15, 1940, Munk spoke to the soldiers at the barracks in Næstved. There he spoke about the Christian duty not to be passive spectators in the presence of injustice.

In the speech there were several calls for physical resistance: "If any physical resistance against the evil can be called a sinful breach of Jesus' holy and divine commandment of love and forgiveness, well then, there can be situations where God demands this sin of us." The speech contained the usual swipe at the Danish government and democracy and a statement that after the occupation of Czechoslovakia "Hitler was no longer Hitler. There is no Prince of Peace halo about his brow."[262] Hitler was still the same– it was Munk's belief in him that was shaken.

Three days later he spoke about the same subjects at a student meeting in Gerlev. He spoke rhetorically, as if the students had asked him if they should; "...go after the Germans with bread knives, carry out acts of sabotage, cut telephone wires, and blow up bridges." Munk answered himself: "...in no way. That chance has passed, it's gone." He finished the speech by saying that perhaps there was an individual to whom he had been sent that evening, to burn into that person's soul "...against democracy and against dictators for Denmark."

Democracy was described as "A great thought, a lofty and bright ideal," which collapsed that day "When the dictator's jackboots trod on Democracy's tree."

---

* "But the power which set the greatest historical avalanches of political and religious nature sliding was, from the beginning of time, the magic force of the spoken word alone." *Mein Kampf*, Adolf Hitler, complete and unabridged English translation, p.136, Reynal & Hitchcock, New York, 1941.

[260] Adolf Hitler, op.cit., p. 525.

[261] Adolf Hitler, Min Kamp. H. Hagerups Forlag, Copenhagen 1934, p. 110.

[262] Kaj Munk, *Mindeudgave. Dagen er inde og andre artikler*
(*Commemorative Edition. The Day Has Come, and other Articles*), Speech to Danish soldiers. NNF 1949, p.167.

About Hitler as the German people's saviour, Munk said: "We rejoiced over each step upward that this people was carried, we still love the Hitler who led them, but he is no longer here. He had promised them, and all of us, peace. Where is that promise now?"[263] Munk recommended new leaders for Denmark, people outside of the old parties; men like Helmer Rosting* and Niels Bukh, instead of the government official that were cozying up to the Germans.

Judging from Munk's speeches up to that time, it could be difficult to tell if he encouraged active or passive resistance to the occupation forces. In 1940 he was presumably still in doubt.

In Sweden Munk was recommended as a candidate for the Nobel Prize. It was Sven Stolpe,[264] who wrote in the *Stockholm Times (Stockholmstidningen)* on October 7, 1940, that Kaj Munk was that: "Man in world literature who at this time most deserves to receive the Nobel Prize.... Kaj Munk has, in a time when Denmark lies paralyzed, given his people a new concept of greatness and distinction, and his mere existence among the Danish people is a greater source of power than armies or the National Guard."[265] It was a grand salute and a nice thought from a Swedish colleague.

In a speech in Odense on November 4, 1940, Munk spoke about God and about evil. In the first half of the speech the subject was evil. The devil was clever at disguising himself, "... but as with all perverse characters, so it is with him. No matter how long they perform so elegantly and beguilingly– someday they'll drop their mask. Instead of the fine merchant in ideals we will suddenly see a very ordinary, coarse, and very brutal burglar."[266] Nobody was in doubt that it was Hitler he spoke about. Nor were the Germans in doubt. It was a dangerous statement about Europe's most powerful man.

---

* Helmer Rosting (1893-1945), Nazi sympathizer, and director of the Danish Red Cross from 1943 to 1945. He committed suicide in 1945.

[263] Ibid., Speech at Gerlev pp. 174-187.

[264] Sven Stolpe (1905-1996), Swedish author and literary critic, wrote the book *Kaj Munk, The Poet and the Prophet (Kaj Munk, Diktaren och profeten)*. Stockholm 1944.

[265] *Det stod i Avisen (It Was in the Newspaper)*, edited by Kai Berg Madsen. Carit Andersen Publisher 1945, p.46.

[266] Kaj Munk, *Commemorative Edition*, op. cit., Where is God (Hvor er Gud) p. 202.

Munk's Christmas letter to his teacher and friend Martinus Wested is marked by what had happened in Denmark in 1940:

> *These are difficult times. Criminals control the world while honorable people run their errands... the Farm Denmark lies cozy in dishonor, sells its products at a profit, and thinks that Hitler is a clever man.... These Danish Nazis, who for German money will buy Denmark a new future, are even worse than the parliamentarians.*[267]

If there were Danes who thought that Hitler was a clever man, then Munk had probably influenced many them with his numerous articles and admiring remarks about the German dictator throughout the thirties. Munk was a man who was read and listened to. With respect to selling products to the Germans, in August 1940, in the speech at Gerlev, Munk had written: "Denmark can trade with Germany because it is just external things that we deal with and not things that touch our soul."[268]

That was a bizarre argument for trade with an occupying force. Later Munk would see these relations quite differently.

Munk dreamed of a united Scandinavia when "the crisis" was over, a "Nordic Empire,"[269] and yet there was a warning from Munk in July 1941: "There is once again a call for volunteer military help from Denmark to Finland." He truly wished that Finland could win back its territory, also with the help of volunteers, but not right then, as "Denmark, our Mother, requires all of us now for her own needs. The Danish youth have an obligation to understand that."[270] Munk realized that soon the young would be needed in the struggle for freedom that he finally realized was coming.

On March 8, 1941, Prime Minister Stauning spoke at the Student Union about Denmark and Europe. The speech seemed

---

[267] Letter from Kaj Munk to Martinus Wested. Christmas 1940, The Royal Library.

[268] Kaj Munk, op. cit., The Speech at Gerlev pp. 174-187.

[269] Kaj Munk, ibid. Scandinavianism, pp. 242-247.

[270] Kaj Munk, ibid. No volunteers to Finland now!, p.247.

to indicate that the Prime Minister had already given up on the idea that Danish policy could have any influence on what was to take place in Europe: "Developments during the war show that Germany has now taken the position as the central power; and that it will also determine certain main guidelines, both cultural and economic, for the future." He also thought that the German planned economy was better than "...the liberal society, which to a great degree builds on egoism– that is business and social egoism.... It is unhealthy and unwise to resist the changes that time and events carry with them." For Stauning this meant, "adjusting," when the time came, and at the same time following a policy "... that can carry us unharmed through the turbulence of the present time, and into the new era that awaits us."[271]

Nor were there any bright refrains to hear at the Midsummer Festival at Skamlingsbanken on June 22, 1941, where Munk was the main speaker. That very morning Germany had attacked the Soviet Union with three million men. Munk spoke about the difficult times, the war, and the downtrodden Denmark:

> *I stand here now, and things have happened in the world that mean that what I would have said yesterday, would be wrong to say today. We see that one of our neighbor nations, Finland, is again drawn into a bloody conflict. Our thoughts are torn. We no longer know what to think, what to wish for, or what to pray for." At the end he said that if life demanded it, then our boys would "...do no less than the Finnish boys...."*

---

[271]"Stauning on Denmark's place in the new Europe", *Lolland-Falsters Folketidende*, 10 March 1941.

Again there is an undertone of fighting spirit. The article said that Munk was greeted "... with enthusiastic applause as soon as he appeared...."[272]

In June of 1941, after the attack on The Soviet Union, the Germans demanded that all leading communists in Denmark be interned, an order that was followed immediately with the help of the so-called "communist law."[273]

The play *Pilate* (*Pilatus*),[274] which Munk wrote in 1917 while he attended the Cathedral School in Nykøbing Falster, was printed in 1937, and used as Christmas gifts to his friends. The play is about Pilate's deliberations before sentencing Jesus. Pilate's wife Julia warns him, saying that she had learned in a dream that Jesus was innocent, but Pilate condemns him to death. On July 4, 1941 *Pilate* was performed in the open air on Bispetorvet in Aarhus. Kaj Munk was present at the premiere where there was an audience of 4000.

Beside the review of *Pilate* in *Jyllands-Posten*, there was an article about the technical preparations in connection with this arrangement in the middle of the city. It explained that the city of Aarhus had gone to great lengths to insure that the play would be a good theater experience. Bispetorvet was an area with heavy traffic, so to minimize noise traffic was routed away from the square.

Only streetcars were allowed to run there, and the rails were kept well greased "... and all the streetcars that Aarhus had gotten so cheaply from Germany, which unfortunately were rather narrow in track width, were allowed to stay home at the depot. They screech so terribly in the curves."[275] That the journalist would mention the German streetcars with their "narrow track width" and screeching would not normally be part

---

[272] "6000 attend the meeting at Skamling" *Kolding Folkeblad*, 23 June 1942.

[273] *Danmarks Historie* (*History of Denmark*). *Politikens Forlag* 1966. Volume 14, p.118.

[274] Kaj Munk, *Pilatus* (*Pilate*). A play in 4 acts (under the pseudonym Harald Cajus, Private edition). NNF 1937.

[275] "*Pilate* was a great and beautiful experience" *Jyllands-Posten*, 5 July 1941.

of a review of a play; but Denmark was occupied and in this way a discreet kick could be given to the occupying forces.

That *Pilate* could be performed at this time, when neither the Danish government nor the German occupation forces were at all kindly disposed towards Kaj Munk, was perhaps due to the play's content. Did the German censor find the play anti-Semitic? It was, after all, about Jews who demanded that Jesus be crucified. Svend Aage Nielsen wrote about the performance in Aarhus:

> *There is no indication that the occupying forces had any objections to this– or even subjected this play, written by a nationally known dramatist, to any ban or censorship. Is it because the occupiers don't think that people will get worked up by plays that are effective in confirming their prejudices?*[276]

In Denmark it was only in the theater that plays about Jews that were performed. In Germany it wasn't theater, but cruel reality. The German historian Wolfgang Benz wrote that on July 31, 1941, SS Obergruppenführer Reinhard Heydrich[277] was formally ordered by Herman Göring to find a "final solution" to the European Jewish question.[278] The so-called "Endlösung" had thus been adopted before the infamous "Wannsee-Conference" in Berlin, January 20, 1942; a conference that Benz believed did not have the authority to make such a comprehensive decision. Fifteen people participated in the conference that was led by SS Obergruppenführer Reinhard Heydrich.

It was SS Obersturmbannführer Adolf Eichmann who kept the minutes.[279]

It was thus most likely Herman Göring who, in July 1941, gave the order that would eventually result in the murder of six million Jews. In the same year, on October 1, after a request by

---

[276] Svend Aage Nielsen, "Om ungdomsdramaet *Pilatus*" (About the youth play *Pilate*), in the anthology: *På Lolland jeg den hented* (*I got it on Lolland*). Poul Kristensens Forlag Herning 1998, pp.22-23.

[277] Reinhard Heydrich (1904-1942) head of Reichssicherheitshauptamt (Reich Main Security Office)

[278] Wolfgang Benz, op. cit., pp.219-221.

[279] Adolf Eichmann (1906-1962), SS-Obersturmbannführer.

the Foreign Minister to the King, the German Foreign Minister Joachim von Ribbentrop received the Danish Great Cross with Diamonds of the Order of Dannebrog– 17 months after the German attack on Denmark, April 9, 1940.[280] Göring had already received the same Order on July 25, 1938.[281]

A number of well-known people in Denmark who resisted the occupation were quickly placed under the control of the German authorities. Editor Kaj Holbech wrote to Munk on February 28, 1942 with a warning:

> *Last Monday the German minister [Cecil von Renthe-Fink (?)],[282] informed the Danish Foreign Ministry that they were very concerned about the campaign of agitation that had been started from the Danish side, and that they were particularly unhappy with la Cour, Falk Hansen, Hal Koch, Kaj Munk, and Arne Sørensen. The ministry was informed that these men would be kept under special surveillance!*

Then Holbech described in detail the case of la Cour, who was jailed by the Germans, and that several members of the government threatened to resign if he was not turned over to the Danish authorities. At the end of the letter he hinted that telephone service was unclear, and that the postal service "... is, honestly speaking, rather careless with the mail these days... for example the envelopes have been crumpled, or accidentally ripped up. That of course can happen in a post office if they're just a bit too busy."[283] The German intelligence service was everywhere. Kaj Holbech was active in the resistance and editor of the illegal publication *The Free Danes* (*De Frie Danske*). The Gestapo murdered him on October 14, 1944.

In the book *In the Middle of the Enemy's Camp* (*Midt i Fjendens Lejr*), the Danish South Schleswig spokesman in Berlin,

---

[280] *Handbook for the Royal Kingdom of Denmark. Kongelig dansk Hof- og Statskalender.* Year 1941.

[281] *Handbook.* Ibid. Year 1939.

[282] Cecil von Renthe-Fink (1885-1964), German envoy to Denmark, 1936-1942.

[283] Letter to Kaj Munk from editor Kaj Holbech (1901-1944). Billed-Bladet. KMF Archives.

Jakob Kronika, shows, in a short section, that Munk and his critical view of the German occupation forces was known at the highest levels in Berlin: "July 25, [1942] – In Goebbels' Ministry, at a small "tea circle" gathering, surprisingly harsh statements were made about our poet-pastor Kaj Munk!"[284] It was unbelievable that in the middle of WWII, in the Ministry of Propaganda in Berlin, people were concerned about a Danish parish pastor. Munk was under surveillance by the Germans and not just in Copenhagen, but also in the German capital. Neither the King nor the Danish politicians could frighten the Germans, but the "Living Word" could. As seen in the earlier quotation from *Mein Kampf*, it was only "The Living Word " that could bring about great changes. The living word was a tool that Munk mastered. For that reason he was seen as dangerous.

Munk's play *Niels Ebbesen* is about the freedom fighter Niels Ebbesen, who in 1340 rebelled and killed the German Count Gerhard the 3rd of Holstein, the "Bald Count." Count Gerhard held a part of Denmark as collateral and was an unpleasant master to live under. The theme in *Niels Ebbesen* is historical, but the play describes the Occupation. In the play, Munk covers everything– the opportunists, the collaborators, and the woman who fraternizes with the enemy– as well as the unaggressive resistance man Niels Ebbesen who kills Count Gerhard, a symbol for Hitler.

No one who read *Niels Ebbesen*, or saw the play performed, or heard Munk read it aloud, could have misunderstood the message.[285] The play was a direct incitement to get rid of Hitler, and to resist the German occupation forces.

Fearing that the Germans would take action, the publisher promptly distributed the book to the bookstores. The play was to come out on April 9, 1942, but already by April 8 the Germans had received a court order to confiscate the book. The next day, when they went to the publisher to confiscate the books, there were only 1,000 left out of an edition of 15,000.

Niels Ebbesen was performed at the Swedish Dramatists' Studio (Svenska Dramatikers Studio) in Stockholm on September 14,

---

[284] Jacob Kronika: *Midt i Fjendens Lejr* (*In the Middle of the Enemy's Camp*), Gyldendal 1966, p.84.
[285] Kaj Munk: *Niels Ebbesen*. NNF 1942.

1943, with Ingmar Bergman as director. This Swedish performance has until now been considered the play's first showing; but in an article in the *Christian Daily* (*Kristeligt Dagblad*) on August 4, 2004, Selma Mouritsen points out that the teachers at Ollerup High School had performed *Niels Ebbesen* on February 27, 1942. Selma Mouritsen, who had seen the performance, quotes from the High School's yearbook from 1945 where the principal, Tage Haastrup Petersen, wrote that every year the teachers at Ollerup would perform a play in February. Munk's numerous readings of *Niels Ebbesen* had given him the idea to perform that play in 1942. An inquiry to Munk for permission to perform the play was well received. *Niels Ebbesen* had not yet been published in book form but was in the works. Munk's goodwill went so far that when he received the first proofs from the publisher, he sent them on to the principal at Ollerup so that they could begin rehearsals. About 1,000 people saw the performances. Tage Haastrup Petersen sent a report on the performance to Munk. Later he received a greeting from Munk in which, among other things, he had written: "I am pleased and encouraged that you have become a spokesman for my voice. God bless your work."[286]

Despite war and occupation, *Niels Ebbesen*, Munk's resistance play, had its Danish premiere performance at Ollerup High School in the middle of the Occupation. The performance at Ollerup set a precedent, for a month later on March 27, 28, and 29 the teachers and students at Støvring High School performed *Niels Ebbesen*. 200 audience members who had been bussed in from Aalborg saw the performance on the 28th. In response to the High School's inquiry to Munk to get permission to perform the play, he answered: "Yes, you certainly can. And you have my blessing that you can get its message across."[287]

Despite Munk's criticism of the politics of the coalition government, and his call for resistance, he knew how difficult it was for the ministers to lead the country and people through

---

[286] Selma Mouritsen, "*Niels Ebbesen* had its premiere performance in Denmark", Kristeligt Dagblad, 4 August 2004.
[287] Støvring High School's Yearbook, 1942, p.61. Local Historical Archives in Støvring.

the period of occupation. In March of 1942 he wrote in *Jyllands-Posten* about the difficult balancing act of the government:

> *Moreover, with respect to what is required to lead a free people who is under occupation, it is surely not just tricks. For honest people there will be many difficult conflicts of conscience to struggle with. It will require strength to stand firm, and sometimes even greater strength to give way. Such men may well need the declared confidence of the people for support, but they also need their criticism– to urge them forward in the right direction.... They need to have persons among the people who can say the things that they want to say but because of their position cannot.*[288]

In July 1942 a much-discussed summer meeting was held at Askov High School, with Hal Koch and Kaj Munk as speakers. Munk talked about the German butchers and had harsh words for the occupation forces. At a meeting after the speech with J. Th. Arnfred, Askov's principal, Munk was warned about his aggressive position. Kaj Munk was not satisfied with the passiveness of the High School's personnel and called Arnfred a "cottonhead."[289] During his stay at Askov, Munk spent the night at the home of high school teacher Bo Bojesen Rud, who had arranged the meeting. Bojesen Rud had previously written a book about Munk.[290]

There is a duplicated role booklet– "*Shakespeare's HAMLET*, retold by Kaj Munk– Askov High School 1942-43."[291] On the last page of the booklet there is a note saying that it was duplicated at Askov High School during the winter of 1942-43, with permission of high school teacher Bo Bojesen Rud.

---

[288] Kaj Munk, Commemorative Edition. Op. cit., Unity (Sammenholdet) NNF, pp.266-270.

[289] Bjarne Nielsen Brovst, op. cit., pp. 204-207.

[290] Bo Bojesen Rud (1897-1968), high school teacher and author, wrote *Kaj Munk. Critical studies over a heroic and dramatic poetry, with remarks by Kaj Munk.* NNF 1938.

[291] Author's archive.

The previously mentioned performances of the resistance play, *Niels Ebbesen,* were appropriate for the time, but to plan and perform Munk's most controversial play during the Occupation, which the critic Svend Erichsen in 1938 called "Munk's Nazi-Hamlet," seems very strange. No mention of a performance of *Hamlet* in 1942-43 has been found in Askov High School's yearbooks or archives. Presumably the play was not performed at the high school.

Munk had been a much sought-after speaker for many years, but during the war years he was in so much demand that he often had to say no. He even had a printer make up a handwritten "rejection letter," so that he only had to write the date on it. Munk was said to be an excellent reader, and in connection with his speeches he often read aloud from *Niels Ebbesen.* While the play could not be performed in Denmark, its message could be spread through readings.

Those Danes who Munk considered way too passive received a rough treatment in a speech he gave at a clerical conference in Tommerup on September 2, 1942. He spoke about the Devil who exploits man's desire to be well off:

> *On April 9, the Devil came to the Danish government and said, 'I need a few drops of human blood for your signature on this little document, then you'll all be well off in Denmark, while the whole world writhes in suffering.' And now we are well off. And the whole world writhes in suffering.*

About the German dictator, Munk continued:

> *Who is this Mr. Hitler? Nothing's bad about Mr. Hitler. For us he is just a very ordinary conqueror. Surely history had big plans for that man. The words he spoke sounded powerful in Christian ears as well: The willingness to sacrifice, the awareness of the call, the Almighty. Christ says: By their fruits you will know them. The lies follow in the path of truth– using the same words.[292]*

---

[292] Kaj Munk, Op. cit., The speech at Tommerup, pp. 280-290.

Munk had earlier admitted that he had been mistaken about Hitler. Now his view of Hitler had changed so radically that he called him a liar. Was this a hint of an apology for his earlier admiration of the German dictator?

In a lecture at the Christian Academics Society (Kristelige Akademikeres Forening) on November 7, 1942, Munk again touched on the plight of the Jews:

> *Where is the church when Jesus' own countrymen are chased across the plains like game running from dogs? I don't have to stand here and incite to civil war– no, God help us, it's already here when Danish men are thrown into jail by Danish police because they won't be anything else but Danes.[293]*

It became gradually more difficult for Munk to get his message out to the people. He had earlier given a copy of three sermons to Arne Sørensen. With the help of Christensen's Printing in Struer they were printed by a publishing house established for just that purpose: "Easter Lily Publishers" (Forlaget Paaskeliljen). *Three Sermons* was released on May 20, 1943 in an edition of 26,500 copies, with Munk's name on the front page. Not until ten days later did the court in Holstebro order their confiscation. The results were meagre. All together the Germans managed to get back about 400 copies.[294] The contents were the three sermons; "John and Jesus," "The Christ Child and Stephen," and "Christ and Denmark." In the sermon on "John and Jesus," Munk spoke about Herod, who committed adultery: "... and even in our country there is a Herod, who fornicates with foreign gods...." John the Baptist, who was jailed and executed, provided another opportunity to talk about the resistance:

> *And now you, my countrymen, who have been thrown into the prisons of the state's power for that which had called upon you with the voice of truth, I pray to God that you will be*

---

[293] Bjarne Nielsen Brovst. Op. cit., p. 221.
[294] Ove Marcussen: *Kaj Munks Bøger* (*Kaj Munk's Books*), N.C. Roms Forlag Copenhagen 1945 p. 60.

strong and faithful toward your belief that you have acted correctly. If any of you are unsure and doubtful, then in the name of the Lord, I forgive your sin. From the church it shall be said to you: The Lord of Truth has let His face shine upon you, may He give you His peace! Amen.

In the last sermon, "Christ and Denmark," he spoke about all that we should cherish:

You shall be faithful to the sacred ideals of democracy: do not betray your conscience, do not resort to violence against other religions, except the religions of violence, grant all people true justice, and shun like a pest the persecution of the defenseless.

In the first sermon, Munk blessed those who fought against the occupation; in the second sermon he characterized the "sacred" and cherished ideals of democracy as the opposite of what Nazism had practiced since 1933.

These three sermons could not have been pleasant reading for the Nazis, and they reacted promptly when they got hold of a copy. In the *National-Socialist* paper, the three sermons were described on June 11, 1943 under the heading, "A smear campaign under the cloak of Christianity." The writer wondered if the pastors did not understand the new times and the new thoughts, which are "... a practical expression of charity." About the *Three Sermons* it was stated that "... they are only available through the numerous underground channels that at this time are undermining Danish society and are only sold to 'a circle of friends,' and the very faithful anglophiles, and friends of the Soviets." From the last sermon in the piece, "Christ and Denmark," the Nazi magazine quoted the following:

Lead us to fight along with the shackled Norway in the Nordic struggle against that idea that is the opposite of all of ours, lead old Denmark forward to its new spirit.... We, who can see that vision, will offer ourselves for that. We promise that we will. May God hear our oath, and He Himself say amen.

The Nazi editor commented on the quotation this way: "After the last sentence one would expect that Mr. Kaj Munk, besides inflaming others, will himself follow the dangerous path. With the knowledge that we have of Kaj Munk's 'courage,' we doubt very strongly that he will do that." The man that fought alone, a person with Munk's personal courage was, for the Nazi group mentality, an unknown concept.

At a large school meeting in Viborg, Munk spoke about "Denmark and Norway." Before he began to speak, he turned to Knud Kristensen, Member of Parliament, who had just arrived.[295] Although they disagreed on many things, Munk had been pleased with many of his recent remarks: "I think he is a leader the Danish farmer can be proud of. Thank you, Knud Kristensen! (Loud applause). "[296]

---

[295] Knud Kristensen (1880-1962), Secretary of State 1940-1942. Refused to enter the Scavenius government 1942-1943, foreman for Venstre's parliamentary group 1942-1945.

[296] "En Fører de danske Bønder kan være stolte af" (A leader the Danish farmers can be proud of), Viborg Stifts Folkeblad, 15 June 1943.

Chapter 12

"... learn to kill in the name of Jesus"

There was a young woman, Elsebet Kieler,[297] who was active in "Free Denmark's Student Union," but as a Christian had qualms about the resistance's use of violence and liquidations. She wrote to Munk to ask his opinion on these things. In her letter she talked about the different books she had read in search of answers for her problem. She received an answer from Munk on June 3, 1943. His letter is often quoted in Munk literature, as it is here:

> *Dear Miss Elsebet, burn all that literature, it's so trivial at this time, or just a millstone around your neck– and learn to use a machine gun. It is a Christian duty to help widows and orphans, and one way you can do that is by shooting the thieves who would attack them. But it is not Christian to let others bear the struggle and torment of defense while sitting back in a state of Nirvana. That is opium and depravity. Now become a Christian and learn to kill in the name of Jesus. Your devoted Kaj Munk.*

As a postscript he wrote: "Those who live by the sword will die by the sword. Yes, exactly! It's a good thing that Christians too can use the sword." He wrote on the back: "It's rubbish that we should hide God's words in our heart. God's words shall not be hidden anywhere. Long live Absalom!"[298]

That was a very substantial challenge that Elsebet Kieler was not completely in agreement with. In a four-page letter, dated June 15, 1943, she challenged Munk. Here is a short extract:

> *Dear Pastor Munk! It was very friendly of you to answer my letter, so I probably should not bother you with additional protests. If it wasn't that my entire confirmed soul rebelled against your maxim: 'to kill in the name of Jesus!' I am thinking, for example, about the*

---

[297] Elsebet von Führen Kieler (1918-2006), M.A.

[298] Jørgen Kieler, *Hvorfor gjorde I det? (Why did you do it?)* Gyldendal 2001, volume 1, p.183.

words of Luke: 'A good person shows the best of his heart's treasure– as it is from the heart's treasure that the mouth speaks' (for that reason it is good to keep the word of Jesus in your heart). It's a bad example for widows and orphans, and no help to insure their present welfare, to break God's commandments. It is taking a monstrous authority to end a person's life, and not really knowing what you're doing– it is in more than one way a deed of darkness. And to return to the real subject: 'to kill in the name of Jesus.' That's probably what the Jews were thinking about with the Kingdom of the Son of man, who with His legions would establish a world empire for His chosen people. Jesus said, 'My kingdom is not of this world,' and he forbade Peter to pick up the sword.... It was the same delusion that Absalom and the crusaders were lost in, but they were still savages in Christian skin.[299]*

Elsebet Kieler believed that by using violence against the violent we would just be putting ourselves in the same class as those we condemned, and she asked: "What do we gain? What happens to the compassion in our Christian discourse? Isn't it just false heroics and delusional behavior?"

This exchange of letters, and also earlier correspondence that is found in Munk's archives– for example letters from Danish volunteers in the Finnish-Russian war– shows that Munk was someone that the young had faith in and could seek advice from concerning existential questions. That Elsebet Kieler wasn't completely satisfied with his advice is another matter.

Martinus Wested had already dealt with the subject of the war between Finland and Russia in a newspaper article in March 1940. He wrote that the sense of responsibility for God and man might make it necessary to kill. He asked if the Finns: "Weren't just as heartless in this bloody harvest? Can you really murder in God's name?" But the Finns were driven into war out of duty: "There is a higher regard than even the regard for human life, and even the bloodiest massacres can, with brutal necessity, take place in God's name and honor...Christian morality cannot be drawn up with a ruler."

---

[299] KMF

Wested concluded: "We know at least one people with a genuine popular Christianity– the Finns."[300]The concept that it could become necessary to "kill in the name of Jesus," was something that the previously radical anti-militarist Wested now had in common with his friend and pupil Kaj Munk.

---

[300] Martinus Wested, "Guds Kraft" (God's Power), Lollands Tidende, 19 March 1940.

Chapter 13

No Victory without a Struggle

A lot had happened in 1943. An important turning point in the war was the defeat of the German army at Stalingrad on 2 February. Germany's military fall was within sight, and it was going downhill for the Fascists in Italy. On July 24, 1943, Mussolini was deposed by the Fascist council and imprisoned. German soldiers freed him on September 12. With German help, he tried to establish a fascist republic in northern Italy, "The Italian Social Republic," in Saló by Lake Garda.[301] Among the soldiers who freed him was Peter Schwerdt, who would be one of Kaj Munk's murderers.[302] Munk mentioned the fall of Mussolini in the poem, "The God of all Fronts" (Alle Fronters Gud):

> Defenseless towns of Abyssinia,
> You, smashed along the road to peace,
> While your emperor kneeled in his church,
> Sent prayers to the deaf arches!
> Those, who sent you bombers, flee
> Now from *their* ruined homes and scream.
> He, who princes drove from their domains,
> A refugee now, back in his own land.[303]

Is there a trace of satisfaction in this poem over the fall of the tyrant, the dictator Mussolini, who Munk so admired earlier? Munk had already criticized the Italian attack on Abyssinia in 1935, and their treatment of the Jews.

---

[301] Wolfgang Benz: *Geschichte des Dritten Reiches*. Verlag C.H. Beck, Munich, 2000,pp. 205-207.

[302] Bjarne Nielsen Brovst: *Kaj Munk, krigen og mordet* (*Kaj Munk, The War and The Murder*) p.269.

[303] Kaj Munk: *Korrekturtryk – Den Skæbne ej til os* (*Galley proof –That Fate is Not for Us*). Poems, A. Rasmussen Printers, Ringkøbing, 1943, pp.47-48.

The poem above is from the collection *That Fate is Not for Us* (*Den Skæbne ej til os*), which the censor certainly would not have approved. After September 8, 1943 all books and leaflets had to be approved by the government. For that reason Munk had this poetry collection printed as a "proof," and sent it out privately to his friends, stamped "2nd. Proof 7/9." The poems were written before the coalition government resigned.[304]

In one of the poems, "Law is Life" (Lov er Liv), Munk defends his position with respect to the political conditions in Denmark in the war year 1943:

> You throw words of acid at my face,
> And fearfully avoid the ace of spades.
> "Your words in Denmark have no weight,
> For you are enemies against our people's
> state."
> Alas. You make a grotesque and horrible
> mistake,
> For now it's you who fail the people's
> state
> Fleeing from yourselves before full sail,
> And me, who had so fervently foretold
> your fate.[305]

Munk was not satisfied with the coalition government. He used the Danish word for democracy, "People's State," a neutral expression! But you make a mistake, he wrote, "... now it is you who fail...." The word "now" means that now it is the opposite, that before it was Munk who failed. It seems to be an admission. In March 1943, it was Munk who had encouraged the vote for Dansk Samling[306] in *The Moment (Øjeblikket)*, when he wrote:

---

[304] Ibid. This poetry collection was finished September 7, 1943, but was not for sale. It was later printed and sold illegally.
[305] Ibid., p.49.
[306] Dansk Samling was founded in 1936 by Arne Sørensen. It participated in the resistance. The organization, which was against parliamentarianism

".... In Denmark's fateful hour we cannot support the Scavenian parties in their abandonment of the people's state*."[307] Did Dansk Samling want a "People's State"? They received only three seats in the election of March of 1943.

In the second verse of "Law is Life," Kaj Munk admits that he had previously lashed out hard against democracy; and if it becomes necessary, he would do it again, if he were still alive. Whatever he and his old opponents might have thought earlier, now the old disagreements should be swept from their thoughts with a smile, and they should fight together to free occupied Denmark.

> Yes, before I swung down with my flail
> To beat grain to the stable floor.
> And shall I live, the time will come again
> -perhaps- to strike down hard against its core.
> But what we before this time could think,
> You, countrymen! Oh, let's wipe off
> with a smile.
> What must now be asked, is this one thing:
> Where were you on April ninth?[308]

In the next verse (the poem contains nine verses), he wrote that we must uphold the law (the constitution), for that is what holds us up. Whether it is good or bad, we can discuss that after the war, and we will call traitors those who make "monkey-shines" with illegal rules for incarceration and the like. "We Christians don't believe in death, but on the deep words from Nazareth...." Here too Munk wrote that we had to put our lives on the line. It was cowardly to expect a victory without a fight.

---

and party rule, was part of the government in 1945. It was not represented in parliament after 1947.

*Erik Scavenius (1877-1962), member of the Social Liberal Party, Danish Prime Minister November 1942-August 1943. He was anti-military, and believed that cooperation with the Germans was the best policy for Denmark during the occupation.

[307] Kaj Munk encourages voting for Dansk Samling. *Øjeblikket* (*The Moment*), March 1943. *Øjeblikket* was published by Dansk Samling.

[308] Op.cit., p.49.

The increasing sabotage, the strikes, and the other forms of disobedience toward the occupying forces heightened the tension. Sunday morning, August 29, 1943, at 4.00 a.m., the Germans declared martial law in Denmark. The Danish military was disarmed and interred. The exercise of power was taken over by the German military.

Munk, who had heard about the enactment of martial law, said in the beginning of his sermon on the same day: "Today is a day of pride for Denmark.... We breathe a sigh of relief, we greet each other with congratulations... if we will ourselves, it's the best that has happened to us: that we are in God's hands."[309] Now we could stop this giving in and double play. Now we stood in the open against our enemy. That there would be suffering, that blood would flow, Munk did not doubt. But that had always been a part of being "a child of God."

The next day, August 30, there was an official declaration. Prime Minister Scavenius had tendered his resignation to the King, and had resigned. The relationship to the occupying forces approached a state of war.

In July of 1943 the Foreign Ministry had sent a directive to the news media not to publish articles by Munk.[310] The irritating pastor in Vedersø should keep quiet and not encourage people to resist. The Danes had clearly given the coalition government their support in the election on March 23, 1943.

In a very critical poem, "The Concealed Spirit" (*Den skjulte Aand*) from 1943, Kaj Munk, in one of the verses, reproaches the Danish authorities for their cooperation with the Germans:

> Government, parliament, courts, police,
> You who should have shed light in the dark,
> But quickly found a mouse hole to hide in,
> And aid the strangers 'gainst their countrymen,
> Isn't Denmark's spirit here today?[311]

---

[309] Kaj Munk: *Commemorative Edition, Sermons.* Sermon in Vedersø Church, 29 August 1943, NNF 1963, p.3.
[310] Per Stig Møller, *Munk.* Gyldendal 2000, p.313.
[311] Kaj Munk, *Korrekturtryk,* Op.cit.p.45.

This type of an accusation against the country's leaders and authorities was doubtless one of the reasons that led to Munk's unpopularity in certain circles after the Second World War.

Munk's one-act play *Before Cannae* (*Før Cannae*) was published in 1943.[312] In the play, which takes place the evening before the battle at Cannae, the Roman general Fabius Maximus, who would prefer to avoid battle, goes to the enemy camp to speak with Carthage's general Hannibal. When Fabius' offer of peace is so scornfully rejected by Hannibal, Fabius says: "Then I give you my condolences for the victory tomorrow." Many have interpreted the play as being about current events, dressed in historical costume. Per Stig Møller suggests that perhaps the Roman and Hannibal could have symbolized Churchill and Hitler.[313] At the premiere performance in Oslo, in June of 1945, the two protagonists wore black-tie, another suggestion that the play was about current events. At the performance at the Kammarteatern in Helsinki in 1953, Fabius was dressed as Montgomery, and Hannibal as Erwin Rommel.[314]

At the same time that the persecution of the Jews was on the rise in Germany and the countries it occupied, Munk continued to draw attention to their treatment. He had defended them since 1933 with increasing intensity.

In a sermon from 1941 Kaj Munk had talked about the close connection between Christians and Jews, and against the Nazi theories that Jesus was not a Jew but an Aryan:

> *Jesus was born in a very definite country and of a very definite people. Jesus was a Jew. His ancestral history was the history of the Jews, his poets were the prophets, and his way of speaking followed the Jewish tradition.... and Jesus knew that his people were chosen by God.*

---

[312] Kaj Munk, *Før Cannae (Before Cannae)*. Special edition of Bogrevyen. Samlerens Forlag, Copenhagen 1943.

[313] Per Stig Møller, Op. cit., p. 536.

[314] Harald Mogensen, *Kaj Munk paa Teatret (Kaj Munk on the Theater)*, NNF 1953, p.64.

Munk did not believe that Jesus was interested in conquest, repression, or power, "... not a world conqueror, but a world savior, that's why God had chosen the Jewish people, to give that gift to mankind."[315]

On the night of October 1, 1943, the Germans, on orders from Berlin, started to round up Danish Jews. They were to be assembled and sent to the concentration camp at Theresienstadt. The German envoy G.F. Duckwitz, who was knowledgeable about shipping, sent a warning (with the approval of SS-Gruppenführer Dr. Werner Best*) to his Danish acquaintances, including the Social Democrat Hans Hedtoft, about the planned action against the Jews. [316] This warning made it possible for many Jews to escape to Sweden, and for others to hide until an escape was possible. Within days a network was established that arranged escape for the persecuted over the straits. That many of the refugees had to pay for the trip does not detract from this voluntary and exceptional action. Out of over 7,000 Jews in Denmark, the Germans were only able to detain 472. The others were either in Sweden or in hiding in Denmark.[317]

Dr. Best received numerous protests from different organizations and politicians. The Bishops protested with a Pastoral Letter, "The Position of the Danish Church on the Jewish Question," which was read aloud in most churches on Sunday, October 3rd.[318] Munk admired the efforts made to help the Jews; "Nothing else has made me feel so good since April 9 as this."[319] Munk's two Jewish translators– Erwin Magnus and Walter Berendsohn– escaped from Copenhagen to Sweden in 1943.

---

[315] Kaj Munk, *Commemorative Edition*, Sermon on the King's birthday, 26 September 1941, NNF 1963, pp. 304-305.

*Dr. Werner Best (1903-1989), German plenipotentiary in Denmark, 1942-1945.

[316] *Tyskere imod Hitler* (*Germans against Hitler*) *Five Diplomats in Copenhagen*. The German Republic's Embassy in Copenhagen, 1999, pp.14 ff.

[317] *Danmarks Historie.* (*History of Denmark*) Politikens Forlag 1966, volume 14, pp.178 ff.

[318] Erik Thostrup Jacobsen, *Som om intet var hændt* (*As if nothing had happened*) Odense Universitetsforlag 1991, p.147.

[319] Niels Nøjgaard, *Ordets Dyst og Daad (Power and Action in the Word).* NNF 1946, p.398.

The newspapers were forbidden to print Munk's articles, and publishers could not release his books. He had so far, however, not been prevented from speaking. He tried, through the Bishop of Copenhagen, to arrange a speech there and had an agreement to give a sermon at Helligaandskirken (Church of the Holy Spirit) on Sunday November 21, 1943. Munk was already in Copenhagen when Dr. Best, on Saturday afternoon, banned the church service with Munk as a preacher.

Kaj Munk wanted to speak anyway, but the local pastor did not want to start a "church war." Shortly after this unsuccessful arrangement Munk received an invitation to speak at Copenhagen's Cathedral on December 5. For good reasons the preacher's name was not announced.[320] This time Munk did make it to the pulpit. In his sermon he said that if "Those in power" do not want politics talked about in church, then they would have to practice Christian politics, and if they didn't "... then the church would not be the church of Jesus if it kept quiet. It is said that silence in the face of sin is the devil's language." Munk also touched on the relationship to the Jews:

> When here at home a certain group of our countrymen is persecuted just because of their heritage, then it is the Christian duty to speak up: this is contrary to the constitution in God's Kingdom, the rule of compassion, and it is repulsive to the free Nordic mind... if it happens once more, then with God's help we will lead our people to revolt.

He praised the youth "... who are ready to risk life, limb, and honor for their country, and for what they believe in."[321] It was a direct homage to the resistance, and a challenge to the occupiers. Munk's desire to get his message out to as many as possible was fulfilled. His sermon in the Cathedral was printed and illegally distributed in 40,000 copies.[322]

---

[320] Ibid. p.399.

[321] Kaj Munk, op. cit., 2nd. Sunday in Advent, Frue Kirke, December 5, 1943, NNF 1963, pp. 349-355.

[322] Bjarne Nielsen Brovst, op.cit., p. 305.

Munk's next-to-last sermon, and the most widely discussed, was held on New Year's Day 1944, in Vedersø Church. The altar candles were not lit. The organ was not played. After one hymn, Munk gave his sermon, standing on the church floor next to the pulpit without his vestments. After the sermon he finished the service with The Lord's Prayer.

In this sermon Munk explained the reason for the unusual service: He could not ascend the pulpit that day as his heart was full of sorrow and pain because some in the parish had begun to work for the Germans. After August 29 the Danes were, in his opinion, at war with Germany.

"When a Dane voluntarily helps a German now, then it is an act of treason." And when "... people in the parish sin, then the parish has its house of God so it can be denounced." Munk also said that for months he had not been able to go to sleep without thinking; "Will they come after you tonight?" But Munk could not hate the Germans. "The Saviour has taught us the prayer: Forgive them– for they know not what they do. However, that does not mean that it is a Christian thing to help them build their fortifications. And it is not a Christian act to sell to the Germans, at a high price, eggs and bacon that our own poor workers in the cities need so badly." He said that the Germans had brought the scandal of Jewish persecution to our Nordic land. He praised the saboteurs, both for their respect for human life, and for their participation in the resistance movement. They were the ones who had taken it upon themselves "... to show Denmark's face."[323]

If some of the Danish food reached hungry "widows or orphans" in Germany, wasn't that a "Christian act"? After August 29 it was treason to help the Germans. Hadn't it been treason since April 9, 1940? The German goals were the same before and after August 29. Munk had, after all, already complained about the cooperation between the Danes and the Germans, also in a letter to the teacher Martinus Wested on May 5, 1940: "What pains me most are those not so very 'Danes', who have already obediently put on Germany's harness, or even done it with enthusiasm."[324]

In the late thirties Munk had bought the "Sap" farm, which lay close to his forested estate "Lokkelykke." It produced agricultural

[323] Kaj Munk, op.cit., New Year's day 1944, pp. 356-359.
[324] Letters from Kaj Munk to Martinus Wested. The Royal Library.

products, of which a portion most likely had ended up in Germany, just like from the other farms in occupied Denmark. Had Munk himself done that which he said was wrong for others?

That Munk had also thought about that side of the problem is clearly seen in a dedication in 1942: "Well, where are we headed? And this harvest, which is abundant, rich and good. It's the Devil's gift to those who idolize him? God's hand is heavy upon us. Now the Germans can hold out a while longer."[325]

On Sunday, January 2, 1944, there was another service in Vedersø Church where Munk gave an "evangelical sermon with both warmth and sorrow."[326]

No manuscript has been found for that sermon. It would be Munk's last.

---

[325]   From a dedication in *Foraaret saa sagte kommer* to teacher Martinus Wested, 15 September 1942. County Library, Maribo, Kaj Munk collection.

[326] Bjarne Nielsen Brovst, op.cit., p.348.

Chapter 14

"... to give up life for Life"

In the poem "The Hidden Spirit" (Den skjulte Aand) from 1943, Munk puts his faith in those who are fighting for freedom. In the last verse he is convinced that the Old Danish spirit will triumph:

> That people who now, as through a thousand
> years,
> Had the courage to give up life for Life,
> And for their love have given up themselves,
> That Denmark, thanks to God, we know,
> Will stand as long as stars 'cross Heaven
> flow.[327]

Munk's numerous calls for resistance against the occupying powers, and his anti-German articles and poems, had been an on-going thorn in the side of Dr. Best and his associates. Kaj Munk, Ole Bjørn Kraft,[328] and many others were on the German hit list. Carefully chosen "specialists" were assigned to carry out the assassinations. The attempted assassination of Ole Bjørn Kraft on December 30, 1943 was a warning of what could happen.

In the evening of January 4, 1944, a car drove into the courtyard of the parsonage in Vedersø. While one man stood watch at the door, three others entered and asked for Munk. They claimed to be police detectives. Munk was told that he was under arrest and that he would have go with them. Lise Munk packed a bag for him. Munk said goodbye, hugged his wife, and said, "Trust in God, Lise." He got into the car with the other four– where a fifth was waiting.

---

[327] Kaj Munk, *Korrekturtryk – Den Skæbne ej til os,* p.46.
[328] Ole Bjørn Kraft (1893-1980), journalist, conservative politician, held several cabinet positions.

They drove off from the parsonage, and everything happened quickly. When they got to Hørbylunde outside of Silkeborg the car pulled over and Munk was ordered out. He was killed with three shots to the head, and fell into the ditch where they left him. To make the murder look like the liquidation of an informant, the murderers left a note on the body that said: "You pig have anyhows worked for Germany." (Du Svin har alligevell arbejdet for Tyskland) The mistakes in the writing indicated that the note had not been written by a Dane.[329]

The circumstances surrounding the murder of Kaj Munk are described in detail in *Kaj Munk, the War and the Murder, (Kaj Munk, krigen og mordet)* by Bjarne Nielsen Brovst.

During the Occupation Munk had turned down many offers of help to go to Sweden or England. But he would not leave Denmark. He encouraged others to resist, to risk their lives in the struggle. What was demanded of others must be demanded of himself. For that reason a man like Munk could not flee.

The Germans informed the press that Munk's murder could only be covered to the same extent as that of a Nazi and informant who was shot in Slagelse. That was the reason that most papers carried only a short notice about Kaj Munk's murder. The more extensive commemorative articles came out after liberation, May 5, 1945. Many illegal publications, probably all of them, carried extensive obituaries and articles where Munk was described as the great inspirer for the freedom fighters.

Before Munk's coffin was taken from the hospital in Silkeborg, his friend, Pastor Herluf Aagaard, held a service in the chapel. Then the hearse drove to Vedersø Church. At the funeral on January 8 there were about 3000 people in attendance. Pastor Niels Nøjgaard held the graveside committal service and the casting of earth. The coffin, covered by a Danish flag donated by the parish youth and a cross of heather from Munk's own moorland, was then lowered into the ground.[330]

Among the many wreaths and bouquets sent to the funeral, there was one with a red silken ribbon[331] with the following text

---

[329] Bjarne Nielsen Brovst, op.cit., pp.357 ff.
[330] Ibid., pp. 406 ff.
[331] The ribbon is in the Munk family archive.

in gold colors: "Thank you for your valor" (Tak for din Daad), followed by the symbols of a star, hammer, and sickle– a salute from the communists in Aarhus.[332]

Munk's murder did not dampen the National Socialists' hatred of him. In October of 1943 he had published the children's book *The Stories of Jesus (Jesus' Historier)*[333] and in December *The Acts of the Apostles (Apostlenes Gerninger)*.[334] The latter was to be a part of *The New Testament Retold by Danish Poets (Det Nye Testamente gengivet af danske Digtere)* to be published by Westermann.[335]

These books were then mentioned in the Nazi magazine *The National-Socialist*, on February 25, 1944, under the heading "Offensive Bible stories replace authors' and publishers' heretofore golden "national" smear campaign!" Munk was described as,

> *The late, clever Pastor Kaj Munk" who had written a Bible story for children- "... of such a 'quality' that even the establishment's press, which was normally ready to grovel for even the worst nonsense from Vedersø, had trouble justifying its existence.*

Munk's book, *The Acts of the Apostles*, was mentioned with a note saying, "It was met with silence."

The magazine wrote that now it was the Bible's turn. "The publisher Westermann has hired a consortium of Soviet friends to

---

[332] Munk had once, possibly twice, sent 10,000 crowns to a communist resistance group in Aarhus, with the instructions that the money was to be used for the resistance, not for communist propaganda. The salute mentioned here could be proof that this story is true. For good reason there are no receipts or other documentation. Niels Nøjgaard: *Ordets Dyst og Daad*, Nyt Nordisk Forlag Arnold Busck, Copenhagen 1946, p.398.

[333] Kaj Munk: *Jesus' Historier (The Stories of Jesus)*. Nyt Nordisk Forlag Arnold Busck, Copenhagen 1943.

[334] Kaj Munk, *Apostlenes Gerninger (Acts of the Apostles)*. Nyt Nordisk Forlag Arnold Busck, Copenhagen 1943.

[335] *Det ny Testamente gengivet af danske Digtere (The New Testament, retold by Danish poets)*, Westermann Forlag, Copenhagen. December 1944. For this edition Munk had retold the *Acts of the Apostles*, and the *Gospel according to Luke*.

produce a retelling of– The New Testament– should we laugh or cry?" The "Soviet friends" were Marcus Lauesen, Johannes Wulff, and Tom Kristensen. The journalist thought that none of them were known for "... having a very Christian mentality."

Munk was now personally out of reach; but the illegal press was increasingly using his articles, speeches, and poems. He was still a dangerous enemy for the Germans and was treated as such.

However, Munk was certainly not forgotten in the authorized Danish press either. Had the authorities slacked off on their restrictions? Despite censorship, and a scarcity of paper, in 1944 publishers were able to send out several of Munk's books in new press runs, totalling 169,000 copies. [336]

Since 1940, Munk had been subjected to frequent censorship by the foreign ministry's press bureau. During the war this bureau determined what could be written and published, and was forced into a balancing act between the desire to maintain tolerable conditions, and the hard line set down by the Germans. This often resulted in strange requests. When Munk's memoirs, Silently Comes the Spring (Foraaret saa sagte kommer) came out in 1942, publishers and newspapers were told that they could not mention the book, and bookstores could only display one copy in their windows![337]

In May of 1945, Germany surrendered in a war that had already been lost. On May 5, 1945 Denmark was again a free country. In the days that followed newspapers printed entire pages about Munk, with articles and obituaries. He was now, and not without reason, Denmark's champion of liberty. Very few had spoken out so openly against the occupiers and the collaborators.

At a memorial service in Copenhagen's Cathedral on August 23, 1945, Munk's widow, Lise, together with four of their children, the Queen, the Crown Prince and Princess, prime ministers from Norway and Sweden, and several Danish ministers, were present. The Norwegian Bishop Eivind Berggrav gave the keynote speech, and said, among other things, "What a person is becomes evident when great things hang in the balance. Take note of this, all of you, who have anything to say about his personal greatness and his weaknesses... he speaks, and will always speak, with his deep, fervent, loving and passionate words, this God's champion, through

---

[336] Ove Marcussen, *Kaj Munks Bøger* (*Kaj Munk's Books*).
[337] Niels Nøjgaard, op.cit.,p.382.

the generations to come."[338] Berggrav also spoke about Munk's importance for Norway during the war.

Ten years later Jens Kruuse wrote in an article about Munk's death: "It was the very magnitude of that horrendous act that endowed it with a significance and splendor like no other death in those years when the harvest was so rich."

Munk's death would not now, or in the future, be called unreasonable: "It was tragic, and that means necessary, correct— a consummation.[339]

---

[338] *Kaj Munk Papirer* (*The Papers of Kaj Munk*), NNF 1948, p.50.
[339] "Kaj Munks Død- en tragisk Nødvendighed" (Kaj Munk's Death- A tragic necessity). Ph.D. Jens Kruuse, Jyllands-Posten, March 1, 1954

SECOND PART — APPENDIX

After Kaj Munk's death
1944-1988

The second part of this book contains a brief review of the material written about Munk in Switzerland and Germany during the period 1944 -2007. Several items, however, are only listed in the index. The German titles have not been translated into English.

After Munk's death, and in particular after the end of WWII, many books were written about him and his own works were reprinted. In 1948-49 *Kaj Munk Mindeudgave* (*Kaj Munk Memorial Edition*) in 9 volumes was published. Munk was also translated into several languages, including German.

With the exception of the translated plays which were available as duplicated parts, the first of the Munk translations into German done during WWII were published in neutral Switzerland

Kaj Munk: *Bekenntnis zur Wahrheit* [*Bekendelse til sandheden*] was published by Evangelische Verlag AG Zollikon/Zürich in 1944. The book contains 12 sermons from Munk's collection of sermons: *Ved Babylons Floder* (*By The Rivers of Babylon*).[340] Laure Wyss did the translation.[341] She lived in Sweden for a time during WWII so she might have made the translation from the Swedish edition of *Ved Babylons Floder,* which was published under the title *Hoppet förbliver* by Svenska Kyrkans Diakonistyrelses Bokförlag i 1942. In *Bekenntnis zur Wahrheit*, Munk's first German language publication, the introduction finishes with:

> *Through his extensive authorship he will, as heretofore,*
> *speak to the Danish people, and continue his work as a*

---

[340] Kaj Munk: *Ved Babylons Floder*, Danish sermons 1941. NNF 1941. The original Danish edition contained 24 sermons. John M. Jensen, Lutheran pastor, translated 15 of these sermons in 1945. They were published by the Lutheran Publishing House under the title *By The Rivers of Babylon.*
[341] Laure Wyss (1913- 2002), journalist and author. See biographies.

sentinel and comforter. And in the following sermons he will
speak to us as well.[342] (a.t.)

On September 6, 1944 Munk's play *Niels Ebbesen* had its
premiere at the Zürich Schauspielhaus.

It was later performed several places in Switzerland.[343] In
one review it was suggested that it was sympathy for Munk's
fate, and the play's contemporary relevance, rather than its
poetic value, that was the basis for its performance. But that the
play was well written was recognized. The review finished by
mentioning that at the time Switzerland was the only place with
German language theaters where a play like that could be
performed. The reviewer wrote that Switzerland was a
sanctuary for German theater. Switzerland could handle that
task because it had become the forced refuge of "... a group of
eminent actors who were well above our own theatrical level."
[344](a.t.) In that "group" of German and Austrian refugees there
had most likely been several Jewish actors.

After the performance in Zürich *Niels Ebbesen* was released
in book form[345] in a translation by Otto Maag.[346] In the
beginning of the book are two pages of corrections and
supplements which the publisher explains is because Maag had
translated the play from an English edition but later had the
opportunity to compare it with the original Danish. Magg
believed that the resulting changes were necessary to give a
better understanding of the play. Which English translation
Maag used is not stated in the book. It could have been an
unprinted manuscript but could also have been what is most
likely the first published edition in English: *Niels Ebbesen.*
Historical Drama in Five Acts, translated by Erna Voight and H.

---

[342] Kaj Munk, *Bekenntnis zur Wahrheit.* Evangelische Verlags AG
Zollikon/Zürich. 2 edition 1944, p. 8.

[343] Harald Mogensen: *Kaj Munk paa Teatret.* NNF 1953, p. 61.

[344] Kaj Munk, "Niels Ebbesen". Review by N.N. in Schweizer Bücherzeitung,
October 1944.

[345] Kaj Munk, *Niels Ebbesen.* Translated by Otto Maag. Artemis Verlags AG,
Zürich 1944.

[346] Otto Maag (1885-1960). See biographies.

Orlo Miller: *The Scandinavian News*, September 1942, February 1943, London, Ontario.

A third publication in German in 1944 was Maria Bachmann-Isler's[347] translation of Kaj Munk's memoirs, *Foraaret saa sagte kommer*, which was given the German title of *Fragment eines Lebens*.[348]

The publisher was able to get Christmas Møller,[349] a well-known politician during WWII, to write a preface. Christmas Møller was the foreman for the Danish Council (Det Danske Raad) in London from 1942 til 1945.[350] The Council's task during the war was to facilitate communication between the Allies and the Danish resistance movement. In the preface Christmas Møller wrote that Munk's writings occupied a special place in Danish literature: "If his language had been one of the world languages, then he would have been known as one of the greatest dramatists." (a.t.)

In 1944 the German author Max Tau[351] founded "Neuer Verlag, Stockholm." The publisher was to be a home for exiled authors where their works, and the works of others, could be published in German. In 1945 Neuer Verlag published *Dänische Predigten von Kaj Munk (The Danish Sermons of Kaj Munk)*, which contains twelve sermons translated by the German refugee Edzard Schaper.[352] They are from Munk's collection of sermons *Med Ordets Sværd (With the Sword of the Word)*,[353] *3 Sermons*, the famous "illegal" sermon on 5

---

347 Maria Bachmann-Isler, translator. No information.

348 Kaj Munk, *Fragment eines Lebens*. Translated by Maria Bachmann-Isler. Artemis Verlags AG. Zürich 1944.

349 John Christmas Møller (1894-1948), conservative Danish politician, lived in England 1942-45.

350 *Hvem Hvad Hvor (Who What Where)*. Politikens Aarbog 1948, p. 49.

351 Max Tau (1897-1976), author, immigrated to Norway 1938, fled to Sweden 1942. Lived in Norway after1945. After the war he worked as a cultural ambassador between Germany and Scandinavia.

352 Edzard Schaper (1908-1984), author. See biographies.

353 Kaj Munk, *Med Ordets Sværd (With the Sword of the Word)*, Danish sermons 1941-42, 2. Collection. NNF 1942.

December 1943 in Copenhagen's Cathedral,[354] and Munk's beautiful sermon over his stepmother Marie Munk.[355]

Dänische Predigten came out in a 2nd printing in 1947. The above-mentioned sermon over Marie Munk was held on the 6th Sunday after Easter. It was printed in a German edition under the title "Am siebenten Sonntag nach Ostern."

Ebbe Neergaard's[356] book *Vildt afsted over Himmel og Jord. Kaj Munk, en Digter mellem to Verdenskrige* (*Headlong over Heaven and Earth. Kaj Munk, a poet between two world wars*) was published in 1945 by Artemis Verlags AG, Zürich and translated into German by Maria Bachmann-Isler under the title: *Kaj Munk, Ein Dichter zwischen zwei Weltkriegen*. The book is about Munk's life and works.

The following year another book by Munk was published in Switzerland. It was Munk's cheerful tale about Danish hunters, *Liv og glade Dage* (*Life and Happy Days*) from 1936, translated by Elsa Carlberg[357] under the title *Glückhafte Tage*.[358] As in the Danish edition, this book was illustrated with drawings by Ib Andersen. It was the fourth and last publication by Artemis. A letter from the publisher to Erwin Magnus on May 24, 1946, in which they thank him for his letter, indicates that they planned to continue working with Munk's works. In the letter the publisher wrote that they would negotiate a possible edition of Munk's *The Word* (probably in cooperation with Nyt Nordisk Forlag Arnold Busck, Copenhagen), and they asked if Magnus was interested in translating the play.[359] The publisher was apparently not aware that Magnus had already translated *The Word* in 1932. It has not been possible to find any additional correspondence between Magnus and Artemis. Magnus died the following year, 1947, and as

---

[354] Kaj Munk, *Mindeudgave, Prædikener*. Second Sunday in Advent. Frue Kirke in Copenhagen 5 December 1943. NNF 1963, pp. 349-355.

[355] Kaj Munk, *Ved Babylons Floder*, s. 51.

[356] Ebbe Neergaard (1901-1957), M.A. in English and German, author.

[357] Elsa Carlberg, translator. No information.

[358] Kaj Munk: *Glückhafte Tage*. Mit Federzeichnungen von Ib Andersen. Artemis Verlags AG. Zürich 1946.

[359] Letters of 24 May 1946, from Artemis Verlag, Zürich to Erwin Magnus. Private archive Michael Freud-Magnus.

far as I have been able to find out, Artemis has not published any books by Munk with Magnus as the translator

At the international PEN Club's meeting in Copenhagen on June 3, 1948 the decision was made to re-establish the Club's German Branch. One of the German participants, author Johannes R. Becher[360] from Berlin, was asked to speak.

He began his speech by saying that he appreciated being allowed to speak in a country that had been so deeply violated by his countrymen. Becher continued: "I cannot begin this speech without first mentioning Kaj Munk, the Danish pastor who was murdered by the Nazis."[361] With that remark everyone in the room stood up. The communist Johannes R. Becher's relationship to the clergy is in this connection of minor importance. The Danish pastor Kaj Munk, who risked his life, and lost it, in the fight against Hitler's National Socialist Germany, had won his deepest respect.[362] (Becher was a prominent cultural celebrity in post-war East Germany and in 1954 was appointed Minister of Culture in the DDR). The next day the Dutch and Belgium delegation to the PEN Club laid flowers at Kaj Munk's commemorative plaque at the Royal Theater. It was particularly in the smaller European countries that had shared a common fate with Denmark that Kaj Munk's name and life was known.

Munk's *Jesus' Historier (Stories of Jesus)* told for children was translated into German[363] and French[364] by Gudrun Cavin[365] in

---

360 Johannes R. Becher (1891-1958), author. See biographies.

361 "A German's tribute to Kaj Munk in PEN". Lollands Tidende 4. 6. 1948.

362 A. O. Schwede: "Kaj Munk und Niels Ebbesen". Standpunkt, Evangelische Monatsschrift. Berlin DDR. February 1980, p. 39. Archiv Günter Wirth. Konrad Adenauer Stiftung, Bonn. The article included part of Becher's speech.

363 Kaj Munk: *Jesus-Geschichten*. Translated by Gudrun Cavin. "Rocailles" Verlag Genf. Switzerland 1949.

364 Kaj Munk: *Histoires de Jésus racontées aux enfants*. Translated by Gudrun Cavin. Éditions-Rocailles Genève, Schweiz. 1949. 2. edition 1950.

365 Gudrun Cavin, translator. See biographies.

1949-50. She had previously written a book about Munk: *Kaj Munk- Dramaturge, prophète et martyr.*[366]

Of the many Germans who had written about Munk, Rolf Italiaander[367] was probably the only one who had actually met him. In the 1945 edition of the magazine *Ausblick* published by "Deutsche Auslandsgesellschaft", there was an article about Munk where Italiaander wrote the following about the meeting:

> *Many years ago, during my first bicycle trip through Denmark (1932?), I had a chance to become acquainted with Kaj Munk. It was at a film lecture about Knud Rasmussen. The passionate, lively, dark haired man was so different from the usual inside and outside blondes. After this first and rather remarkable meeting I began to study his life. For me it has become a passion to write about this strange man who is unjustly so little known in Germany.*[368] *(a.t.)*

In 1957 *Knaurs Schauspielführer,*[369] written by the dramatist Verner Arpe, was published. It had a preface by that giant of the German theater Gustaf Gründgens.[370] In *Knaurs Schauspielführer* Arpe has a section about Munk's dramas. He writes about *En Idealist, Cant, Puslespil, Diktatorinden* and *Niels Ebbesen. Diktatorinden*, which he had translated into German for Englind, he called Kaj Munk's most interesting Danish historical drama. *Ordet*, which he most likely had translated himself, and *Smeltediglen*, two of Kaj Munk's best known plays, are not mentioned.

---

[366] Gudrun Cavin: *Kaj Munk. Dramaturge, prophète et martyr.* Editions Labor et Fides, Genève,Schweiz 1946.

[367] Rolf Italiaander (1913-1991), author, translator.

[368] Rolf Italiaander: "Kaj Munk in der Spur Martin Luthers". Ausblick, Mitteilungsblatt der Deutschen Auslandsgesellschaft, October 1954, pp. 42-44.

[369] Verner Arpe: *Knaurs Schauspielführer.* Droemersche Verlagsanstalt Th. Knaur Nachf. München-Zürich 1957, pp. 291-293.

[370] Gustaf Gründgens (1899-1963), German dramatist. Leader of Preussisches Staatstheater in Berlin 1934-45, and of Deutsches Schauspielhaus in Hamburg 1955-63.

A collaboration between Dr. Christian Mettin, Städtische Bühnen Lübeck, and Odense Theater's leader, director Helge Rungwald,[371] led to the performance of Munk's drama *Kærlighed* at the Kammerspiele in Lübeck, premiering on February 18, 1958. This play is about a pastor who preaches Christianity to his congregation even though he is not a believer and is in love with his best friend's wife. Thyra Dohrenburg [372] translated the play into German under the title *Liebe*. Rungwald had prior experience with this play, *Kærlighed*, as he had directed a successful performance of it in 1949 at the Odense Theater, and in 1950 at the Aarhus Theater.[373]

There was widespread praise from the German critics for Munk, Rungwald, and the German actors. Among the actors there was particular praise for the two main roles, Ingeborg and pastor Kargo, played by Enzia Pircher and Robert Casapiccola.

Besides their discussion of the play, the German critics also wrote about Munk's tragic death during the occupation. Lise Munk had considered attending the performance but did not believe that she could deal with the emotional pressure of seeing Munk's play performed in Germany.[374]

Berlingske Tidende had sent the critic Svend Kragh-Jacobsen to the premier in Lübeck, and he had a favorable opinion of the German performance:

> *Kaj Munk's first play performed in German[375] received a fine and promising reception at its premier at the Kammerspiele in Lübeck Tuesday evening... there were fourteen curtain calls before the emotional evening was over.*

---

[371] Helge Rungwald (1906-60), Danish actor, director of the Odense Theater from 1936 til 1960.

[372] Thyra Dohrenburg (1898-1972). See biographies.

[373] Harald Mogensen: *Kaj Munk paa Teatret.* NNF 1953, p. 40.

[374] Jens Kruuse: "Kaj Munk i Hansestaden". *Jyllands-Posten* February 20, 1958.

[375] Svend Kragh-Jacobsen had apparently not been known that *Ordet* had been performed in German in Schwerin in 1935.

About one scene, where the pastor appears with his superiors, the dean, and the bishop, Kragh-Jacobsen writes: "There was real drama in this scene between three excellent actors, and the translator Thyra Dohrenburg had hit the mark precisely with the lively and insightful Munk lines which here were at their best."[376]

On May 11, 1958 Rungwald arranged a single performance of *Liebe* at the Odense Theater. To have the play performed in German in Denmark in 1958 was daring. The occupation was long from being forgotten. But the well-attended performance received high marks. *Politiken's* critic wrote:

> *The German cast's effective routine and good timing was an asset to Rungwald's genuine and very earnest direction. The performance held the audience in its grasp from beginning to end – German or not German; it was definitely understood and taken to heart.*[377]

During an international conference for Nordic literature in 1958 professor Siegfried Beyschlag[378]gave a lecture about Kaj Munks dramatic works, in particular *Das Wort* (*Ordet*). The lecture was an interpretation of *Ordet* and in particular dealt with the spiritual changes in the person of Johannes. Beyschlag also touched briefly on similar changes in other characters in some of Munk's plays: Herod in *En Idealist*, Grundtvig in *Egelykke,* and Professor Mensch in *Smeltediglen*. He called *Ordet* one of the most distinctive plays in Scandinavian drama in the 20th century, and believed that Munk, with these plays, had given renewed strength to poetry and life well beyond the Nordic countries.[379]

---

[376] "14 curtain calls in Lübeck after the Munk- premier". By Svend Kragh-Jacobsen. *Berlingske Tidende* February 19, 1958.

[377] "Kaj Munk in German". By H. E. (Harald Engberg). *Politiken*, May 13, 1958.

[378] Dr. Siegfried Beyschlag (1905-1996), Germanic philologist, has written about older German and Nordic literatur. Employed at the University of Copenhagen as professor in German language, literatur, and folklore 1942-46. Research projects at the Royal Library, Copenhagen 1946-48.

[379] Siegfried Beyschlag: Kaj Munks dramatisches Werk, zumal "Das Wort". Eine Studie. Nach einem Vortrag auf der 2. Internationalen Studienkonferenz für nordische Literatur zu Lillehammer im Juli 1958.

In connection with a "Dänische Woche", a recent obituary over Munk was read on Radio Bremen on May 29, 1961. The author, Edzard Schaper, mentioned earlier, wrote the text and read it aloud. About Munk's preaching style, Schaper said that it was a

> *Fascinating mix of sincere personal disclosure, elaborate, contrived, and pure naiveté, flaming joy of confession, subtle irony, half conscious simplicity, and intentional coarseness... The permanent and everlasting testimony for Denmark, for freedom, and for evangelical freedom under the cross! And the Gestapo always had a few bullets left over for that.[380] (a.t.)*

On January 4, 1964, the 20 anniversary of Munk's death, Freies Berlin (Radio Free Berlin) sent a broadcast of a commemorative program about Kaj Munk: "Widerstand im Glauben" (Resistance in Faith).

A young theologian, Uwe Nabersberg,[381] had read Munk. Nabersberg had discussed Munk with Arnim Juhre,[382] the editor of the *Evangelischer Rundfunkdienst* in Berlin, and that resulted in the commemorative broadcast for which Uwe Nabersberg wrote the manuscript. It included Munk quotations as well as Nabersberg's commentary, and a narrative of Munk's career. Arnim Juhre believed that Nabersberg used German language books about and by Kaj Munk that were published in Switzerland while writing his manuscript.[383] The radio program was produced with one voice as narrator, another for the quotations, and a third for the commentary. The manuscript has been published in book form.[384]

Printed in *Orbis Litterarum. Revue internationale d´etudes Litteraires*, Tome XIV. Fasc. 2-4. Copenhagen 1959, pp. 223-229.

[380] Manuscript in KMF.

[381] Uwe Nabersberg. No information.

[382] Arnim Juhre (born1925 in Berlin), author, publisher's spokesperson, poet, dramatist and essayist, has written radio plays.

[383] Conversation with Arnim Juhre 19 June 2006.

[384] *Spiele für Stimmen - ein Werkbuch*. Herausgeber Arnim Juhre. Jugenddienst Verlag, Wuppertal-Barmen 1965, p. 65-73.

Negotiations in 1964 between Nyt Nordisk Forlag Arnold Busck and Friederich Wittig Verlag about plans to publish a German edition of Kaj Munk were abandoned.[385]

In 1964 a doctoral thesis was presented at the University in Vienna: *Zeitaktuelle dänische Dramatik des 20. Jahrhunderts und ihre Inszenierung* (*Contemporary Danish drama in the 20 century, and its direction*) written by Manfred Klein.[386] The thesis filled 294 pages, of which 75 were about Munk's dramas.

The theater publisher Klaus Lensch[387] from Hamburg had been in Denmark in 1962 to negotiate with dramatists and theater publishers on the translation and rights for Germany for various Danish plays. Through a reading of Thyra Dohrenburg's translations of Nordic literature he had developed an interest for this language area. The publishing company that Lensch had founded would promote Scandinavian drama to the German theater.

He also obtained the rights in Germany for several of Munk's plays. In a catalog that Lensch distributed in 1966 there were five plays by Munk: *Brandung* [*I Brændingen*], *Das Wort* [*Ordet*], *Ein Idealist* [*En Idealist*], *Liebe* [*Kærlighed*], and *Vor Cannae* [*Før Cannae*], all translated by Thyra Dohrenburg who had furthermore translated 34 of the catalog's 60 titles.[388]

In an interview in *Berlingske Aftenavis* Lensch spoke about the work with the translation and catalog:

> *The preparations have gone on for three years now, and for Dohrenburg's part six years. If we can't make a breakthrough now then I don't see much hope for an exchange of drama between Denmark and Germany.*[389]

---

[385] Letter to NNF from F. Wittig. Friederich Wittig Verlag on 11 January 1964. KMF.

[386] Manfred Klein, Ph.D. See biographies.

[387] Klaus Lensch (1929-), author, journalist and theater publisher.

[388] Catalog 1966. Klaus Lensch Theaterverlag. Ahrensburg bei Hamburg.

[389] *Nordisk dramatik til Tyskland, Østrig og Schweiz (Nordic drama to Germany, Austria, and Switzerland).* By Gunnar Martin Nielsen. Berlingske Aftenavis 19 January1966.

The big breakthrough did not happen for Munk's works.

On May 18, 1963 *Vor Cannae* was read aloud at the Städtische Bühnen Dortmund in connection with "Auslandskulturtage der Stadt Dortmund, Deutschland - Dänemark." Dortmund Theater performed Kjeld Abell's play *Die letzte Szene [Dronning gaar igen]*, and the program brochure contained a long article about Munk and Abell.[390] On January 19, 1966 *Vor Cannae* was read and performed in Hessischer Rundfunk. But other than that the attempt to have Munk played in the German theater was not successful. Thyra Dohrenburg and Lensch had made an outstanding effort, but to no avail. Thirty years would go by before one of Munk's plays would be performed in Germany.[391]

The first book about Munk written by a German author and published in Germany came out in 1970 in East Germany. It was pastor Alfred Otto Schwede's[392] book *Verankert im Unsichtbaren*.[393] The title is taken from Munk's sermon "Forankret i det usynlige" (Rooted in the Invisible) from the 7th Sunday after Trinity, 1942.[394]

In the book's postscript Schwede tells how, as a soldier in Berlin in January 1944, he found a crumpled page from a newspaper in the hall at the Stettiner Bahnhof in Berlin. It was a page from the *Sydsvenska Dagbladet Snällposten*. Schwede could read Swedish, and from a portion of an article he learned that the Danish pastor Kaj Munk, who he had read before the war, was dead.

---

[390] Städtische Bühnen Dortmund. Program. Schauspielhaus 1962-63. KMF.
[391] *Er sitzt am Schmelztigel*. 1996 in Essen.
[392] Alfred Otto Schwede (1915-1987), pastor and author. See biographies.
[393] Alfred Otto Schwede: *Verankert im Unsichtbaren. Das Leben Kaj Munks*. Evangelische Verlagsanstalt Berlin DDR 1970.
[394] Kaj Munk: *Med Sol og megen Glæde*. NNF 1942, p. 249.

Is your father home?
Illustration from Sydsvenska Dagbladet – Snällposten, 7 January
1944, which Alfred Otto Schwede found on a street in Berlin. Drawn
by Anders Sten. Reproduced with permission of the Sten family.

Schwede mentions an illustration on the same page that shows two children opening a door, and outside there are two SS men who ask "Is your father home?" But Schwede's memory was mistaken. It was death who stood outside the door.[395]

---

[395] Sydsvenska Dagbladet Snällposten.Friday, 7 January 1944, front page, and p. 7.

Upon returning home from captivity after the war he was given books about Munk by Swedish and Danish acquaintances. Schwede's research resulted in articles and lectures about Munk and in 1970 his book *Verankert im Unsichtbaren* was published.

Schwede was not uncritical towards Munk. In his discussion of *Smeltediglen* he writes that Munk sat in Berlin and wrote about Jews, Nazis, Christians, opportunists, and whatever else the German people might have comprised at that time in 1938. But it should be noted, Schwede wrote, that Munk did not write about the resistance movement against Hitler. There were no workers among those characters that Munk described.[396]

About Munk's disappointment over Hitler's actions, Schwede asked:

> *Hadn't Kaj Munk read Hitler's Mein Kampf? Or had he, years ago, purposely decided to ignore what was there in black and white? And why had he, in particular, failed to see it when so many others had been able to understand the book?*[397] *(a.t.)*

Schwede was certainly correct. Until late in the thirties Munk was not interested in reading anything that could tarnish his ideal image of Adolf Hitler, and when he finally experienced the realization of National Socialism it was too late to read the program.

In the following story from the time when Germany was divided, Schwede's book about Munk played an important role. What might seem comical today could, at the time, develop into a serious affair. In the early seventies, Kaj Munk's son Arne Munk, together with his mother Lise Munk, brother Helge, and nephew Christian, were in a car on the way home from Austria. The route went through East Germany, over Berlin, to the border at Helmstedt where they would leave the DDR and enter the Federal Republic of Germany. They had to wait six hours

---

[396] Alfred Otto Schwede: *Verankert im Unsichtbaren. Das Leben Kaj Munks.* Evangelische Verlagsanstalt Berlin DDR 1970, p. 217.

[397] Alfred Otto Schwede: *Verankert im Unsichtbaren. Das Leben Kaj Munks.* Evangelische Verlagsanstalt Berlin DDR 1970, p. 226.

before getting permission to cross the border. The irritation over the long wait resulted in Arne Munk informing the East German border guard that he now had proof that the DDR was a police state.

Alfred Otto Schwede
(1915-1987)
The Schwede Family's private archive

That was something he should not have said. And it led to a thorough inspection of Arne Munk, his passengers, and his car.

They confiscated a copy of *Berlingske Tidende* because it had a picture of a skimpily clad woman, and that type of thing was forbidden in the DDR. A book on a shelf under the rear window drew the attention of the guards, and they demanded to see it. Arne Munk explained to them that it was about his father.

It was Schwede's book about Kaj Munk. It was soon discovered that both Schwede and the publisher were from the DDR, and were well known. When the police read on the back of the book that Kaj Munk had been murdered by the Nazis in 1944 and had been an anti-fascist, then everything changed completely. Arne Munk, together with his passengers and car, was at once directed back onto the correct road, and with no further problems was able to leave the DDR.[398] Schwede's book about Munk had been helpful simply by being there.

The first and so far only German doctoral thesis on Kaj Munk was written in 1979, and was published in book form the following year.[399] The author was pastor Th.D. Christian Eisenberg[400] from Braunschweig. Eisenbergs interest in Munk began with a vacation experience in Denmark when, as a 16 year old, he spent time in Jutland with a friend of his mother.[401] During an auto tour she talked about the famous pastor Kaj Munk, who she had heard preach.

Eisenberg did not forget that story, and when he was searching for a subject for his doctoral thesis he chose Munk, and the title became Die politische Predigt Kaj Munks.[402] Through his many stays in Denmark Eisenberg developed a good knowledge of the Danish language and culture. In May of 1996 he gave a lecture in Rødby about Dietrich Bonhoeffer and Kaj Munk. Eisenberg lectured at the University of Copenhagen in April 1996, once again about "Dietrich Bonhoeffer and Kaj Munk - two theologians during WWII", and in May 1998 about "Kaj Munk's relationship to Hitler-

---

[398] Conversation with Arne Munk 6 August 2006.

[399] Christian Eisenberg: *Die politische Predigt Kaj Munks*. Peter D. Lang Frankfurt am Main 1980.

[400] Christian Eisenberg (1940-1999). See biographies.

[401] Jytte Breum (1914-2005), teacher.

[402] "Beretningen om en modig præst tændte hos ung tysker" (The story of a courageous pastor inspired a young German). John Karlsen in Folketidende 13 January 1998.

Germany". The lectures were given in Danish. In the anthology Dansk rebel og international inspiratory, Eisenberg wrote a chapter on "Kaj Munk's political sermons."[403] In the book På Lolland jeg den hented' (I Got it on Lolland), which came out on Munk's 100th birthday in 1998, Eisenberg had written about "Kaj Munk's relationship to Hitler's Germany."[404]

Th.D. Christian Eisenberg (1940-1999)
Photo Ib Geertsen
Author's archive

---

[403] *Kaj Munk - Dansk rebel og international inspirator*. Akademisk Forlag København 1995, pp. 112-126.
[404] *Kaj Munk 1898-1998 - På Lolland jeg den hented'*. Poul Kristensens Forlag Herning 1998, pp. 44-48.

At a theological seminary in Braunschweig where he was a research assistant, he had lectured about Munk. He had also contributed an article about Munk to the Jahrbuch der Gesellschaft für Niedersächsische Kirchengeschichte 1995. Eisenberg has translated Før Cannae and several of Munk's poems into German. He lectured about Munk numerous places in Germany.

At the Danish Kaj Munk Institute's summer seminar in Vedersø in 1998, Eisenberg spoke about his thesis: Kaj Munk's political sermons.

Isabel Sandig and Ralf Gottesleben performing
"He sits at the Melting-Pot"
Photo Thomas Heiser
Sandig/Gottesleben archive

1989-2007

On November 9, 1989, the wall between the German Democratic Republic and the Federal Republic of Germany came down. And thereby was not only Germany reunited, but all of Europe became more closely integrated. Throughout the 20th century November 9th had been a fateful date for Germany; Kaiser Wilhelm 2nd's abdication in 1918, Hitler's attempted coup in Munich in 1923, and the escalation of Jewish persecution on Kristallnacht in 1938.

And Munk had had a premier performance twice on that date. The first time was in 1933 with *De Udvalgte* at the Royal Theater. The second time was in 1996 with the German premier of the play *Er sitzt am Schmelztiegel* in the protestant church in Essen-Bergerhausen. As mentioned earlier, in 1939 Munk wrote about *Smeltediglen*: "In twenty years it will be played in Germany, and loved there." It took 57 years, but it finally happened.

It was pastor Paul Gerhard Schoenborn[405] from Wuppertal who had translated *Smeltediglen*. Schoenborn showed Kaj Munk's play to a fellow pastor, Dieter Schermeier,[406] who was very knowledgeable about the theater. He knew two young professional actors, Isabel Sandig[407] and Ralf Gottesleben,[408] and when they read the play they decided to perform it. Dieter Schermeier directed the play in which the two actors, with the help of hand held masks and simple figures in masonite, played all of the roles. A seemingly impossible task but performed to perfection. They have now performed *Er sitzt am Schmelztiegel* over 100 times.

A very comprehensive program brochure has been produced for these German performances of Smeltediglen. It starts with Schoenborn's translation of B. S. Ingemann's hymn "Den store mester kommer"(The Great Master is coming), where in the 3rd line is written "Han sidder ved smeltediglen" (He Sits at the

---

[405] Paul Gerhard Schoenborn (1934-), pastor. See biographies.

[406] Dieter Schermeier (1937-), pastor.

[407] Isabel Sandig (1969-),German actress, educated in drama, voice, and dance from Berliner Schule für Bühnenkunst.

[408] Ralf Gottesleben (1963-), German actor, studied drama in Wuppertal, had also studied piano.

Melting-Pot). Four articles follow, respectively, by Isabel Sandig and Ralf Gottesleben, Dieter Schermeier, Susannah Heschel, and Paul Gerhard Schoenborn.[409]

The play was performed in the former concentration camp at Dachau in November 1999:

> In remembrance of the Jews, among others, a play about Jewish persecution, written by a Danish pastor and dramatist who was murdered by Germans on January 4, 1944 during the German occupation of Denmark, is performed in a German concentration camp by German actors.[410]

Outside of Germany the play was performed in May of 2001 in Munk's hometown of Maribo in the parsonage of the parish cathedral, and in Aabenraa in February 2002.

In Aabenraa the performance was arranged by the Deutsche Zentralbücherei and was played in the hall of the Deutsches Gymnasium. The newspaper *Der Nordschleswiger* had a very positive review of the performance, where Kaj Munk's son, Arne Munk, was present in the audience. Under the heading "Schmelztiegel", the journalist, who wrote short articles under the by-line "dm.", described the thoughts that went through his head upon hearing the historical introduction by library director Nis-Edwin List-Petersen before the play. And, dm. continued,

> There were also other thoughts running through my mind, as almost side by side in the audience sat Arne Munk, and the son of the former leader of the DNSP-N,[411] Jens Möller. [412] Probably both of them were thinking about their fathers, each

---

[409] The program was printed in German in 1996.

[410] "Kaj Munk spilles i Dachau". By Søren Daugbjerg and John Karlsen. *Lolland-Falsters Folketidende* 13 November 1999.

[411] Deutsche Nationalsocialistische Partei - Nordschleswig.

[412] Jens Möller (1894-1951), Veterinarian and politician, leader of the German minority, a prominent Nazi in south Jutland.

on their side of the conflict. The symbolism was palpable– not just on the stage![413] *(a.t.)*

One of the masonite figures used by Isabel Sandig and Ralf Gottesleben when they perform "Han sidder ved Smeltediglen". The figures were made by pastor Dieter Schermeier, and were originally used in church services for confirmation classes.
Author's photo

---

[413] "Kaj Munk Schauspiel fesselte". *Der Nordschleswiger* - Deutsche Tageszeitung in Dänemark. 15 February 2002.

In 1996 Schoenborn's book *Alphabete der Nachfolge - Märtyrer des politischen Christus* was published, in which Kaj Munk is mentioned together with Dietrich Bonhoeffer, Oscar Romero and others.[414]

A copy of Schoenborn's translation of *Smeltediglen* is held in the archives of the Holocaust Museum Yad Vashem in Jerusalem.

The Melting-Pot was to be just the beginning of Schoenborn's translation work. Translations of several of Kaj Munk's works were done in the following years, and he planned an edition of the plays in book form. Schoenborn came into contact with another translator, Rolf Lehfeldt,[415]who had studied Munk for many years. Their collaboration resulted in *Kaj Munk - Schauspiele*[416]. That book contains the plays *Ein Idealist, Das Wort, Er sitzt am Schmelztiegel*, and *Die Herren Richter* translated by Schoenborn, and *Cant, Niels Ebbesen* and *Vor Cannae* translated by Lehfeldt. There is also an introduction by Arne Munk, Kaj Munk's son: "Der Dramatiker Kaj Munk und die geistige Situation seiner Zeit", as well as a short explanation of each play and Schoenborn's postscript on Munk, "Leben und Werk". The postscript aids in understanding Munk and his plays in a country where he is not well known. About these "aids", Arnim Juhre wrote in a review:

> In this way a history book of a special nature has evolved, a commentary on the legacy of a martyr who, as pastor and author, was also an important dramatist.[417] (a.t.)

Kaj Munk-Schauspiele was published in March of 2003, but was first presented officially at a reception at Flensborghus in Flensborg on August 11 of the same year. On that occasion Arne

---

[414] Paul Gerhard Schoenborn: *Alphabete der Nachfolge– Märtyrer des politischen Christus*. Peter Hammer Verlag. Wuppertal 1996, pp. 48-78.

[415] Rolf Lehfeldt (1928-2002). See biographies.

[416] *Kaj Munk-Schauspiele*. Aus dem Dänischen von Rolf Lehfeldt und Paul Gerhard Schoenborn. Mit einem Essay von Arne Munk. Herausgeber Sydslesvigsk Forening . ATEdition im LIT-Verlag, Münster 2003.

[417] Arnim Juhre: "Der Vermächtnis eines Märtyrers". Das Gespräch aus der Ferne. Hamburg 2003.

Munk paid tribute, and spoke about how, 70 years after Erwin Magnus' first efforts, it was finally possible to present some of Munk's drama to the German public. About the translator Arne Munk said:

> *There is not a shadow of a doubt that it was these two men, Rolf Lehfeldt and Paul Gerhard Schoenborn– regardless of how different they may be– whose sterling contribution has pleased my father in that corner of heaven where he sits at his writing desk.[418]*

Pastor Paul Gerhard Schoenborn (1934-)
Private photo

---

[418] Quoted from Arne Munks manuscript. www.kajmunk.dk

The book was published with the support of the Kaj Munk Commemorative Fund among others. Co-translator Rolf Lehfeldt did not live to see the finished book. He died in April of 2002.

For their efforts in spreading knowledge of Kaj Munk to the German speaking countries Schoenborn and the two actors, Isabel Sandig and Ralf Gottesleben, received the Kaj Munk Prize in 2002. It was the first time the prize had been awarded to Germans. The presentation took place on January 4, 2004 at the Flensborghus in Flensborg.419

The book was published with the support of the premier in Schleswig-Holstein's reserve fund and the Kaj

The publication of *Kaj Munk - Schauspiele* resulted in it being discussed in two radio programs. The first program was in the Westdeutscher Rundfunk Program Three on June 13, 2003. The program's host and Schoenborn talked about and quoted Munk. The program was written by Hannelore Becker-Willhardt, who also wrote a review of the book in the magazine *Gegen Vergessen- Für Demokratie*,420 which was published by an association with the same name. The second program was on February 12, 2004 in *RTL Morning Magazine* "Rundfunkmission der Evangelisch-methodistischen Kirche", with the title "Menschen die bewegen– Kaj Munk", in which *Kaj Munk - Schauspiele* is also mentioned. The text was written and read by Anja Kieser. Hartmut Handt read the quotations.

The celebration of Munk's 100th birthday on January 13, 1998 was a continuation of this renascence that Munk had achieved in the eighties and nineties. The event was mentioned in newspapers and magazines not just in Denmark, but in several countries. On January 10, 1998 Schoenborn had written an article "Kaj Munk - Pastor, Poet, Gegner Hitlers, Märtyrer" in *Der Nordschleswiger*, and *Flensborg Avis* carried a full-page photo of Munk, together with a poem, "Hommage til Kaj Munk - by Rolf Lehfeldt". Here is the last stanza:

---

419 "Tyskere får mindepris for første gang" (Germans win the memorial prize for the first time). Flensborg Avis 2. 1. 2004. "Tak for kulturelt brobyggeri". *Flensborg Avis* 5. 1. 2004.

420 Information für Mitglieder, Freunde und Förderer des Vereins "Gegen Vergessen-Für Demokratie e.V.". Berlin Dezember 2003.

Dit guldhjertes renhed var viljen til alt
hvad troskab mod ordet har lidt.
Så glæden mig tynger, når jeg beder en tak
ved et danskhedens kors af granit.[421]

(Your golden heart's purity was the will to all
That faith to the Word had suffered.
So joy weighs me down, when I offer my thanks
At a Danish cross of granite.)*

A special celebration of the day with respect to the relationship between Munk and Germany was a memorial service in Toreby kirke on Lolland, January 11, 1998.

The parish pastor and Kaj Munk researcher Svend Aage Nielsen had invited Arne Munk to preach. The German cultural attaché, the first secretary at the German Embassy, Boris Ruge, had asked if he might participate.

As neither the Munk family nor the pastor were opposed, Boris Ruge participated as an official representative of the German Embassy. In his sermon Arne Munk spoke directly to the cultural attaché in German. It was a very deliberate strategy, as Boris Ruge both spoke and understands Danish perfectly. The ceremony was suddenly elevated to an almost international level. Arne Munk said that some might want to interpret Boris Ruge's participation, as a representative of the German nation, as an act of contrition, but that was not at all the case. It was not the Germans, and not even Hitler's Germany, that was the problem, but rather mankind. He finished by quoting from his father's play *Niels Ebbesen*:

A great day of freedom will come sometime– I believe it, and I will believe it– when our neighbor and we live side by side to each other's benefit. For that reason both our peoples shall endure.[422]

---

* Refers to the cross of granite placed at the site of Munk's assassination near Hørbylunde.

[421] *Flensborg Avis* January 13, 1998. Kultur, p. 8.

[422] Kaj Munk: *Niels Ebbesen*. NNF 1942, p. 79.

Rolf Lehfeldt (1928-2002)
Photo Martina Metzger
Flensborg Avis photo archives

The service in the packed church in Toreby drew attention and was reported in a large part of the press, also abroad.

At the Danish Central library in Flensborg a commemorative exhibition with photos and texts on Munk's life and work was held from February 3 to 28 1998.[423] In connection with the exhibition there was a lecture evening where the exhibition was discussed, and Arne Munk spoke about "Kaj Munk as a father."[424]

The Danish minority's theater in Flensborg, where Munk's plays had often been performed in Danish, celebrated him with "An evening with Kaj Munk." That was the title of four evening exhibitions in November 1998 in "The Little Theater." The exhibition's first part was a mix of recitals, solo singing, and choral singing of Munk's texts. Among the texts was Munk's poem "The 15 small coffins", about the 15 children in a Danish kindergarten who were killed in a bombing raid during WWII.

The exhibition's second part was a performance of Munk's play about the poet Johannes Ewald: *Ewalds Død*. "An evening with Kaj Munk" was arranged by Else Fanø and Rolf Lehfeldt.[425]

A feature article in February 1998 by the former high school teacher from Berlin, Reinhart Behr, now living on Fyn, was titled "Two men against Hitler", and the subtitle was:

> *Bertolt Brecht and Kaj Munk were both authors, born 100 years ago, and fierce opponents of Hitler. Brecht had always been one, Kaj Munk became one! And that is all they have in common. Or is it?[426]*
>
> *It's not always popular to point out Kaj Munk's political position before the occupation, his long enduring and naive belief that Mussolini, and even Hitler, lived up to his ideals. Kaj Munk will, despite his problematic statements, always enjoy great respect, as he was ready to give of himself, even to the last tragic sacrifice. Brecht on the other hand seems like an anti-hero, for some outright cowardly. Fortunately we live in*

---

[423] Søren Daugbjerg: Commemorative Exhibition for Kaj Munk 1898-1998. 28 Plaques with photos and text.

[424] Hans Chr. Davidsen:"Djævle blev brugt i pædagogikken"(The Devil was used in education) and "Til minde om Munk" (In memory of Munk). Flensborg Avis 4 November 1998.

[425] Hans Chr. Davidsen: "Stærkt og overbevisende" (Powerful and convincing). *Flensborg Avis* 7. 11. 1998.

[426] Reinhart Behr (1928-2003). See biographies.

another time. Confronted with a new barbarism we might need
them both, the firebrand [Munk] and the analyst [Brecht].[427]

Behr's text in German is in a somewhat different form, and supplemented with a comparison between Kaj Munk's *Ordet* and Brecht's *Leben des Galilei*, printed in the magazine *Vorschein*.[428]

Ph.D. Niels Vilhelm had presented this comparison between Kaj Munk and Brecht in an earlier article: "Kaj Munk og Bertolt Brecht."[429] Arnim Juhre discusses this subject briefly in his review of *Kaj Munk Schauspiele*.[430]

Kaj Munk- Leben und Wirken, written by the German teacher Kurt Bratmann431 in 1998, was intended to be a brochure for German tourists. It was never printed, but a copy is available for visitors at the Vedersø Egnsmuseum (district museum).

In October 1998 a dissertation by Matthias Wulsten was presented at the Christian Albrechts Universitet in Kiel[432]: *Die dramatische Zeitdichtung Kaj Munks als Reaktion auf den und geistige Auseinandersetzung mit dem Faschismus*. It is about Munk's attitude toward fascismen as seen in his plays *Sejren, Han sidder ved Smeltediglen* and *Niels Ebbesen*. Wulsten does not believe that *Smeltediglen* can be seen as a true anti-Nazi play. He does not find any real renunciation by Munk of fascism.[433]

Kaj Munk's one-act play *Før Cannae* was published in 2000 in Dresden in a limited edition of just 90 numbered copies. The

---

[427] Reinhart Behr: "To mænd mod Hitler" (Two men against Hitler). Feature article in *Berlingske Tidende* February 10, 1998.

[428] Reinhart Behr: "Die gesellschaftliche Verantwortung des Schriftstellers". Vorschein, Blätter des Ernst-Bloch-Archivs. Nr. 17, Hamburg, Mai 1999, Seite 137 bis 144.

[429] *Kaj Munk - Dansk rebel og international inspirator*. Akademisk Forlag, København 1995, p. 60-72.

[430] Arnim Juhre: "Der Vermächtnis eines Märtyrers". Das Gespräch aus der Ferne. Hamburg 2003.

[431] Kurt Bratmann (1937-), teacher. See biographies.

[432] Matthias Wulsten (1959-), M.A.

[433] Matthias Wulsten: *Die dramatische Zeitdichtung Kaj Munks als Reaktion auf den und geistige Auseinandersetzung mit dem Faschismus*. Kiel 1998, p. 62 ff.

translation and typographical arrangement was by Kai Kromer.[434] The book contains both the Danish and the German text in a handsome layout. Graphic artist Peter Wagler illustrated it with 8 drawings. The motives are taken from the Dresdener Schlachthof, which has since disappeared. *Vor Cannae* is a beautifully executed edition for book collectors.[435]

During a seminar on ecclesial history with the theme "Evangelische Märtyrer im 20. Jahrhundert" at Humboldt Universitetet in Berlin in 2002, Kristina Krüge wrote a seminar paper: "Kaj Munk- Mit Gottes Hilfe das Volk zum Aufruhr bringen".

A play composed of excerpts from Kaj Munk's sermons, the play *Niels Ebbesen,* and the poem "Mester med den tunge Tornekrone" was performed by the St. Georg Gemeinde Goslar on the Day of the reformation in 2002. The play's title *Der Stein an der A 15* refers to the granite cross at the place where Munk was found murdered. Translations by Schoenborn, Lehfeldt and Henkys were used. The text can be seen at www.kajmunk.dk.

The high school teacher Dr. Gottfried Lorenz[436] did what is presumably latest translation of *Smeltediglen* into German in 2002. Lorenz did this translation, with commentary and notes, solely for his use in teaching at the high school in Glinde near Hamburg. It was impossible, Lorenz wrote, while researching Norwegian, Swedish, and Danish literature about these three countries' relationship to Germany during WWII, not to be confronted with Munk. The encounter with Munk's work, and the interest for it, resulted in the translation of Smeltediglen, which Lorenz had dedicated to his high school pupils in the years 2002 and 2003.[437] The translation exists only in manuscript form.

On Sunday, March 30, 2003, 11.30 a.m., under the title "Stop the War", Prinz Regent Theater in Bochum in Nordrhein Westfalen held a matinee in protest against the war in Iraq. The first performance in the matinee was Munk's *Vor Cannae*, read by the actors Christian Ebert and Uwe Rohde, with Stefan Nölle as

---

[434] Kai Kromer (1969-), printer. See biographies.

[435] Kaj Munk: *Vor Cannae - Før Cannae.* Satzverlag Dresden 2000.

[436] Gottfried Lorenz, Dr. (1940-). See the biographies.

[437] Kaj Munk: "Er sitzt am Schmelztiegel". Aus dem Dänischen von Gottfried Lorenz. Glinde 2002, s. II til IV.

director. Rolf Lehfeldts translation was used. The performance was in support of "Doctors without Borders."[438]

That *Før Cannae*, 60 years after its creation, could still be used in political protest shows that Munk's one-act play had not lost its relevance.

On May 15, 2004, Schleswig-Holsteinisches Landestheater held the premiere in Rendsborg of *Die Erde brennt*, with a recital of scenes from Kaj Munk's *Smeltediglen* and *Niels Ebbesen*, chosen by the dramaturge Regina Härtling, and read by four actors. The performance was also given in Slesvig and Flensborg. The performance's title, *Die Erde brennt*, is taken from the introduction that Munk wrote in the Folketeatret's program brochure for *Smeltediglen* in 1938, where he began with the sentence: The Earth is burning.

The German texts were from the book Kaj Munk - Schauspiele, with translations by both Schoenborn and Lehfeldt. It was the theologian Dr. Hans Joachim Pruszak who had brought Kaj Munk's drama to the attention of Regina Härtling.

The dubbed over German version of Carl Th. Dreyer's film of Munk's *Ordet* (*The Word*) was shown on the German cultural channel "Arte" on June 28, 2006. On "Arte"s website there was a lengthy discussion of the film and its instructor.

A Catholic association, Amateurbühne Münster-Ost e.V. (The largest amateur theater in Nordrhein-Westfalen) put Munk's *Das Wort*, in Schoenborns translation, on the program in 2006. The directors were Stephanie Doms and Petra Neuhaus. The premier performance was on August 26, 2006. The play was performed five times before a full house.

During Hitler's reign the play *Ordet* was, as mentioned earlier, performed in 1935 in Schwerin. After 71 years *Ordet* was again performed in Germany, in a relatively peaceful Europe, reborn through a trial of suffering and terrible mistakes.

The mistakes and suffering have not been forgotten. At a town meeting in Garbsen by Hannover on November 9, 2006 about the international resistance against Nazi Germany, there were two speakers. Superintendent Gisela Fähndrich spoke about the Portuguese diplomat Aristides de Sousa Mendes, who helped many

---

[438] Prinz-Regent-Theater. info@prinzregenttheater.de

Jews escape from Germany, and pastor Christian Voigtmann who spoke about Kaj Munk. On November 19, Germany's national day of sorrow, Volkstrauertag,[439] Christian Voigtmann recited the lecture about Munk in the church in Garbsen.

Isabel Sandig and Ralf Gottesleben celebrated their tenth year with Smeltediglen with a performance on February 10, 2007 in the protestant church in Essen-Bergerhausen, where the German premier had been performed on November 9, 1996.[440]

---

[439] Volkstrauertag, introduced in 1920, a German day of memory for the fallen in WWI. During the Nazi period it was called "Heldengedenktag". After 1945 it was also a day of memory for the victims of Nazism and WWII. Source: *Brockhaus Enzyklopädie* 1974, volume 19, p. 708.
[440] Press release.

Postage stamp with Kaj Munk that was never printed. Drawn by Henning Pihl.

In 1945 the Minister of Transportation approved a suggestion from the Freedom Fund to print a stamp to raise funds for the victims of the resistance and their survivors. The stamp was later printed, but with other motifs.

From "Frimærke Nyt" (Stamp News), October 1945

Biographies

Sources given in parentheses.

Arpe, Verner

Stage manager, actor, author. Born 1902 in Hamburg, died 1979 in Stockholm. Swedish heritage on his mother's side. Immigrated to Sweden 1937. His German citizenship was annulled in 1943. Became Swedish citizen in 1948. Worked as a translator and dramaturgist for the theater publisher Englind in Stockholm from 1939 until he was fired in 1943 under pressure from the German legation. This was another example of Nazi Germany's influence in a neutral country. After1945 he was a cultural ambassador between German speaking countries and Scandinavia. In 1957 he wrote Knaurs Schauspielführer, in which several of Munk's plays are discussed.

(Handbuch des deutschsprachigen Exiltheaters. Band 2. Biographisches Lexikon der Theaterkünstler. Teil 1 A-K. K. G. Saur München 1999).

Baldus, Alexander

Author, translator, critic. Born in Koblenz am Rhein 1900, died 1971. Lectured on Scandinavian literature, and translated St. St. Blicher and Marie Bregendahl. Discussed Munk in radio programs and articles. Posthumous papers are found in the Stadtarchiv Koblenz. A Book collection is in the Stadtbibliothek Koblenz. In a letter to Lise Munk on 4 August 1951 it appears that he was working on a Munk biography to be included in a work titled: "Dänischen Dichtung von Georg Brandes bis Kaj Munk." Baldus had written and spoke about Munk in several articles and radio programs. See under theses, books, and articles.(page 257)

(Letters to Lise Munk, 4.August,1958. KMF/2. colophon in Nordische Dichtung der Gegenwart. Verlag Die Egge. Nürnberg. 1948, p. 55./ 3. Information from the Stadtarchiv Koblenz about the author's archives).

Becher, Johannes Robert

Author and politician, born in Munich 1891, died in Berlin 1958. Member of the German parliament for the Communist Party before 1933. Fled to Czechoslovakia in 1933, lived from 1933 until 1945 in Moscow. Minister of Culture in the DDR (East Germany) 1954-58. He spoke about Munk at a meeting of the PEN Club in Copenhagen in 1948.

(1. Wolfgang Benz and Walter H. Pehle: Lexikon des deutschen Widerstandes. S. Fischer Verlag Frankfurt am Main 1994, p. 333).

Behr, Reinhart

Professor, mathematician, and physicist. Born in Hamburg 1928, lived from 1930 until 1988 in Berlin, died in Ulbølle on Fyn in 2003. Taught in Berlin until 1988, and then lived in Denmark. In Berlin he was for a time a member of the town council for the "Alternativen Liste" (the Green Party). Has written articles where he compares Munk to Brecht. Author of "Oh, dieses Dänisch" about pitfalls in the Danish language. (Reinhart Behr: "Über mich". Kurze Biographie. August 2003).

Berendsohn, Walter Arthur

Ph.D., literary historian, born in Hamburg 1884, died in Stockholm 1984. Professor at the university in Hamborg 1919-33, lived for a while in Denmark, fled to Sweden in 1943. He was the first person to begin collecting and archiving German language immigrant literature from the period 1933-1945. During his stay in Denmark he wrote many articles in the *Højskolebladet* (Cultural magazine, founded in 1876 by the Union of Folk High Schools in Denmark) about WWI and the German Folk High Schools. Berendsohn wrote about Scandinavian authors, including H.C. Andersen, Martin Andersen Nexø, August Strindberg, Selma Lagerlöf and Knut Hamsun. In 1938 he translated Munk's Smeltediglen into German.

(Steffen Steffensen: På flugt fra nazismen. Tysksprogede emigranter i Danmark efter 1933. C. A. Reitzels Forlag København 1986, p. 255 ff./ 2. Internationales Germanistenlexikon 1800-1950. Band 1: A-G. Walter de Gruyter. Berlin-New York 2003, p. 142).

Bratmann, Kurt

Teacher, born 1937 in Blankenburg in Harzen. After finishing school he became a teacher in Bad Berensen and Tarmstedt in Niedersachsen. He became interested in Munk after a stay in West Jutland/Vedersø. That interest led to the earlier mentioned Munk biography. (Information from Kurt Bratmann. AA).

Cavin, Gudrun

Author, translator. Born in Denmark, married to the pastor at the cathedral in Geneva, Albert Cavin. Wrote a biography about Munk in French, and translated Jesus' Historier into German and French.

(Letter to Lise Munk from Gudrun Cavin 1946. KMF).

Dohrenburg, Thyra (married name Jakstein)

Translator, born 1898 in Berlin-Schöneberg, died 1972 in Ry, Jutland. Married in 1922 to Stadtbaurat Werner Jakstein, Altona (born 1876 in Potsdam).

Translations for Klaus Lensch probably began around 1960. She had earlier translated other Scandinavian authors.

(1. Heiratsurkunde, Steglitz 1942, letters from probate court in Skanderborg 2005/ 2. Klaus Lensch, Hamborg).

Eisenberg, Christian

Th.D., born 1940 in Braunschweig, died there in 1999. He studied theology in Göttingen and Tübingen, archival assistant at Landeskirche Braunschweig, 1977 pastor in Braunschweig. From 1981 scientific assistant at the Prediger Seminar der Evangelisch-Lutherischen Landeskirche in Braunschweig. Th.D. 1980 from Christian Albrechts University in Kiel, defending his thesis: Die Politische Predigt Kaj Munks. His thesis was published in book form by Peter D. Lang GmbH, Frankfurt am Main 1980. ISBN 3-8204-6823-4.

(Annemarie Eisenberg).

Klein, Manfred

Born 1937 in Castrop-Rauxel, studied theater, German, music and philosophy at the university of Wien. Studied theater history and Scandinavian literature at the University of Copenhagen during the winter semester 1961-62. Ph.D. in 1964 defending his thesis: Zeitaktuelle dänische Dramatik des 20. Jahrhunderts und ihre Inszenierung.

(Manfred Klein's autobiography in dissertation).

Kromer, Kai

Printer, born in 1969 in Dresden. Independent printer in Dresden, primarily of rare or limited editions. Developed an interest in Denmark before 1989. Attended Askov Højskole and participated in political activities in Denmark (SF). This connection to Denmark resulted in an interest for Kaj Munk. Kromer was fluent in Danish, and he translated and published Vor Cannae in 2001.(Kai Kromer).

Lehfeldt, Rolf

Ph.D. in economics., author, deputy mayor in Flensborg, born 1928 in Magdeburg, died 2002 in Flensborg. Despite his German heritage Lehfeldt joined the Danish minority where he was active in many areas. He has written about and translated several of Munk's works into German.

(Flensborg Avis, obituary from April 3-4, 2002).

Lorenz, Gottfried,

Ph.D., High school teacher, born 1940 in Steinau/Oder (Schlesien), studied history, German, Scandinavian and sociology at the universities in Kiel, Göttingen and Saarbrücken. Doctoral thesis was on a subject from German-Scandinavian history from the Thirty Years' War. He translated *Smeltediglen* in 2002.

(Gottfried Lorenz).

Magnus, Erwin

Translator, author, literary advisor, born 1881 in Hamburg, died 1947 in Copenhagen. He was married 3 times: 1. Elna Magnus, nee Nathansen, the niece of Henri Nathansen, 2. author Margareta Freud-Magnus, sister of Lilly Freud-Marlé, 3. pianist Käthie Birch.

He wrote a book about the cinema: Lichtspiel und Leben, Filmplaudereien. Dürr und Weber m. b. H., Berlin SW 11, 1924. Magnus was also the author of a small book: Asta Nielsen und die Sprechbühne about the famous Danish actress. Georg Brandes wrote the book's preface.

Magnus gave up independent production and became primarily occupied with translation. In a letter to Peter Freuchen he wrote: "...I would rather be a first class translator than a third class author".[441] He was the first to translate Jack London into German (35 volumes). Among Nordic authors he translated Bjørnstjerne Bjørnson, Knut Hamsun, Halldór Laxness, and Oehlenschläger. Also Jacob Paludan, Georg Brandes, Herman Bang, Thit Jensen, Agnes Henningsen, Sophus Michaëlis, Leck Fischer and Soya.

Magnus came to Denmark in 1934 through Austria and Poland, and fled to Sweden in 1943. After may of 1945 he again lived in Copenhagen.

(1. Steffen Steffensen: På flugt fra nazismen. Tysksprogede emigranter i Danmark efter 1933. C. A. Reitzels Forlag København 1986. s. 46-47./ 2. Gitta Magnus./ 3. Michael Freud-Magnus).

Michelsen, William

Ph.D., He was a High school teacher (1913-2001), and brother of Birgit Michelsen, who in 1943 was a private teacher for Kaj Munk's children.

Maag, Otto

Theologian, author, journalist and translator, born in 1885 in Mannheim, died 1960 in Basel. Pastor in Heidelberg, moved to Basel in 1927.

(UB Basel: Basler Literarisches Archiv: Maag, Otto).

---

[441] Letter to Peter Freuchen 5 January 1939. The Royal Library.

Schaper, Edzard

Author, Born in 1908 in Ostrovo/Posen, died in 1984 in Bern. Lived in Denmark (Christiansø), Finland and Sweden, where he worked as a translator.

(Biography and bibliography at www.bautz.de/bbkl).

Schoenborn, Paul Gerhard

Theologian, born 1934 in Bochum, pastor in Duisburg-Rheinhausen-Friemersheim 1963, student pastor in Wuppertal 1973, and from 1981 pastor with responsibility for adult education there. Pensioned in 1995 for health reasons. While pastor for German tourists in west Jutland he became interested in Munk. In 1995 he wrote his first article about "Der dänische Pfarrer Kaj Munk". Since then he has written a long series of articles that have been published in several European countries. He has also produced educational material about Munk. In the local Museum in Vedersø there is a four page brochure about Munk, written by Schoenborn in German, English, Dutch, and Danish. His lecture on Munk's play Ordet is often combined with a showing of Carl Th. Dreyer's film from 1955, dubbed in German. He has talked about Munk in Germany and Austria, and lectured on the same subject in universities in Germany, and academies in Austria.

(Information from Paul Gerhard Schoenborn).

Schwede, Alfred Otto

German theologian and author, born 1915 in Haynsburg, Kreis Zeitz, died 1987 in Berlin Hohen-Neuendorf. Traveled in 1938 to Sweden. To avoid internment at the outbreak of WWII he returned to Germany and fought in the war, and was a prisoner of war, captured by the Americans. Upon returning home he took his last exams and became a pastor in Haynsburg, Uthleben by Nordhausen and later in Brandenburg-Görden until 1961, after which he lived off his writing. Schwede produced a large number of his own books, including several travel books about Denmark. He has translated many books into German, in particular those by Scandinavian authors. Of Danish authors, he has translated St. St. Blicher, Søren Kierkegaard, J. P. Jacobsen, Martin A. Hansen and

Leif Panduro. Schwedes book on Munk, Verankert im Unsichtbaren, was published in 1970.

(1. "Uns gefiel es so". Dieter Mehlhardt sprach mit Alfred Otto Schwede, Potsdamer Kirche DDR 5. 11. 1983/ 2. „Brücken nach Skandinavien" Ein Gespräch Dr. Günter Wirths mit dem Schriftsteller. I „Standpunkt" Berlin DDR. Heft 11, 1977./ 3. "Book pastor in DDR". Article of the deceased pastor Erling Kristiansen (1930-2003), Flensborg Avis 6 April 2001/ 4. Christiane Fleischer, Evangelische Verlagsanstalt GmbH, Leipzig, letter of 7 January 2003).

Wyss, Laure
Born 1913 in Biel, Switzerland, died 2002 in Zürich, teacher, journalist, and author. 1958-1967 editor at the Swiss TV. Resided in Sweden during WWII. He has, among other things, translated books and documents concerning the role of the Scandinavian church in the resistance to the German occupation forces in 1940-1945. (Limmatverlag, Schweiz).

Works by Kaj Munk published in German in books, magazines, and parts.

Chronological by the year of the translation's publication or printing.

Cant (Cant) Schauspiel von Kay Munk. Also Einzig berechtigte Übertragung aus dem Dänischen von Erwin Magnus. Archivexemplar. Gustav Kiepenheuer Bühnenvertriebs GmbH. Berlin Charlottenburg 1932. Copy of parts, 111 pages A-5.

Kaj Munk: *Ein Idealist. (En Idealist)*, translated by Erwin Magnus 1932. This translation has not been found.

Kaj Munk: *Das Wort (Ordet)*. Translated by Erwin Magnus 1932. Performed in Schwerin in 1935. Parts/translation has not been found.

Kaj Munk: *Ein Idealist (En Idealist).* Einige Eindrücke aus den Leben eines Königs. Berechtigte Übertragung aus dem Dänischen von Verner Arpe. Gustav Kiepenheuer Bühnenvertriebs GmbH. Berlin-Dahlem. Undated (1938-43?). Copy of parts, 250 pages A-4.

Kaj Munk: *Brandung (I Brændingen).* Translated by Verner Arpe, undated (1938-43?). This translation has not been found.

Kaj Munk: *Am Anfang war das Wort (Ordet).* Translated by Verner Arpe, undated (1938-43?). A part with no title: "Am Anfang war das Wort" berechtigten Übertragung aus dem Dänischen von Verner Arpe is found at Gustav Kiepenheuer Bühnenvertriebs GmbH. Berlin. Has not been available for this book.

Kaj Munk: *Die Diktatorin (Diktatorinden).* Translated by Verner Arpe, undated (1938-43?). This translation has not been found.

Kaj Munk: *Bekenntnis zur Wahrheit.* Evangelische Verlag AG Zollikon/Zürich 1944. This volume contains the sermon collection Ved Babylons Floder from 1941 translated by Laure Wyss. 2. Edition 1945. 83 pages.

Contents: In parentheses, Danish title and page number in Ved Babylons Floder:

Der reiche Mann und der arme Lazarus
(Valdemarsdag, p. 69)
Einladung zum Gastmahl
(Anden Søndag efter Trinitatis, p. 76)
Die verlorene Drachme
(Tredie Søndag efter Trinitatis, p. 83)
Petri Fischzug
(Femte Søndag efter Trinitatis, p. 97)

Neue Gerechtigkeit
(Sjette Søndag efter Trinitatis, p. 104)

Speisung der Viertausend
(Syvende Søndag efter Trinitatis, p. 110)

Falsche Propheten
(Ottende Søndag efter Trinitatis, p.116)

Klage über Jerusalem
(Tiende Søndag efter Trinitatis, p. 126)

Pharisäer und Zöllner
(Ellevte Søndag efter Trinitatis, p. 132)

Ephata
(Tolvte Søndag efter Trinitatis, p. 139)

Der barmherzige Samariter
(Trettende Søndag efter Trini   tatis, p. 145)

Am Erntedankfest (Høstprædiken, p. 156)

Kaj Munk: *Fragment eines Lebens* (*Foraaret saa sagte kommer-Erindringer*). Artemis Verlags-AG Zürich 1944. Preface by John Christmas Møller. Translated by Maria Bachmann-Isler. 424 pages.

Kaj Munk: *Niels Ebbesen*, Artemis Verlags-AG Zürich 1944. Translated by Otto Maag (Autorisierte deutsche Übersetzung). 71 pages.

Dänische Predigten von Kaj Munk. Neuer Verlag Stockholm 1945. Preface by Olle Nystedt. Translated by Edzard Schaper from the collections Ved Babylons Floder 1941, *Med Ordets Sværd* 1943, 3 Prædikener 1943, and Munk's sermon in Copenhagen Cathedral May 12, 1943. 112 pages.

Contents: In parentheses, Danish title, book, and page number.

Am 25. Sonntag nach Trinitatis (25. Søndag efter Trinitatis. Med Ordets Sværd, p. 62)

Am 1. Sonntag im Advent (1. Søndag i Advent. Med Ordets Sværd, p. 70)

Allerheiligen (Allehelgensdag. Med Ordets Sværd, p. 37)

Busstag (Munks prædiken i Københavns Domkirke, 5 December 1943. Bjarne Nielsen Brovst: Kaj Munk, krigen og mordet Centrum 1993, p. 305)

Am Neujahrstag (Kristus og Danmark. 3 Prædikener, p. 17)

Am sechste Sonntag nach Ostern (Sjette Søndag efter Paaske. Ved Babylons Floder, p. 51)

Am zweiten Sonntag nach Heilige Drei Könige (2. Søndag efter Hellig 3 Konger. Med Ordets Sværd, p. 119)

Am dritten Sonntag nach Heilige Drei Könige (3. Søndag efter Hellig 3 Konger. Med Ordets Sværd, p. 126)

Am dritten Sonntag im Advent (Johannes og Jesus. 3 Prædikener, p. 6)

Am dritten Sonntag der Fastenzeit (3. Søndag i Fasten. Med Ordets Sværd, p. 169)

Am 18. Sonntag nach Trinitatis (18. Søndag efter Trinitatis. Med Ordets Sværd, p. 18)

Am Erntedankfest (Høstprædiken. Ved Babylons Floder, p. 156)

Kaj Munk: Glückhafte Tage. Artemis Verlag Zürich 1946. Munk's hunting letters Liv og glade Dage from 1936, translated by Elsa Carlberg with illustrations by Ib Andersen. 130 pages.

Contents: In parentheses title and page number in the Danish edition.

Jägerbrief an einen Jagdfeind
(Jægerbrev til en Jagtfjende, p. 7)
Die weisse Frau von der Heide
(Den hvide Dame paa Heden, p. 15)
Ajax (Ajax, p. 25)
Der Kampf um den Balg (Kampen for Bælgen, p. 29)
Das Heidekirchspiel (Hedesognet, p. 41)
Eine Frau aus dem Volke (En Kvinde af Folket, p. 48)
Ewigkeit und Frühling (Evigheden og Vaaren, p. 60)
Jener Sommer und jener See (Den Sommer og den Sø, p. 70)

O Herbst! (Oh, Efteraar! p. 79)

Aber wie ist's denn im Winter? (Men saa Vinteren da,   p. 84)

Posten auf der Fuchsjagd (Paa post for en Ræv, p. 89)

Sie schoss wie ein Teufel (Hun skød som en Djævel, p. 98)

Der Pascha der Heide (Hedens Pasha, p. 108)

Die Seele der Kleinstadt (Smaabyens Sjæl, p. 116)

Johan vom Havbierge (Johan fra æ Havbjerge, p. 128)

Du hast mich heimgesucht bei Nacht. Abschiedsbriefe und Aufzeichnungen des Wiederstandes 1933 bis 1945 von Helmut Gollwitzer, Käthe Kuhn und Reinhold Schneider. Gütersloher Verlagshaus, Gütersloh 1951. 8. Auflage 1994. About Munk on pages 36-37. Although the book is primarily about the German resistance movement, room had been found for a short biography of Munk, and quotations from two sermons. The source is given as "Bekenntnis zur Wahrheit".

Hans Peter Johannsen: *Deutsche und dänische Dichter der Gegenwart.* Westholsteinische Verlagsanstalt Boyens & Co. Heide Holstein 1957, pages 231-233, about Kaj Munk and his work. On pages 234-248 chapters XXXIII and XXXIV from the Swiss edition of Munk's memoirs "Fragment eines Lebens. Erinnerungen" are reproduced. Artemis Verlag. Zürich 1944.

Kaj Munk: "Herz, was begehrst du noch mehr" (Vestjylland) Translated by Thyra Dohrenburg. Monthly magazine "Merian. Monatsheft der Städte und Landschaften". Forlaget Hoffmann and Campe. Hamburg 1960, pp. 22-24.

Calendarium spirituale '65 Evangelischer Almanach. Evangelische Verlagsanstalt Berlin DDR 1964, on pages 46-50 contains "Meister mit der schweren Dornenkrone" (Mester med den tunge Tornekrone) translated by Peter-Paul Sänger, together with an article he wrote about Munk.

H.W. Bähr: *Die Stimme des Menschen.* Briefe und Aufzeichnungen aus der ganzen Welt 1939-1945. R. Piper & Co Verlag München 1966 (1st edition 1961). Excerpts from Tre prædikener by Kaj

Munk, pp. 232-235. The texts are probably taken from the translation by Laure Wyss in Kaj Munk: *Bekenntnis zur Wahrheit.* Evangelische Verlags AG Zollikon/Zürich. 1944. The excerpts are from the following sermons: 13. søndag efter trinitatis (*Mindeudgave, Prædikener*, p. 159), 23. søndag efter trinitatis (*Mindeudgave, Prædikener*, p. 202), 4. søndag efter hellig tre konger (*Mindeudgave, Prædikener,* p. 261. Laure Wyss translated the first sermon. It is not known who translated the others. They were not included in *Bekenntnis zur Wahrheit* or in *Dänische Predigten von Kaj Munk.*

Kaj Munk: *Ein Idealist (En Idealist)* Schauspiel in 8 Bildern. Adapted by Svend Methling. Aus dem Dänischen von Thyra Dohrenburg. Klaus Lensch Theaterverlag, Ahrensburg bei Hamburg. Publisher's catalog 1966. Parts, 49 pages A-4.

Kaj Munk: *Brandung* (*I Brændingen*). Schauspiel in 5 Akten. Aus dem Dänischen von Thyra Dohrenburg. Klaus Lensch Theaterverlag, Ahrensburg bei Hamburg. Publisher's catalog 1966. Parts, 96 pages A-4.

Kaj Munk: *Das Wort* (*Ordet*) Schauspiel in 4 Akten. Aus dem Dänischen von Thyra Dohrenburg. Klaus Lensch Theaterverlag, Ahrensburg bei Hamburg. Publisher's catalog 1966. Copy of parts. 68 pages A-4.

Kaj Munk: *Liebe* (*Kærlighed*). Drama in sechs Bildern. Aus dem Dänischen von Thyra Dohrenburg. Klaus Lensch Theaterverlag, Ahrensburg bei Hamburg. Publisher's catalog 1966. Parts. 60 pages A-4.

Kaj Munk: *Vor Cannae* (*Før Cannae*). Eine Studie. Aus dem Dänischen übersetzt von Thyra Dohrenburg. Klaus Lensch Theaterverlag, Ahrensburg bei Hamburg. v 1966. Parts 11 pages A-4.

Die Reise nach Bethlehem. Weihnachtsgeschichten aus unserer Zeit. Udgiver Arnim Juhre. Gütersloher Verlagshaus Gerd Mohn

Gütersloh 1967. Pages 6-10 contain among other things Kaj Munk's "Ernste Weihnacht" (Alvorlig Jul) Translated by Thyra Jakstein (Dohrenburg).

Deutsches Pfarrerblatt. Herausgegeben vom Verband der Evangelischen Pfarrervereine in Deutschland e. V. 1. Ausgabe März 1969, on pages 142-143 are found Kaj Munk's "Die Aufgaben des Pfarrers heute" (Præstens Gerning i Dag), with a short biography "25. Todestag Kaj Munks", translated and written by Thyra Dohrenburg.

"Der christliche Erzähler". Schriftenmissionsverlag Gladbeck 1969. The magazine carried Kaj Munk's "Bei Ivers wird ein Kind getauft" (Et bitte Barn bliver døbt hos Ivers) on pages 254-257 and 280-281, together with a short biography "Kaj Munk", translated and written by Thyra Dohrenburg.

Sven Danielsson: *Nordische Weihnacht*. Weihnachtserzählungen aus Dänemark, Schweden, Norwegen und Finnland. Verlag Die Arche Zürich 1970. Contains Kaj Munk's: "Weihnachten" (Jul) Lukas 2, 1-14, p. 181-186. Translated by Ursula von Wiese. A Christmas sermon broadcast on Denmark's Radio in 1942.

Frühlicht erzählt von dir. Neue geistliche Lieder aus Skandinavien. Ausgewählt und übertragen von Jürgen Henkys. Edition 1175. Strube Verlag GmbH. München 1990. ISBN 3-921946-12-8. On page 9 is Henkys' translation of "Du ved det nok mit hjerte" ("Du weißt, mein Herz, schon lange").

Evangelisches Gesangbuch. Ausgabe der Evangelischen Kirche in Österreich 1994, ISBN 3-85073-335-1 Number 623 contains Jürgen Henkys' translation of "Du ved det nok mit hjerte" in a slightly different form ("Du weißt, mein Herz, du weißt es").

Hans Klüche: *Jütland*. Edition Erde - Reiseführer 1996. On pages 48 and 178 of this extensive travel guide there is a mention of Munk. On pages 163-164 and 179 Munk's article "Vestjylland" is quoted ("Herz, was begehrst du noch mehr". Merian).

Kaj Munk: *Vor Cannae- Før Cannae*. Satzverlag. Dresden 2000. The book contains both the German and the Danish text. Illustrated by Peter Wagler. Printed in 90 numbered copies. Translation, typography, and arrangement by Kai Kromer. 36 pages. ISBN 933354-05-6

Kaj Munk-Schauspiele. Aus dem Dänischen von Rolf Lehfeldt und Paul Gerhard Schoenborn. Mit einem Essay von Arne Munk. Herausgeber Sydslesvigsk Forening . ATE-Verlag. Münster 2003. Contains the plays: Ein Idealist, Das Wort, Er sitzt am Schmelztiegel, Die Herren Richter, translated by Schoenborn, and Cant, Niels Ebbesen and Vor Cannae translated by Lehfeldt. 390 pages. ISBN 3-89781-039-5

Works by Kaj Munk that have been translated into German, Printed and not printed.

Plays:

To the extent possible these are listed chronologically by their year of publication in Denmark, or by the year of their original performance. Where the year of publication differs from the year of creation, the latter is given in brackets. German title, translator, and the year of publication are given in parentheses.

En Idealist 1928. [1923-24] (Ein Idealist- Erwin Magnus 1932/ Thyra Dohrenburg 1960-66/ Verner Arpe 1938-43/ Paul Gerhard Schoenborn 2003).

I Brændingen 1929. [1926] (Brandung- Verner Arpe 1938-43/ Thyra Dohrenburg 1960-66).

Havet og Menneskene 1948. [1929]. (Das Meer und die Menschen- Paul Gerhard Schoenborn 2005, manuscript, not printed).

Cant 1931. (Cant- Erwin Magnus 1932/ Rolf Lehfeldt 2003).

Ordet 1932. [1925] (Im Anfang war das Wort - Ervin Magnus 1933/ Am Anfang war das Wort- Verner Arpe 1938-43/ Das Wort- Thyra Dohrenburg 1960-66/ Paul Gerhard Schoenborn 2003).

Kærlighed 1948. Performed in 1935. [1926] (Liebe- Thyra Dohrenburg 1960-66).

Diktatorinden 1948. Performed in 1938. [1937] (Die Diktatorin- Verner Arpe 1938-43).

Han sidder *ved Smeltediglen* 1938. (Professor Mensch und das Christusbild- Walter A. Berendsohn 1938/ Er sitzt am Schmelztiegel- Paul Gerhard Schoenborn 2003/ Gottfried Lorenz 2002, manuscript, not printed).

Fugl Fønix 1939. [1926] (Vogel Phönix- Paul Gerhard Schoenborn 2004, manuscript, not printed).

Niels Ebbesen 1942. [1940-42] (Niels Ebbesen- Otto Maag 1944/ Rolf Lehfeldt 2003).

De Herrer *Dommere* 1942. (Die Herren Richter- Paul Gerhard Schoenborn 2003).

Før Cannae 1943. (Vor Cannae- Thyra Dohrenburg 1960-66/ Christian Eisenberg 1996?/ Kai Kromer 2000/ Rolf Lehfeldt 2003).

Articles, sermons, and poems: Listed chronologically by year of creation. "Not printed?" is a presumption. This is followed by the source.

"Elifelet" sermon 1920. ("Eliphalet"- Thyra Dohrenburg, not printed?). Mindeudgave, Prædikener, p. 22.

"Mester med den tunge Tornekrone..." 1921 („Meister mit der schweren Dornenkrone..."- Peter-Paul Sänger 1964/ Jürgen Henkys 1994). Mindeudgave, Digte, p. 59.

"Det moderne Menneske og Døden". Article 1931. ("Der moderne Mensch und der Tod"- Thyra Dohrenburg, not printed?). Mindeudgave, En Digters Vej og andre Artikler, p. 43.

"Tro" sermon 1932. ("Glaube"- Thyra Dohrenburg, not printed?). Mindeudgave, En Digters Vej og andre Artikler, p. 50.

"Kortner og Jannings i "Patriot"" Anmeldelse 1932. ("Kortner und Jannings in "Patriot""- Thyra Dohrenburg, not printed?). Med Sol og megen Glæde, p. 176.

"Om Miraklet" article 1932. ("Über das Wunder"- Thyra Dohrenburg, not printed?). Mindeudgave, En Digters Vej og andre Artikler, p. 61.

"Gud er ingen 'Virkelighed'" article 1935. ("Gott ist nicht 'Wirklichkeit'" Thyra Dohrenburg, not printed?). Mindeudgave, En Digters Vej og andre Artikler, p. 151.

"Johan fra æ Havbjerge" article 1936. ("Johan vom Meerhügel"- Thyra Dohrenburg, utrykt?/ "Johan von Havbierge" Elsa Carlberg i bogen "Glückhafte Tage 1946"). Mindeudgave, En Digters Vej og andre Artikler, p. 159.

"Birthe" short story 1937. ("Birthe"- Thyra Dohrenburg, not printed?). Mindeudgave, En Digters Vej og andre Artikler, p. 293.

"Præsten i Menigheden." Article 1937. ("Der Pfarrer in der Gemeinde"- Thyra Dohrenburg, not printed?). Mindeudgave, En Digters Vej og andre Artikler, p. 320.

"Undervejs". Article 1937. ("Unterwegs"- Thyra Dohrenburg, utrykt?). Mindeudgave, En Digters Vej og andre Artikler, p. 332.

"Lette Bølge, naar du blaaner." Article 1938. ("Leichte Woge, wenn du blaust..."-Thyra Dohrenburg, not printed?). Mindeudgave, Dagen er inde og andre Artikler, p. 14.

"Et bitte Barn bliver døbt hos Ivers" 1938. ("Bei Ivers wird ein Kind getauft"- Thyra Dohrenburg 1969). Mindeudgave, Dagen er inde og andre Artikler, p. 26.

"Ved Smeltediglen." Folketeatrets program 1938. ("Am Schmelztigel"- Thyra Dohrenburg, not printed?). Mindeudgave, Dagen er inde og andre Artikler, p. 48.

"Du ved det nok, mit hjerte..."* 1938 ("Du weißt, mein Herz, schon lange..."- Jürgen Henkys 1990). The film about Christiern II by Kaj Munk, NNF 1938, p. 39.

"Alvorlig Jul". Article 1938. ("Ernste Weihnacht"- Thyra Dohrenburg 1967). Mindeudgave, Dagen er inde og andre Artikler, p. 72.

"Vestjylland". Article 1939. ("Herz, was begehrst du noch mehr"- Thyra Dohrenburg 1960). Mindeudgave, Dagen er inde og andre Artikler, p. 86.

"Hvor gaar vi hen?". Article 1940. ("Wohin gehen wir"- Thyra Dohrenburg, not printed?). Mindeudgave, Dagen er inde og andre Artikler, p. 155.

"Nok frygte, men ikke forfærdes". Sermon 1940. ("Sich fürchten zwar, doch nicht erschrecken"- Thyra Dohrenburg, not printed?). Mindeudgave, Prædikener, p. 297.

"Præstens Gerning i Dag". Article 1941. ("Die Aufgaben des Pfarrers Heute"- Thyra Dohrenburg 1969). Mindeudgave, Dagen er inde og andre Artikler, p. 247.

"Kristendom og Tolerance". Article 1941. ("Christentum und Toleranz"- Thyra Dohrenburg, not printed?) Saa fast en Borg, p. 73.

Ved Babylons Floder. Sermon collection 1941. (Bekenntnis zur Wahrheit- Laure Wyss 1944).

Du ved det nok, mit hjerte
du ved, at Gud er stor;
men stor er og hans fjende,
så tit du det erfór.

Velan! så får du kæmpe
og tro trods fald og brud,
at stor er vel Guds fjende,
men større er dog Gud.

You must know this, my heart
You know that God is great;
But great as well his rivals are,
As you have learned of late.

Rise up! Now you must fight
Have faith though down and broken,
That great might be God's rivals,
Though greater yet is God.

(* see note above,p.263)

"Forankret i det usynlige". Sermon 1942. ("Im Unsichtbaren verankert"- Thyra Dohrenburg, not printed?). Mindeudgave, Prædikener, p. 316

"Jul". Radio sermon 1942 ("Weihnachten"- Ursula von Wiese). Mindeudgave, Prædikener, p. 229.

3 Prædikener. Forlaget Paaskeliljen, Struer 1943, contains "Johannes og Jesus", "Jesusbarnet og Stefanus" og "Kristus og Danmark" (Drei Predigten - Paul Gerhard Schoenborn 2002, not printed/ Sermon "Kristus og Danmark" is given the title "Am Neujahrstag" translated by Edzard Schaper 1945). Mindeudgave, Prædikener, p. 321.

Jesus' Historier. Children's book 1943. (Jesus-Geschichten - Gudrun Cavin 1949).

"Nytaarsdag 1944". Sermon. ("Neujahr 1944"- Thyra Dohrenburg, not printed?). Mindeudgave, Prædikener, p. 356

Who translated what of Kaj Munk into German

German titles in parentheses

Arpe, Verner:
    Plays:
    En Idealist (Ein Idealist). AA
    I Brændingen (Brandung)
    Ordet (Am Anfang war das Wort)
        Diktatorinden (Die Diktatorin)

Bachmann-Isler, Maria:
    Memoirs:
    Foraaret saa sagte kommer (Fragment eines Lebens)

Berendsohn, Walter A.:
    Play:
    Smeltediglen (Professor Mensch und das Christusbild)

Carlberg, Elsa:
    Hunting stories:
    Liv og glade Dage (Glückhafte Tage)
    Contents in the section: Works by Kaj Munk published in German in books, magazines, and parts.

Cavin, Gudrun:
    Children's book:
    Jesus' Historier (Jesus-Geschichten)

Dohrenburg, Thyra:

Plays:
En Idealist (Ein Idealist)
I Brændingen (Brandung)
Ordet (Am Anfang war das Wort)
Kærlighed (Liebe)
Før Cannae (Vor Cannae)
Sermons and articles:
"Elifelet" (Eliphalet)
"Det moderne Menneske og Døden"
(Der moderne Mensch und der Tod)
"Tro" (Glaube)
"Kortner og Jannings i "Patriot""
(Kortner und Jannings in "Patriot"")
"Om Miraklet" (Über das Wunder)
"Gud er ingen "Virkelighed""
(Gott ist nicht "Wirklichkeit")
"Johan fra æ Havbjerge" (Johan von Meerhügel)
"Birthe" (Birthe)
"Præsten i Menigheden"
(Der Pfarrer in der Gemeinde)
"Undervejs" (Unterwegs)
"Lette Bølge, naar du blaaner"
(Leichte Woge, wenn du blaust...)
"Et bitte Barn bliver døbt hos Ivers"
(Bei Ivers wird ein Kind getauft)
"Ved Smeltediglen" (Am Schmelztigel)
"Alvorlig Jul" (Ernste Weihnacht)
"Vestjylland" (Herz, was begehrst du noch mehr)
"Hvor gaar vi hen?" (Wohin gehen wir)
"Nok frygte, men ikke for færdes"
(Sich fürchtenzwar, doch nicht erschrecken)
"Præstens Gerning i Dag"
(Die Aufgaben des Pfarrers Heute)

"Kristendom og Tolerance"
(Christentum und Toleranz)
"Forankret i det usynlige"
(Im Unsichtbaren verankert)
"Nytaarsdag 1944" (Neujahr 1944)

Eisenberg, Christian:
    Play:
    Før Cannae (Vor Cannae). AA.

Henkys, Jürgen:
    Poems:
    "Mester med den tunge Tornekrone...
    "(Meister mit der schweren Dornenkrone...)
    "Du ved det nok mit hjerte"
    (Du weißt, mein Herz, schon lange...)

Kromer, Kai:
    Play:
    Før Cannae (Vor Cannae)

Lehfeldt, Rolf:
    Plays:
    Cant (Cant)
    Niels Ebbesen (Niels Ebbesen)
    Før Cannae (Vor Cannae)

Lorenz, Gottfried:
    Plays:
    Smeltediglen
    Er sitzt am Schmelztiegel). Forf. arkiv.

Maag, Otto:
    Play:
    Niels Ebbesen (Niels Ebbesen)

Magnus, Erwin:
    Plays:
    En Idealist (Ein Idealist)
    Cant (Cant). AA
    Ordet (Im Anfang war das Wort)

Schaper, Edzard:
    Sermons:
    Serman collection (Dänische Predigten von Kaj Munk). Con
    tents in the section: Works by Kaj Munk published in Ger
    man in books, magazines, and parts.

Sänger, Peter-Paul:
    Poem:
    "Mester med den tunge Tornekrone"
    (Meister mit der schweren Dornenkrone...)

Schoenborn, Paul Gerhard:
    Plays:
    En Idealist (Ein Idealist)
    Ordet (Das Wort)
    Havet og Menneskene (Das Meer und die
    Menschen)
    Smeltediglen (Er sitzt am Schmelztiegel)
    Fugl Fønix (Vogel Phönix)
    De Herrer Dommere (Die Herren Richter)
    Sermons:
    3 Prædikener (Drei Predigten)

Wiese, Ursula von:

Sermon:

„Jul" (Weihnachten) Radioprædiken.

Wyss, Laure:

Sermons:

Ved Babylons Floder (Bekenntnis zur Wahrheit), sermon collection. Contents in the section: Works by Kaj Munk published in German in books, magazines, and parts.

Dissertations, books, and articles about Kaj Munk in German.

Chronological by year of publication.

Die dänische Literatur der neuesten Zeit (1871-1933) von Helge Kjaergaard dänischer Lektor a. d. Universitet Greifswald. Levin and Munksgaard, Ejnar Munksgaard, Kopenhagen 1934. A discussion of En Idealist, I Brændingen, Cant og Ordet, pp. 233-234.

Kaj Munk. Ein Dichter zwischen zwei Weltkriegen. Ebbe Neergaards book "Vildt afsted over Himmel og Jord. Kaj Munk, en Digter mellem to Verdenskrige". Artemis Verlags AG, Zürich 1945, translated by Maria Bachmann-Isler, 379 pages.

"Kaj Munk" article by Alexander Baldus in "Welt und Wort. Literarische Monatsschrift" Tübingen 1952, Volume 4, pp. 267-268.

"Kaj Munk in der Spur Martin Luthers", an article by Rolf Italiaander in "Ausblick" Mitteilungsblatt der Deutschen Auslandsgesellschaft, October 1954, pp. 42-44.

Knaurs Schauspielführer von Verner Arpe. München-Zürich 1957, pp. 291-293.

Discussion of the plays En Idealist, Cant, Diktatorinden (translated by Arpe), Puslespil and Niels Ebbesen.

Drama zwischen Shaw und Brecht. Ein Leitfaden durch das zeitgenössische Schauspiel, von Siegfried Melchinger. Carl Schünemann Verlag, Bremen. Fünfte Auflage 1963. (First edition 1957). About Munk, p. 358.

Kaj Munks dramatisches Werk zumal "Das Wort" Eine Studie von Siegfried Beyschlag. Nach einem Vortrag auf der 2. Internationalen Studienkonferenz für nordische Literatur zu Lillehammer im Juli 1958 von Printed in *Orbis Litterarum. Revue internationale d'etudes Litteraires*, Tome XIV. Fasc. 2-4. Copenhagen 1959, pp. 223-229.

Die Religion in Geschichte und Gegenwart- Handwörterbuch für Theologie und Religionswissenschaft. J. B. C. Mohr (Paul Siebeck) Tübingen 1960. 1. Auflage bd. IV, spalte 1190. Article about Munk written by G. Tolderlund-Hansen.

Weltkirchen Lexikon. Handbuch der Ökumene. Kreuz Verlag Stuttgart 1960. Spalte 987. Article about Munk written by Mogens Vilhelm Zeuten (assistant pastor for Munk in 1943).

"Freundschaft mit Dänemark" von Emil Sulser. Zürichsee-Zeitung 19 August 1961. Comments on a performance of Niels Ebbesen in Switzerland and on a trip to Denmark. KMF.

"Kaj Munk", A comment and an obituary written and read by Edzard Schaper on 29 May 1961 in Radio Bremen in connection with "Dänische Woche" in Bremen. Copy of manuscript in KMF.

Kaj Munk. Den religiøse Problematik i hans Dramaer af Søren Holm. NNF 1961. Contains lectures by professor, Ph.D. Søren Holm (1901-1971) given during the same year at the universities in Hamburg, Tübingen and Göttingen.

Das moderne Drama. Strömungen-Gestalten-Motive, von Margret Dietrich. Alfred Kröner Verlag, Stuttgart 1974, (first edition 1961), pp. 385-388. Section on Munk contains a short review of *En

Idealist, Cant, Ordet, Sejren, Han sidder ved Smeltediglen and *Niels Ebbesen.*

Zwei dänische Dramatiker des 20. Jahrhunderts", article by Manfred Klein about Kaj Munk and Kjeld Abell in the program brochure for Städtische Bühnen Dortmund. Schauspielhaus 1962-63.

Lexikon der Weltliteratur. Biographisch-bibliographisches Handwörterbuch nach Autoren und anonymen Werken. Fremdsprachige Autoren L-Z, herausgegeben von Gero von Wilpert. Alfred Kröner Verlag Stuttgart 1963. Kaj Munk biography og bibliography, pp. 1263-1264.

Geschichte der Dänischen Literatur von Hanne Marie und Werner Svendsen. 1964 Karl Wachholz Verlag Neumünster. Gyldendal Copenhagen. History of Danish Literature translated into German by Georg Goetz. Pages 468-470 are about Kaj Munk.

"Widerstand im Glauben" (Modstand i tro) and "Ein dänischer Christ im Widerstand" (En dansk kristen i modstand) commemorative program in Sender Freies Berlin on the twentieth anniversary of Munks death, 4 January 1964. Idé Arnim Juhre. The text, which was written by Uwe Nabersberg, is printed in *Spiele für Stimmen- ein Werkbuch* Herausgeber Arnim Juhre. Jugenddienst Verlag, Wuppertal-Barmen 1965, pp. 61-73.

"Kaj Munk. Sein Leben, Wirken und Tod" af Thyra Dohrenburg. Munk-biography, no date. 15 A-4 pages, manuscript, printed? KMF.

Zeitaktuelle dänische Dramatik des 20. Jahrhunderts und ihre Inszenierung (Tidsaktuel dansk dramatik i det 20. århundrede og dens iscenesættelse) af Manfred Klein. Wien 1964. Doctoral thesis comprising 294 pages, of which pages 81-156 are about Kaj Munk.

Calendarium spirituale '65 Evangelischer Almanach. Evangelische Verlagsanstalt Berlin DDR 1964. Peter Paul Sanger has written an article (pages 46-50) about Munk, and translated "Mester med den tunge Tornekrone".

Verankert im Unsichtbaren. Das Leben Kaj Munks af Alfred Otto Schwede. Evangelische Verlagsanstalt GmbH. Berlin DDR 1970 (2. edition.1971), 291 pages.

Bildnisse evangelischer Menschen - Von Martin Luther bis zur Gegenwart. Evangelischer Verlagsanstalt GmbH Berlin DDR 1971. Contains photos and a reference to Kaj Munk, probably written by Alfred Otto Schwede, pp. 252-253. In the 1971 edition Munk is included for the first time. It is a very exclusive company that Munk is surrounded by in the book: Søren Kierkegaard, Martin Luther, Karl Barth, Dietrich Bonhoeffer, Martin Luther King, Rembrandt, the artist Ernst Barlach and many others.

"Das Ende des Pfarrers Kaj Munk", article by Alfred Otto Schwede in "Standpunkt" Evangelischer Monatsschrift Berlin DDR 1975, pp. 105-106.

"Kaj Munk und Niels Ebbesen", article by Alfred Otto Schwede in "Standpunkt" Evangelischer Monatsschrift Berlin DDR. Volume 2 February 1980, pp. 38-39.

Die politische Predigt Kaj Munks, by Christian Eisenberg. Peter D. Lang. Frankfurt am Main 1980. Doctoral thesis.123 pages A-5. ISBN 3-8204-6823-4

"von Beugel- alias Niemöller" article by Alfred Otto Schwede in "Standpunkt" Evangelischer Monatsschrift Berlin DDR. Volume 1 January 1981, pp. 20-21.

Kindlers neues Literatur Lexikon München 1991. Bind 12, s. 64-68. Reference to Munk's plays, and a literature list. Manfred Klein has written on Smeltediglen. The plays: En Idealist, Niels Ebbesen and Ordet are described by Franz J. Keutler.

Biographisch-Bibliographischen Kirchenlexikon Bearbeitet und herausgegeben von Friederich Wilhelm Bautz 1993. Volume 6. The section on Kaj Munk is written by Wolfdietrich von Kloeden and contains a long reference to Munk, with a bibliography and a literature list. Column 353-364. Can be found on the web: www.bautz.de/bbkl

Kaj Munk 1944– 4. January– 1994, sermon by Arne Munk at a commemorative service on 8 January 1994 in Maribo Cathedral in connection with the 50th anniversary of the murder of Kaj Munk. Translated into German by pastor emeritus Th.D. Jørgen Glenthøj and Gudrun Fog. Prof. Dr. Jürgen Henkys' translation of Munk's poem "Mester med den tunge Tornekrone" is included in the pamphlet. Published by Jørgen Glenthøj, Åbyhøj 1994. ISBN 87-89041-05-4

"Kaj Munk– Märtyrer um des offenen Wortes willen", article by Paul Gerhard Schoenborn. Transparent-Extra in Transparent, Essen, 9. årg. (1995) volume 37, pp. 5-24. The article is included in Schoenborn's book "Alphabete der Nachfolge. Märtyrer des politischen Christus".

Jahrbuch der Gesellschaft für Niedersächsische Kirchengeschichte. Bind 93 1995. Afsnittet "Die politische Predigt Kaj Munks" was written by Christian Eisenberg, pp. 179-192.

Alphabete der Nachfolge. Märtyrer des politischen Christus af Paul Gerhard Schoenborn. Peter Hammer Verlag. Wuppertal 1996, 215 pages. About Kaj Munk, pp. 49-78. ISBN 3-87294-737-0

"Mit Gottes Hilfe das Volk zum Aufruhr bringen..." Die Rettung der dänischen Juden und die prophetische Botschaft des Märtyrers Kaj Munk", article by Paul Gerhard Schoenborn. Transparent-Extra in Transparent, Essen, 11. year. (1998) Volume 49, pp. 1-12.

"To mænd mod Hitler" with sub-title: "Bertolt Brecht og Kaj Munk var begge forfattere, født for 100 år siden og indædte modstandere af Hitler. Brecht var det altid, Kaj Munk blev det! Men dermed ophører det, de har fælles. Eller gør det?" Feature article by Reinhart Behr in Berlingske Tidende 10 February 1998.

"Kaj Munk– Leben und Wirken", by Kurt Bratmann 1998, 28 pages A-4.

Die dramatische Zeitdichtung Kaj Munks als Reaktion auf den und geistige Auseinandersetzung mit dem Faschismus af Matthias Wulsten. Masters thesis. Kiel 1998, 114 pages. A-4.

"Blaue Anemone im Nordseewind" by Dirk Schümer, with a commentary on Munk's 100th birthday, Frankfurter Allgemeine Zeitung (FAZ),14 January 1998.

The article was marked by a number of mistakes, which prompted Schoenborn to write a long letter to the editor in which he pointed them out. Schümer had rather unfortunately insinuated that Munk was a crypto-fascist. Johannes Borgen, who in *The Word* calls his sister-in-law back from the dead, was called a village idiot (Dorftrottel). Schoenborn's letter, in a slightly shortened version, was printed in FAZ on 29 January under the heading "Munk ohne Kryptofascismus".

Yet another letter to the editor in reference to Schümer's article was printed in FAZ on 3 February. It was by Dr. Günter Wirth, Berlin, who with an article titled "Eine Munk-Biographie 1970 in einem DDR-Verlag", called attention to A. O. Schwedes book and articles about Munk.

Der Sandburg, by Dr. Hans Joachim Pruszak (1937—). Novel about Kaj Munk, not published, found as author's manuscript only.

"Die geschellschaftliche Verantwortung des Schriftstellers" - aus der Sicht von Bertolt Brecht und Kaj Munk. Reinhart Behr.

Vorschein, Blätter des Ernst-Bloch-Archivs. Nr. 17, Hamburg, May 1999, pages 137 to 144.

"Ein stolzer Tag für Dänemark" Kaj Munk, Schriftsteller und Wiederstandskämpfer. Article by Aldo Keel in Neue Zürcher Zeitung 25/26 September 1999. The title of the article is taken from Munk's sermon in Vedersø church on 29 August 1943. In the section on Munk's death, the article's author, Aldo Keel, points out, in parentheses, that in that special commando group that killed Munk there was a "specialist" from Switzerland. The "specialist" was a member of the SS, Louis Nebel, born in Hochwald in Switzerland (see. Bjarne Nielsen Brovst: "Kaj Munk. Liv og død". Centrum, Aarhus 1984, p. 262.)

"Lebensbilder– Leidensbilder– Vorbilder", article by pastor Hans-Dieter Stolze in Homiletische Monatshefte, Vandenhoeck & Ruprecht, Göttingen, volume 4, 2000. About Kaj Munk, pp. 168-169.

"Kaj Munk– Mit Gottes Hilfe das Volk zum Aufruhr bringen", by Kristina Krüger. Berlin 2002.

Günter Weitling: "Dramen Kaj Munks bleiben von zeitloser Aktualität". Der Nordschleswiger 28.5. 2003. Review of the book "Kaj Munk-Schauspiele" Aus dem Dänischen von Rolf Lehfeldt und Paul Gerhard Schoenborn. ATE-Verlag, Münster 2003.

Die Religion in Geschichte und Gegenwart- Handwörterbuch für Theologie und Religionswissenschaft. J. B. C. Mohr (Paul Siebeck) Tübingen 1998-2005. 4. Auflage bd. III, column 1581-1582. Article about Munk written by Alf Christophersen.

"Kaj Mun– Wahrheitszeuge im Widerstand– Einführung in Leben und Werk des Dichters, Pfarrers und Märtyrers", article by Paul Gerhard Schoenborn. Pfälzisches Pfarrerblatt, 96th annual edition. (2006) volume 5, pp. 189-198.

"Politischer Widerstand und christliches Martyrium– Kaj Munk, Dietrich Bonhoeffer,Oscar Romero und viele andere" article by Paul

Gerhard Schoenborn. Transparent-Extra in Transparent, Essen, 20th annual edition (2006) volume 83, pp. 11-16.

"Pfarrer, Dichter, Märtyrer" article about Kaj Munk by pastor Hans-Dieter Stolze in Kasseler Sonntagsblatt, Christlicher Familienblatt– Evangelischer Sonntagsbote für Kurhessen-Waldeck, 25. März 2007, p. 2.

Works in English by and about Kaj Munk

Five Plays by Kaj Munk
Translated from the Danish by R.P. Keigwin
Nyt Nordisk Forlag Arnold Busck 1964 The American
Scandinavian Foundation
Content: Herod the King; The Word; Cant; He Sits at the
Melting Pot; Before Cannae.

By The Rivers of Babylon
Kaj Munk – 15 sermons, Translated by John M. Jensen
Lutheran Publishing House
Blair, Nebraska 1945

Four Sermons
by Kaj Munk,Translated by John M. Jensen
Lutheran Publishing House
Blair, Nebraska 1944

Niels Ebbesen by Kaj Munk
Translated into English by Arense Lund with Dave Carley
December 2006 (Straight translation and an adaptation)

Niels Ebbesen: Historical Drama in 5 Acts: Translated from
Danish by Erna Voight and
H. Orlo Miller, The Scandinavian News, Sept. 1942-Feb. 1943

Christianity and Resistance in the 20th Century
From Kaj Munk and Dietrich Bonhoeffer to Desmond Tutu
Brill 2006

Kaj Munk: Playwright, Priest and Patriot, translated and edited
by R.P. Keigwin, The
Free Danish Publishing Company, 1944

Scandinavian Plays of the Twentieth Century, Princeton, Princeton University Press for the American-Scandinavian foundation, New York 1944;

The Honourable Justice, translated by R.P. Keigwin, 1952

Egelykke, A drama in five acts, translated by Llewellyn Jones, 1954

Modern Scandinavian Plays, by Strindberg, August, New York, Liveright Pub. Corp. 1954, comprising Kaj Munk's play Egelykke.

Swans of the North: and short stories by modern Danish authors, by Heepe, Evelyn, G.E.C. Gad, Copenhagen 1953, comprising Kaj Munk's: *But it's not like him!*

Archives and collections

Kaj Munk archives and collections —Kaj Munk Society

The Royal Library. Document collection, and Ove Marcussen's Kaj Munk collection.

Kaj Munk Research Center, Institute for Communication, Aalborg University.

Kaj Munk's private archives. www.kajmunk.hum.aau.dk

Lolland Library, Maribo. www.maribobib.dk

The library's Kaj Munk collection contains letters, books, and newspaper clippings.

Kaj Munk Society. Founded 1997. Publishes the magazine MUNKIANA. www.munkiana.dk

At www.kajmunk.dk there is a great deal of information on Munk in Danish, and also a very comprehensive German language section. Edited by Paul Gerhard Schoenborn since 1998. Includes sermons, plays, and other works translated into German.

Acknowledgements

I wish to thank the following for their assistance in archival research, proof reading, and good advice.

Dr. Reinhold Brunner, Stadtarchiv Eisenach
Professor, Ph.D. Søren Dosenrode
Painter and graphic artist Michael Freud-Magnus,
MA Christian Huber, Sigmund Freud Privatstiftung, Wien
Actress Marga Heiden, Schwerin
Gisela Krauß, teacher, Altenfeld
Gerhard Krauß, teacher, Altenfeld
Erik Rosenstjerne Kølle
Organist Henny Lehrmann, Tybjerglille Bakker
Dr. Gottfried Lorenz, Glinde, Hamburg
Psychologist Yrsa Lund
Th.D. Hanne Munk, Vedersø
Professor Arne Munk, Vedersø
Kaj Munk Research Center Aalborg University
Pastor Ole Opstrup, Maribo
Social worker Aksel Poulsen, Errindlev
Pastor Paul Gerhard Schoenborn, Wuppertal
County Library, Maribo
Professor Dr. Günter Wirth, Berlin
Professor Ph.D. Per Øhrgaard, København

And thanks to my wife Brigitta for her assistance with the extensive German correspondence in connection with this book.

Søren Daugbjerg

www.ingramcontent.com/pod-product-compliance
Lightning Source LLC
Chambersburg PA
CBHW031114030726
47496CB00002BA/544